Community Resilie
Environmental Tra.

A highly welcome book containing novel insights on two great challenges of the post-sustainability era – how to build resilience in social and ecological systems, and how to make transitions to ways of living that are good for both people and planet. Brim full of clear analyses and important policy implications.

Professor Jules Pretty OBE, Deputy Vice-Chancellor, University of Essex

In this book, Geoff Wilson applies transition theory – where he has already made a considerable intellectual mark – to the buzzword of the moment, 'resilience'. This book makes a major contribution to our understanding of how community resilience is made, and unmade.

Jonathan Rigg, Durham University

This book discusses the resilience of communities in both developed and developing world contexts. It investigates the notion of 'resilience' and the challenges faced by local communities around the world in dealing with disturbances (natural hazards or human-made) that may threaten their long-term survival. Using global examples, specific emphasis is placed on how learning processes, traditions, policies and politics affect the resilience of communities and what constraints and opportunities exist for communities to raise resilience levels.

Community Resilience and Environmental Transitions contributes towards academic debates that argue that 'social resilience' (the resilience of human systems) is crucial for understanding constraints and opportunities faced by communities in a rapidly changing world. It analyzes specifically how environmental, political and socio-economic transitions affect community resilience and suggests that community embeddedness into the globalized world can both raise or reduce community-level resilience. The book argues that relocalized community pathways (e.g. the burgeoning Transition Towns Movement), in particular, highlight how communities are attempting to recapture lost social and environmental capital to increase community resilience.

Geoff A. Wilson has worked on research topics linked to human-environment interactions for the past 20 years, with extensive research conducted in various geographical settings, including New Zealand, Australia, Germany, Switzerland, and the UK. He has published several books, including *Environmental Management: New Directions for the 21st Century* and is currently Editor of the journal *Geography Compass: Environment and Society*.

Community Resilience and Environmental Transitions

Geoff A. Wilson

 Routledge
Taylor & Francis Group

LONDON AND NEW YORK

First published 2012
by Routledge
2 Park Square, Milton Park, Abingdon, Oxon OX14 4RN

Simultaneously published in the USA and Canada
by Routledge
711 Third Avenue, New York, NY 10017

Earthscan is an imprint of the Taylor & Francis Group, an informa business

First issued in paperback 2012

British Library Cataloguing in Publication Data
A catalogue record for this book is available from the British Library

Library of Congress Cataloging in Publication Data
[CIP data]

ISBN: 978-1-849-71151-7 (hbk)
ISBN: 978-0-203-14491-6 (ebk)
ISBN: 978-0-415-82793-5 (pbk)

Typeset in Times New Roman
by Wearset Ltd, Boldon, Tyne and Wear

Contents

Figures, tables and boxes

Figures

Tables

Boxes

Acknowledgements

Ideas contained in this book are closely linked to my past research and involvement in research projects over many years and are, therefore, bound to leave a long trail of intellectual and other debts. In particular, a book that focuses on thoughts, ideas and theories cannot be successfully written without the help of many individuals who have critically commented on various aspects of the book. My biggest debt of gratitude is to my wife Olivia Wilson who supported this book project throughout, had to endure my long 'absences' while writing, commented on the final draft of the book, and who was asked regularly to comment on lines of thought developed in the book. Especial thanks must go to my postdoctoral assistant Claire Kelly, and also to Helen Briassoulis, Anton Imeson, Michiel Curfs, Sandra Naumann, Rutal Landgrebe, Agostino Ferrara, Gianni Quaranta, and to all other colleagues on the EU-funded €3 million LEDDRA Project, for very stimulating and critical discussions on issues of community resilience. I am particularly grateful to the EU Framework 7 programme for funding LEDDRA and for giving us the opportunity to investigate issues of community resilience and land degradation in diverse case study communities located in China, Morocco, Spain, Italy and Greece, which have provided the empirical basis for some of the examples mentioned in this book.

Special thanks are due to Rob Hopkins, my former PhD student and initiator of the Transition Town Movement, who greatly inspired ideas expressed in this book; my colleague Ian Bailey at the University of Plymouth who provided invaluable constructive criticism on conceptual issues developed in the book over the years (partly linked to our joint Third Year course 'Global Environmental Politics'); James Sidaway who critically commented on approaches used in the book and for stimulating academic discussions (in the sauna and during delicious meals) on many of the political issues raised in Chapters 5–7; and to my brother Peter Wilson for critical comments and stimulating exchanges (while climbing in the Alps) on philosophical issues of transition and resilience. Many thanks also to my PhD students Wendy Miller, Andrew Fox and Huw Thomas who are all currently working on questions related to community resilience and who have enabled me to discuss and test some of my conceptual ideas with them. Especial thanks also to my son Erik who has often lured me away from my desk and kept me fit by constantly beating me at table tennis and tennis (well, he is a top UK junior tennis and table tennis player!).

Ideas for this book were tested at various conferences, seminars and workshops, and I am particularly grateful to all those who commented critically and asked probing questions. This includes the many people who attended and contributed to the session on 'Rural community resilience' at the 2009 Association of American Geographers Conference in Las Vegas (particular thanks to Bruce Scholten) and to the session on 'Conceptualising resilience' at the 2010 Institute of British Geographers Conference in London (especial thanks to Guy Robinson).

A book like this cannot be written without the supportive environment of research-led institutions that also reward 'blue sky' research not directly linked to the generation of overhead income. I, therefore, wish to thank colleagues at the School of Geography, Earth and Environmental Sciences at the University of Plymouth for providing an academically stimulating work environment (especial thanks to Neil Roberts, Ruth Weaver and Jim Griffiths) and, in particular, for enabling me to find the time beyond the duties of teaching and administration to successfully complete this book.

I am also indebted to staff at the cartographic unit of the School of Geography, Earth and Environmental Sciences, in particular Jamie Quinn who produced the figures and who patiently addressed regular suggestions for changes to these figures as the conceptual framework gradually unfolded. I am also deeply indebted to my editors Alison Kuznets (Earthscan) and Michael Jones (Taylor & Francis) for invaluable help with editorial aspects of the book, but also for urging me to complete the book before the agreed (generous) deadline. Finally, I also wish to acknowledge the beautiful landscape of south Devon where I and my family live. It has not only invited me to take relaxing breaks and cycle rides along the coastal footpaths while writing, but has also greatly inspired me to think about the challenges associated with strengthening community resilience.

Abbreviations

CAP	Common Agricultural Policy
GDP	Gross Domestic Product
EU	European Union
LETS	Local Exchange Trading Systems
NGOs	Non-governmental organizations
TTM	Transition Town Movement
UK	United Kingdom
UN	United Nations
USA	United States of America
WTO	World Trade Organization
WW2	World War Two

1 Introduction

The notion of 'resilience' is rapidly gaining ground as both a targeted process of societal development and as a research topic in its own right. Indeed, the notion of resilience may be beginning to replace 'sustainability' as the buzzword of political and policy-making rhetoric. Research has focused on different levels and scales of resilience. One strand has built on concepts established in research on the resilience of ecosystems (Holling, 1973) to understand resilience processes in interlinked social-ecological systems (Gunderson and Holling, 2002; Folke, 2006). Building on this work, in recent years increasing attention has been paid to issues of *social resilience* which attempts to understand how human systems respond to internal and external disturbances. As part of the latter, increasing focus has been placed on understanding the resilience of human communities, especially the analysis of resilience pathways at the *local level* where actions influencing resilience are among the most tangible (Chaskin, 2008; Gow and Paton, 2008). This book will focus on understanding community resilience, with specific emphasis on how complex environmental transitions increasingly shape communities' abilities to respond and react towards disturbances threatening their survival.

Research on social resilience is still in its infancy, and many key questions still remain unanswered (Brand and Jax, 2007; Davidson, 2010). Despite a plethora of publications on resilience, three key arenas of investigation linked to community resilience have received little attention. First, due to the relative novelty of the research field of social resilience, theoretical discussions about processes, drivers and indicators of social resilience are not yet fully developed (Adger, 2000; Davidson, 2010). This book will argue that theoretical concepts such as *transition theory* provide a particularly novel and suitable lens through which resilience pathways at community level can be better understood, especially as transition theory allows detailed analysis of changes in community resilience over space and time based on different models of transitions and pathways of change.

Second, little work exists on the possible interlinkages between community resilience and different forms of human and environmental capital. Folke (2006, p. 260) argued that "efforts to understand [the resilience of social-ecological systems] are still in an exploratory stage and there is opportunity for creative approaches and perspectives". As a result, this book will propose a novel framework focused on a social science approach for understanding community resilience as the conceptual space at the intersection between *economic, social* and *environmental capital*. It will be argued that this approach enables recognition of the importance of community-environmental interactions emphasized in work related to social-ecological resilience issues, but also acknowledging key resilience drivers linked to economic, socio-political, psychological and moral issues, as well as the importance of power relationships in human societies.

Third, while much work has discussed how communities respond and react towards sudden *natural* catastrophes such as hurricanes, earthquakes or volcanic eruptions (e.g. Pelling, 2003; Adger *et al.*, 2005a; Cutter *et al.*, 2008), there is much less work on resilience and 'slow-onset hazards' associated with *anthropogenic* drivers of change such as socio-political or economic change. This is despite the fact that, in recent history, anthropogenic drivers have led to the destruction of many more communities than natural catastrophes. For example, in the twentieth century alone, nearly 190 million people were killed in revolutions, wars and massacres (Pretty, 2007). Building on Berkes *et al.* (2003), this book is, therefore, concerned with discussing community resilience linked to *both* anthropogenic and natural disturbances that may have internal or external causes and that may be sudden or slow-onset disturbances.

There is no doubt that communities around the world are in transition. Drivers of change ranging from globalization, neo-liberal ideologies, to the spread of global capitalism to even the remotest parts of the world are amplified by climate change, population growth and the increasing movement of people within and across countries and continents. All these forces (and many others) act together in complex ways to influence development trajectories and, ultimately, resilience and vulnerability of communities. There is, therefore, increasing evidence that, at the beginning of the twenty-first century, humanity is at a crossroads with regard to environmental and societal transitions. After 10,000 years of environmental modification by agricultural societies, and over 200 years of industrial, social and environmental transformation, many studies point towards 'irreversible' degradation of many of Earth's resources (Blaikie and Brookfield, 1987; Pretty, 2007). Most prominent are environmental and social problems linked to climate change associated with anthropogenic carbon emissions, loss of biodiversity (especially in tropical forest environments) linked to habitat destruction for agricultural and extractive purposes, and large-scale environmental pollution problems associated with consumer-oriented capitalist lifestyles (Wilson and Bryant, 1997; Pretty, 2007). These problems are exacerbated by predicted shortages in energy availability, especially with regard to 'peak oil' scenarios and the need to reduce global carbon emissions (Hopkins, 2008; Mazmanian and Kraft, 2009).

At community level, these disturbances pose enormous challenges about how to tackle environmental and social changes, who should be in charge of making key decisions about possibly altering current 'unsustainable' lifestyles, and what institutional and policy-related mechanisms should be used to influence decision-making processes associated with strengthening resilience processes. In many communities, global climate change is already threatening survival, especially in areas where agricultural production is jeopardized by increasing frequency of droughts (e.g. Australia, parts of Africa; Adger, 2003; Cline, 2007; Kelkar *et al.*, 2008) or where sea-level rise is likely to destroy livelihoods (e.g. coral atolls in the Pacific Ocean) (Barnett and Adger, 2003). In developing countries, destruction of habitats and associated biodiversity reduction by agriculturalists needing to feed still rapidly rising populations (globally about 80 million more people have to be fed every year), or through multinational logging and mining companies often operating in weakly regulated environments (e.g. Papua New Guinea, Democratic Republic of Congo), is further threatening the livelihood base of many poor and politically/economically marginal communities (Bryant and Bailey, 1997; Pretty, 2007). In the developed world, and increasingly in many developing countries, environmental and social threats to communities are often associated with the dissolution of community networks and/or the outmigration of young people (Locke *et al.*, 2000; Hamilton *et al.*, 2004), leading to abandonment of complex environmental management systems (e.g. abandonment of terraced agricultural fields in the Mediterranean; lack of personpower to maintain wet rice terrace systems in south-east Asia), or to pollution problems associated with long-term exposure to threats such as pesticides, herbicides or industrial pollution (Wilson, 2007). In addition to environmental threats, many communities are also facing increasingly complex and severe social, political, cultural and economic disturbances that threaten community survival (Pelling, 2003).

This tension between social and environmental drivers of change and community resilience provides the framework for analysis in this book. How is community resilience influenced by these drivers of change? How can communities respond and adapt to such changes without sacrificing existing pathways of resilience? Who should be in charge at community level or beyond to tackle questions associated with community resilience? How can we better understand the complex interplay of factors, processes and drivers of change at community level, and what policy responses will be needed to raise the resilience of communities? How communities respond to these challenges will be at the heart of this book.

1.1 Resilience, transition theory, and economic, social and environmental capital

Much scientific work has discussed complex interactions with environmental and social drivers of change, both from a historical and contemporary perspective, and has analysed in detail the nature and extent of such interaction in different geographical settings (e.g. Turner *et al.*, 1990; Simmons, 1996; Pretty, 2007). There is an equal plethora of work that has analysed key drivers of environmental and social change and how communities have attempted to respond to and regulate their interactions with such disturbances (e.g. Wilson and Bryant, 1997; O'Riordan, 2001). Some of the most interesting examples include Diamond's (2006) analysis of anthropogenic environmental degradation and community collapse using a variety of case examples such as Easter Island (see Box 4.3), the Anaszasi in North America or Norse settlements on the west coast of Greenland (e.g. Seaver, 1996), or Gunderson and Holling's (2002) 'panarchic cycle' which – using concepts and theories from ecology – attempts to provide a conceptual framework for understanding both transformations in human and natural systems and how human communities can adapt to rapidly changing environmental and social conditions over time (adaptive cycle in human-ecological systems). Gunderson and Holling particularly ask how much redundancy is required by human systems to sustain the capacity to adapt in flexible ways to unpredictable disturbances, how to develop adaptive capacity in a world of rapidly changing information, technology and homogeneity created by globalization processes, and, most controversially, how societies can fundamentally change the basis of popular and scientific ideas to reflect evolutionary, adaptive and responsive perspectives.

One of the most interesting and challenging research approaches to emerge from this work relates to the notion of 'resilience' – the core concept analyzed in this book in the context of *community resilience*. Indeed, since the early 2000s, the notions of resilience and vulnerability have begun to provide an important conceptual framework to understand how communities respond and adapt to environmental and societal changes (Adger, 2006; Folke, 2006). As Chapter 2 will highlight, resilience is about the ability of a system to absorb impacts/disturbance and to reorganize into a fully functioning system, and about post-event adaptive processes. As a result, resilience has become a powerful notion that transcends both the natural and social sciences and that is increasingly used as a basis for policy-making. Community vulnerability, on the other hand, is a function of exposure and sensitivity of a system that is usually not able to cope with risks, hazards and slow or catastrophic change, leading eventually to the disappearance of the system or parts thereof (Cutter *et al.*, 2008).

Another key approach that has recently emerged is related to analyses of environmental and societal transitions (e.g. Aage, 1998; Martens and Rotmans, 2002; Wilson, 2007; Mazmanian and Kraft, 2009). Using *transition theory*, these authors have attempted to unravel changes over time in human-environment interactions, in particular with regard to transitional concepts such as path dependency, social memory and transitional corridors – concepts that have helped better understand the temporal and spatial dimensions associated with different human decision-making processes. Emphasis has been placed on understanding past pathways, present challenges, as well as future transitional processes. Transition theory is a general theory at the heart of which lie general principles, patterns and processes applicable across different fields (Pickles and Smith, 1998; Martens and Rotmans, 2002). Based on its wide-ranging applicability and holistic multidisciplinary approach, transition theory will form the second key approach in this book (see Chapter 3). Transitional concepts such as environmental pathways, social memory, path dependency and transitional corridors will form an important conceptual structure for the analysis presented in this book (see Chapters 4–7).

The third arena of research that informs the approach in this book relates to attempts to understand how human society organizes itself and is structured on the basis of various *capitals*. Bourdieu (1987) and Coleman (1988) popularized the notion of 'social capital', arguing that it is the 'glue' that holds communities together, i.e. the networks of interaction between individuals and stakeholder groups that form a community. Subsequently, other commentators have broadened out notions of 'capital', referring also to human capital (often used in the context of skills and knowledge available in a community), political capital (the inclusiveness of the political process and/or the extent of institutional and democratic processes) and cultural capital (society's historical memory and experience, the arts, or ideological standpoints of a community)[1], economic capital (the monetary and financial basis of a community), and environmental capital[2] (how well endowed a community or society is with natural resources, such as good soils, water or the availability of mineral resources). The interplay of these different capitals is seen by many to provide key explanations about human-environment decision-making processes and pathways (Wilson, 2010). For the purpose of this book, three main capitals will form the basis of the argument: economic capital, social/political/cultural capital and environmental capital. Although there is much debate about hierarchies and interdependencies between social/political/cultural capital, I will argue here – in line with other commentators (e.g. Adger, 2000; Abel *et al.*, 2006; Parnwell, 2007; Cutter *et al.*, 2008) – that the boundaries between the social, political and cultural spheres are blurred and that these form one type of capital characterized by complex social processes, political arenas and cultural factors. I will refer to these hereafter under the broad umbrella of *social capital*.

The argument in this book will be based on the assumption that resilient communities are characterized by well-developed *economic, social* and *environmental capital* (Bebbington and Perrault, 1999; Rigg, 2006; Bodin and Crona, 2008). In a rural community context, for example, Marsden (1999, p. 504) emphasized the importance of "understanding the balance of economic, social and environmental processes which shape the contemporary countryside, and the interrelationships between these in particular localities". Chaskin (2008) similarly argued that community resilience should be seen as a positive adaptive response to adversity where resilient actors (individuals and/or networks) are able to draw on economic, social and environmental capital to adapt successfully and, thus, are able to moderate or avoid the negative consequences that similar threats visit upon less resilient individuals or networks. Let us look in more detail how this book is attempting to understand community resilience and environmental transitions based on these different, but interlinked, approaches.

1.2 Aim of the book: understanding environmental and societal transitions at community level

The aim of this book is to bring together a transition theory approach with the two arenas of investigation of resilience/vulnerability and the three key types of 'capitals' (economic, social, environmental) in a novel way, thereby providing an *analytical framework* that helps better understand resilience and environmental and societal transitions over space and time at community level. Cutter *et al.* (2008, p. 604) argued that there is a need for further research in this arena, as despite various attempts "for describing and assessing resilience, none of [the] metaphorical and theoretical models have progressed to the operational stages where they effectively measure and monitor resilience at the local level". This book partly forms a critique of the often simplistic assumptions formulated in the natural science-dominated literature on resilience that assumes that human systems respond in similar ways to natural systems. Instead, this book will highlight that social resilience in human systems is inherently complex, non-linear and unpredictable, and that processes of social learning mean that a human system can never 'return' to its initial starting point.

The book has four key objectives:

1 To develop a conceptual model that will help anchor notions of community resilience in the context of economic, social and environmental capital over space and time (Chapter 2).

2 Using transition theory, to discuss a temporal and spatial model for environmental transition in different types of communities, ranging from subsistence farming communities to 'super-globalized' communities (Chapter 3).

3 Using examples from my own research in various geographical settings (especially New Zealand, Switzerland, Australia, the United Kingdom (UK), etc.), from preliminary insights of a European Union (EU)-funded project that investigates the relationships between community resilience and environmental degradation (LEDDRA, 2011), and from case studies published in the literature, to analyse how transitional notions of social memory, path dependency and transitional corridors aid or hinder the development of resilient communities (Chapters 4–6). I will discuss examples where communities have managed to strike the 'right' or 'wrong' balance between environmental exploitation and sustainable pathways, thereby resulting in either more resilient or vulnerable communities.

4 To analyse policy implications of different environmental and societal transitional pathways and to discuss how local communities can be made more resilient (Chapter 7).

Building on existing debates about community resilience, a *normative assessment* of 'good' and 'bad' community pathways will be provided. The book will, therefore, not only develop a conceptual model for understanding community pathways of environmental and societal change, but will also act as an explanatory tool and a normative ideal in the context of resilient communities. Throughout the book it will also become clear that any normative assessment of community resilience is imbued with pitfalls linked to cultural preferences about 'good' or 'bad' community pathways (Resilience Alliance, 2007). Although I will attempt to adopt an objective stance with regard to the identification of the 'ingredients' for community resilience (see Chapter 2), inevitably some of the indicators discussed here will not necessarily be applicable in all community settings. This echoes work by Rigg (2006) and Rigg *et al.* (2008) who, for the global South, have rightly cautioned that researchers also need to be careful about approaches used in studies of community resilience. Indeed, what may be an indicator of strong resilience for one individual may not be good for another, for the household, and possibly even less so for the community as a whole (Oudenhoven *et al.*, 2010). Nonetheless, as Chapter 7 will discuss, normative judgements about 'good' or 'bad' environmental pathways can form important baselines for policy action, despite the fact that community resilience will mean different things to different people – in other words, a complex geography of policy needs with regard to harnessing community resilience will inevitably emerge.

The focus for this study will be placed on the *local community* level, as it is at this level that resilient pathways (social resilience) are implemented 'on the ground' (Adger et al., 2005a; Wilson, 2009; see Chapter 2). The justification for this is both analytical and pragmatic. Over the past two decades, there has been a resurgence in attention to community as a critical arena for addressing a range of issues, including environmental and societal pathways of change (Agrawal and Gibson, 1999; Chaskin, 2008). Indeed, many argue that it is important to understand environmental action at the local level first, before scaling-up to regional, national and global environmental decision-making levels (O'Riordan, 2001; Oudenhoven *et al.*, 2010). As Siegle and Borden (2011, p. 30) argued in the context of the most appropriate level for societal change, "it is working together as communities where real change will happen", while Neal (2009, p. 85) argued that "community is one of those routes through which the behaviour and conduct of populations is regulated, and where people learn to regulate themselves". The pragmatic justification, therefore, refers to scale issues and notions of 'open' versus 'closed' systems (see Section 2.4). However, the focus on the community level is also justified by Adger's (2000, p. 348) earlier criticism of previous work on resilience where "the concept of resilience has not effectively been brought across the disciplinary divide to examine the meaning of resilience of a community".

There has been substantial debate about the meaning and constituents of the notion of 'community', about communities as 'open' and 'unbounded' systems rather than 'closed' easily identifiable geographical entities (such as a 'village community'), and that 'community' is largely an attitudinal construct that means different things to different people (Tönnies, 1963; Agrawal and Gibson, 1999). Indeed, Neal (2009), in her study of rural communities in the UK, emphasized that the notion of 'community' has nearly a hundred different definitions. In particular, the recent rise of web-based 'virtual communities' suggests that many communities are no longer defined by geographical space but by internet-based interconnections (Castells, 1996). Although these virtual communities form an increasingly important part of global society, this book will restrict itself to the discussion of resilience and environmental pathways of *geographically bounded* communities (e.g. an 'urban', 'rural' or 'village community' with which residents can still more or less identify through the existence of a community centre with locality-specific services) (see Tönnies, 1963, and Staeheli, 2008, for good discussions about the problematic notion of 'community'). Based on Kumar (2005) and Cutter *et al.* (2008), communities will be seen here as the totality of social system interactions (i.e. an affective unit of belonging and identity and a network of relations) usually within a defined geographical space. However, there are many different communities *within* such spaces (Tönnies, 1963; Kumar, 2005), embedded within complex networks of power and with often highly divergent aims related to environmental pathways (Allen, 2003).

With these caveats in mind, communities can be conceptually treated as 'more closed' systems than analysis of regional-, national- or global-level environmental transitions would permit (see Section 2.4 for a more detailed discussion). Although communities vary immensely with regard to both population numbers and geographical scale of their environmental and societal interactions (e.g. a remote small subsistence farming community comprised of a few families versus an urban community in New York), open systems have more 'escape values' with regard to both in- and outflow of people/resources/energy which makes analysis of the characteristics of resilience and environmental transitions very complex. This book should, therefore, be seen as extending existing work that has attempted to conceptualize environmental/societal transitions and resilience at a local scale (e.g. Smith and Wishnie, 2000; Carrier, 2004), and as a basis for further studies aimed at 'scaling up' questions addressing regional-, national- and global-level resilience (see also Chapter 8).

It is evident that any framework attempting to identify the characteristics of environmental/societal pathways leading to community resilience or vulnerability based on a normative framework needs to acknowledge the importance of a *researcher's positionality* and cultural embeddedness when making value judgements about community transitions. A more reflexive approach will have implications for the construction of knowledge, and particularly requires sensitivity to the relationships between power, authority and positionality. Echoing Demeritt's (2009) recent call, only through a *multi-disciplinary* approach is it possible to fully understand environmental transitions and drive forward constructive agendas for the future. This will have important repercussions for the selection of appropriate methodologies to assess environmental transitions, and it is evident that any investigation of community resilience requires the use of a multi-method approach (see Section 2.5). I, as a middle-aged white researcher from a European background, will inevitably have some idealized notions about what an 'ideal' community should look like, the 'best' environmental/social pathways a community could choose (given adequate resources) and how economic, social and environmental capital could 'best' be harnessed to maximize community resilience. Although I will attempt to remain as objective as possible and to use examples from various geographical and cultural settings to illustrate various points, there is no doubt that some of my assumptions about the characteristics of resilient communities (see Tables 2.1 and 2.2) may not resonate well with all the readers of this book. Inevitably, therefore, some of the arguments in this book will be controversial. Indeed, one of the aims of the book is to stir up debate, and for future commentators to use the book as a platform to refute or refine ideas expressed here, in particular with regard to critical engagement with notions of community resilience, 'ideal' environmental/social pathways of change, and what may constitute 'preferred' community transitions.

My positionality will particularly become apparent in arguments linked to the impacts of globalization and the global capitalist system on community pathways. I will not hide the fact that – in line with many other critical commentators (e.g. Stiglitz, 2002; Castree, 2008b) – this book will also form a critique of how the contemporary global capitalist system and globalization processes often *negatively* affect environmental/societal transitions and community trajectories. In line with authors such as Jones (1997), Mander and Goldsmith (2000), Stiglitz (2002) or Aggarwal (2006), this book will, therefore, adopt an explicitly critical stance towards the negative aspects of both globalization and the increasing embeddedness of many communities into the global capitalist system. I will, therefore, side more with the anti-globalization argument, although I will also concede that many non-globalized communities, facing extreme pressures linked to external drivers such as climate change, may not be in a position to raise resilience without financial (and other) help from the more globalized rest of the world (see Chapter 3). In addition, the environmental philosophy underpinning this book is based on an approach that can best be described as situated between the 'sustainable development' and the 'green romanticism/survivalism' paradigm on Bailey and Wilson's (2009) spectrum of environmental decision-making. This approach, which sees humans more as a malign than benign force shaping environmental transitions, argues that the emphasis on markets, commodification and competition enshrined in the global capitalist system ill-equips many communities to deal effectively or equitably with environmental and other issues, and criticizes Promethean/ecological modernization views predicated on technocentric 'quick fix' solutions. This highlights that it is impossible to talk *dispassionately* about the global forces that increasingly shape community resilience – for better or for worse.

To address these issues, the book will draw on many examples to illustrate how different types of communities (urban and rural communities from both the developed and developing worlds) address resilience. This will include case studies of forced and voluntary migration of communities and how this can impact on community-level environmental/societal transitions (including evidence from my own research conducted in New Zealand in the late 1980s and subsequent work), examples from the burgeoning literature on the 'Transition Town Movement' (the initiator of which was one of my PhD students; see Hopkins, 2008, 2010), or examples from my involvement in a European project (LEDDRA, 2011) investigating interlinkages between desertification and community resilience in countries such as China, Morocco, Italy, Spain and Greece. Inevitably, these 'case studies' (and others referred to in the book) will be selective and will reflect my own research background, networks, research project interlinkages and personal preferences. This will mean that the focus of the book will be more on rural than urban communities (linked to my research focus on rural geography), and more on the developed than the developing world (with a specific focus on Europe, New Zealand and Australia), although I will also attempt to broaden the discussion and case study examples to the developing world. Some readers will, therefore, quite rightly point towards other examples and case studies that may lead to different conclusions – a process which I, again, invite and encourage as part of seeing this book as a basis for further critical studies on questions about environmental/societal transitions and community resilience.

With its specific focus on environmental transitions and community resilience, this book assumes that readers will have some general background knowledge about issues of environmental and social change, human environmental decision-making processes, and how communities may respond to environmental and social threats and transitions. The book will, therefore, particularly appeal to academic specialists and professionals in the fields of environmental/societal transition and community resilience at global and local scales, advanced and/or graduate university students in the social and environmental sciences, and a wide range of national and international scholars or professionals in disciplines including particularly geography, environmental sociology, environmental science, environmental psychology, political science, economics and environmental history.

1.3 Community resilience and anthropogenic and natural disturbances

Before proposing how to conceptualize community resilience in Chapter 2, we first need to be clear about which internal and external forces can influence community resilience. Such forces are referred to in various ways in the literature, including 'threats', 'stresses', 'shocks', 'perturbations', 'disasters', hazards', 'disruptions', 'disturbances', etc. (Folke, 2006; Forbes *et al.*, 2009; Magis, 2010). In this book, I will use the relatively neutral notion of *disturbances*, based on the argument that community resilience is affected by *both* anthropogenic (human-induced) and natural disturbances (Adger, 2000; Resilience Alliance, 2007; Davidson, 2010). Without claiming to be exhaustive, Figure 1.1 shows examples of such disturbances. Natural disturbances are often associated with the notion of 'disasters' and can be classified into weather-related (e.g. naturally induced climate change, cold weather events, hurricanes, droughts/desertification, floods) and geological disasters (e.g. landslides, earthquakes, tsunamis, volcanic eruptions, meteorite impacts). Anthropogenic disturbances include processes associated with human environmental mismanagement (e.g. human-induced climate change, pollution, human-induced desertification, biodiversity depletion), socio-political disturbances (e.g. wars, revolutions, shifts in power/governance structures), economic disturbances (e.g. shifts in global trade, recessions/depressions) and disturbances linked to globalization processes (e.g.

modernization, technological change, loss of socio-cultural values, etc.). In recent years, disturbances associated with energy availability have received increasing attention in the critical literature, especially related to what has been termed the 'peak oil' crisis (the predicted rapid decline in availability of cheap oil) and how communities are able to reduce their dependency on energy sources beyond the immediate locality (Hopkins, 2008; Bailey *et al.*, 2010).

Not all disturbances shown in Figure 1.1 are necessarily negative for community resilience. As Chapters 3 and 6 will discuss in detail, disturbances associated with globalization processes are particularly open to debate, and some processes, such as technological change, can of course also *positively* influence community resilience. The disturbances shown in Figure 1.1 can have both *internal* (i.e. within the community; e.g. local pollution) and *external* causes (i.e. outside the community; e.g. hurricanes, wars), and include both *sudden catastrophic disturbances* (e.g. earthquakes) as well as *slow-onset disturbances* such as climate change or shifts in global trade (Cumming *et al.*, 2005, 2006). The

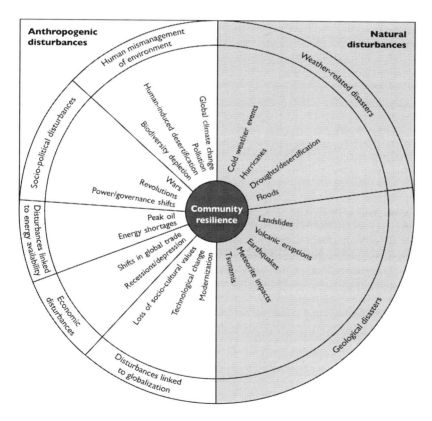

Figure 1.1 Examples of anthropogenic and natural disturbances affecting community resilience. (Source: author)

complexity of disturbances affecting communities suggests that communities are never 'stable', but that they are continuously and simultaneously affected by several disturbances at any point in time. As Chapter 3 will discuss in detail, communities can, therefore, never reach 'maximum' resilience levels but can only strive towards the highest level of resilience achievable within community-specific contexts.

1.4 Structure of the book

The structure of the book will mirror the adopted conceptual approach. Chapter 2 will first provide a framework for understanding community resilience based on economic, social and environmental capital, and will discuss characteristics of resilience/vulnerability applicable in community contexts around the world. The chapter will also include a discussion of community resilience and 'open' and 'closed' systems, with a focus on the conceptual difference between 'geographical' and 'socio-cultural' boundaries of communities, as well as a detailed discussion about methodological approaches to assess community resilience. Chapter 3 will then introduce the notion of transition theory and will explain why it is an important approach for understanding the link between environmental pathways and community resilience. A model will be presented which will suggest that, over time, many local communities around the world have lost resilience based on both increased embeddedness into a globalized world and the global capitalist system, and because of increasing global environmental challenges such as climate change. The chapter will also discuss some relocalized environmental pathways (e.g. the Transition Towns Movement) attempting to re-engage with environmental practices that may raise community resilience.

Chapters 4–6 will then focus on three key transitional concepts and their interlinkages with community resilience. The focus of Chapter 4 will be on 'social memory' and its importance for understanding how the past memory of a community shapes contemporary and future environmental pathways. Several case studies will be examined to illustrate how social memory can both positively or negatively affect environmental trajectories (e.g. New Zealand pioneer settler communities; Australian Aborigines; subsistence farming communities). Chapter 5 will then look at the issue of 'path dependency' and environmental transitions at community level. The focus will be on endogenous constraints and opportunities for individual and community-based environmental decision-making processes and on 'lock-in' effects that make certain community pathways unthinkable and impossible to implement. The chapter will highlight that although many communities would like to change their environmental trajectories, they are often constrained because of path dependency inherent in the community itself through factors such as entrenched customs, habits, conservatism, negative attitudes or lethargic behaviour. Several case study examples from around the world will be discussed to highlight how some communities have managed to radically change their environmental trajectories ('transitional ruptures'), while other examples will illustrate how many communities remain 'stuck' on pathways that may inexorably lead to increased vulnerability. Chapter 6 will build on this discussion by analysing exogenous macro-structural processes (e.g. ideology, economics and politics) and how these can constrain community-level environmental decision-making. The notion of 'transitional corridors' will be analysed and why these corridors are important for understanding community resilience. Specific issues to be discussed will, for example, include transitional corridors influenced by external factors and actors such as the region or the state, governance structures, and global drivers such as neoliberal ideologies or the capitalist system.

Chapter 7 will provide a synthesis of discussions in Chapters 4–6 by investigating more specifically the policy challenge – i.e. how to make local communities more resilient. Policy will be looked at in its widest sense as both an enabling and disenabling force, depending on political structures, the strengths and weaknesses of scalar interlinkages between the community, the region and the nation, and inclusive/non-inclusive governance structures. Case study examples from both the North and South, and from democratic and non-democratic countries, will be used to illustrate the complexities of the policy challenge. Chapter 8 will conclude the book and will point towards avenues for future research.

2 Towards a framework for understanding community resilience

2.1 Introduction

The aim of this chapter is twofold. First, it will provide an analytical framework based on notions of economic, social and environmental capital and how these may help conceptualize resilience at community level (Section 2.2). Second, the chapter will discuss different characteristics of community resilience and vulnerability that may find applicability in any geographical setting (Section 2.3). The aim will particularly be to highlight the complexity of interactions of different characteristics that make up a resilient community and to discuss the importance of interlinkages between economic, social and environmental processes as a basis for understanding community transitions over time (Chapter 3). Section 2.4 will then focus on scalar issues for understanding community resilience, in particular with regard to communities as partly 'open' systems that can obtain skills, services and resources from 'outside' the confines of the physical community boundary. Section 2.5 will discuss how we can 'measure' the resilience of communities by giving methodological insight into a recent EU-funded research project investigating community resilience and land degradation. Section 2.6 will provide concluding remarks.

2.2 Conceptualizing community resilience at the intersection between economic, social and environmental capital

This section will first discuss the notion of 'resilience', both from its roots in ecology and through its subsequent application to social-ecological and social systems (Section 2.2.1). Section 2.2.2 will then highlight how social resilience is linked to economic, social and environmental capital as the three key processes that provide the basis within which community-level responses to disturbances are framed and implemented.

2.2.1 Ecological, social-ecological and social resilience

The notion of 'resilience' has been analyzed from different disciplinary vantage points, and any discussion of 'resilience' needs to acknowledge the subjective nature of the term. Anderies *et al.* (2006, p. 8) highlighted that it is not appropriate to describe resilience-based research as a 'theory', but as a "collection of ideas about how to interpret complex systems". Several approaches have been used to conceptualize resilience and, broadly speaking, three key approaches can be identified. As Folke (2006) highlighted in his analysis of the genesis of resilience as a research topic, during the late 1960s and early 1970s the term focused first on notions of *ecological resilience* (from the Latin 'resilire' = to leap back, rebound or recoil) which was about how ecosystems responded to disturbances, whereby the vitality of a system was not seen to be defined as the ability to reach a 'climax' but rather in terms of evolutionary change (e.g. Holling, 1973). Brand and Jax (2007) highlighted that research into ecological resilience was largely descriptive and non-normative, but that it since has been frequently redefined and extended to promote research across disciplines and between science and policy.

Resilience research between the late 1970s and 1990s began to focus on an extended ecological resilience definition strongly influenced by the theory of complex adaptive systems which investigated whether ecological resilience could be applied to human systems under the umbrella of *social-ecological resilience*. Brand and Jax (2007) argued that this marked the beginning of the notion of resilience as a 'boundary object' between the natural and social sciences. An important part of this research was Gunderson and Holling's (2002) seminal concept of 'panarchy' which took fast/slow resilience dynamics and cross-scale interactions and interdependencies into account, and provided a heuristic model of four nested adaptive cycles of resilience emphasizing cross-scale interplay ranging from periods of exponential exchange, periods of growing stasis and rigidity, periods of readjustment and collapse, and periods of reorganization and renewal (Folke, 2006; Resilience Alliance, 2007). The Resilience Alliance – an international consortium of 15 research groups and institutes from many disciplines who collaborate to explore the resilience of social-ecological systems – have since expanded this work and have suggested several methods and approaches to analyze the resilience of interlinked social-ecological systems (e.g. Cumming *et al.*, 2006; Kinzig *et al.*, 2006; Walker *et al.*, 2006; Resilience Alliance, 2007, 2009). They have particularly highlighted that the delineation between social and environmental systems that marred earlier ecological resilience research is highly artificial (Forbes *et al.*, 2009).

Building on this, the generally accepted *definition of resilience* has been

the capacity of a system to absorb disturbance and reorganize while undergoing change to still retain essentially the same function, structure, identity, and feedbacks ... resilience is measured by the size of the displacement the system can tolerate and yet return to a state where a given function can be maintained

(e.g. Forbes *et al.*, 2009, p. 22041; see also Adger, 2003; Folke, 2006; Walker and Salt, 2006). In other words, "if system identity is maintained over the time horizon of interest under specified conditions and perturbations, we can term the system resilient" (Cumming *et al.*, 2005, p. 978). Resilience, therefore, is an *emergent property* – a relative attribute characterized by responses to disturbances which can only be assessed by looking at changes in a system over time. Qualities of resilience are evident in the notion of *adaptive capacity*, which is generally used to analyze how a system does, or does not, respond to endogenous and exogenous changes and is defined as "the ability of a system to adjust to change, moderate the effects, and cope with a disturbance" (Cutter *et al.*, 2008, p. 600). A system characterized by diversity, potential for change (level of redundancy in the system) and by connectedness (feedbacks, flexibility) usually has better adaptive capacity (Folke, 2006; Resilience Alliance, 2007).

However, the approach used in the social-ecological resilience framework has been criticized for relying too heavily "on the idea that complex system behaviours in multivariate space will typically fall within a stability domain around an attractor" (Cumming *et al.*, 2005, p. 978) – behaviours that may not necessarily be true for the resilience of human systems (Abel *et al.*, 2006; Hastrup, 2009). Oudenhoven *et al.* (2010, p. 163) also argued that " 'measuring' social-ecological resilience is challenging, particularly because in order to clarify features that contribute to it, institutional and organizational processes must be understood as carefully as ecological ones". Folke (2006, p. 254), therefore, rightly argued that research integration on resilience between natural and social science approaches "is still in its infancy". Social scientists have felt particularly uncomfortable with notions of linearity and 'measurable' resilience responses assumed to be equally present in both social and ecological systems. As Adger (2000, p. 347) highlighted, "it is not clear whether resilient ecosystems enable resilient communities". This was echoed by Davidson (2010, p. 1142) who argued that "the Panarchy model implies that in the absence of disturbances, systems will tend toward increasing complexity [but] several problems arise with the transfer of this model to social systems", and that "the application of the [social-ecological] resilience framework to social systems will require improved articulation of the … multiple relationships … between complexity and disturbance in a less deterministic manner than is afforded by ecological systems". As a result, she also argued "the means by which social systems can be readily cast into the ecological terms encompassed by the resilience framework must be critically examined" (Davidson, 2010, p. 1141) – a challenge which this book aims to address. Thus,

> while the structural complexity of both ecological and social systems can be conceived of in similar terms, the feedback processes associated with each are incomparable: social systems are unique in that the tendencies toward complexity, and the responses of individual organisms to those levels of complexity, are defined not solely by structural variables, but by agency.
>
> (Davidson, 2010, p. 1142)

In this sense, the four nested adaptive cycles suggested in the deterministic ecosystems-oriented panarchy cycle (see above) may not occur in a linear fashion in human systems, but simultaneously with strongly overlapping and, at times, contradictory behaviours associated with less predictable human agency.

The result of these criticisms has been an emergent third strand of resilience research focused on the resilience of human systems and communities, referred to as *social resilience* (Adger, 2000; Brand and Jax, 2007; Davidson, 2010). The focus of this book on *community resilience* is, therefore, a subset of research on social resilience defined "as the ability of groups or communities to cope with external stresses and disturbances as a result of social, political and environmental change" (Adger, 2000, p. 347), or, in Cutter *et al.*'s (2008, p. 599) words, is about

> the ability of a social system to respond and recover from disasters and includes those inherent conditions that allow the system to absorb impacts and cope with an event, as well as post-event, adaptive processes that facilitate the ability of the social system to re-organize, change, and learn in response to a threat.

Folke (2006, p. 255) highlighted that social resilience is about the necessity of human systems to learn to manage by change and that it implies that "uncertainty and surprise is part of the game". Social/community resilience can be both preventative (avoiding poor outcomes by developing coping strategies), or it may facilitate recovery after a traumatic event or catastrophe. It is also about whether the worst-off stakeholder group (i.e. economically or politically weak groups within a community) can recover from a disturbance without necessarily reducing the well-being of any other community-based institution or individuals. The notion of social resilience, therefore, assesses how communities develop adaptive capacity to respond to endogenous disturbances (e.g. political upheaval, revolutions) or exogenous threats (e.g. climate change, volcanic eruptions, flooding) discussed in Chapter 1 (Adger, 2000; Magis, 2010). Although understanding human-environment interactions continues to form a crucial component of these approaches, research on social resilience is often based on a 'bottom-up' approach predicated on understanding human drivers and indicators of resilience, of which human-environment interactions are only one of many components. Rival (2009, p. 296), therefore, argued that we need "to question resilience theorists for a lack of attention to power relations, politics, and culture". As a result, social resilience research usually focuses more on the importance of politics, power and socio-economic, psychological and moral parameters than 'traditional' social-ecological resilience research (Adger, 2000; Bonnano, 2004; Cumming *et al.*, 2005).

There are obvious differences between the more ecologically informed notions of social-ecological resilience and those attempting to understand social resilience related, in particular, to issues of linearity/non-linearity (Resilience Alliance, 2007). A key issue of non-linearity, for example, relates to the assumption that human systems can *never* return to their *original* state after disturbance (which ecosystems may be able to do) due to social learning processes and social memory (Adger, 2000; Davidson, 2010; Magis, 2010). In human systems, therefore, adaptations can be both anticipatory or reactive, and depending on their degree of spontaneity they can be ad hoc or planned (Smit and Wandel, 2006). Lebel *et al.* (2006, p. 4), therefore, argued that "the capacity to cope with non-linearities or other forms of surprise and uncertainty requires an openness to learning, an acceptance of the inevitability of change, and the ability to treat interventions as experiments". Similarly, Smit and Wandel (2006, p. 282; emphasis added) argued that

> adaptation in the context of human dimensions of global change usually refers to a process, action or outcome in a system (household, community, group, sector, region, country) in order for the system to *better* cope with, manage or adjust to some changing condition, stress, hazard, risk or opportunity.

This notion of 'better coping' highlights that social learning implies human adjustment processes that propel the post-disturbance system to a different (sometimes 'better') state (Rival, 2009; Oudenhoven *et al.*, 2010). As this book will highlight, this has crucial implications for the 'management' of community resilience (see Chapter 7), as the goal for adaptive capacity after a disturbance should often *not* be to attempt to reinstate the original state but to use learning processes and social memory as a basis for the creation of a *qualitatively different* more resilient community. Thus, while technological adaptation to a disturbance is usually seen as an easier process (e.g. engineering solutions towards sea-level rise), human attitudinal and behavioural adaptation is much more complex and usually takes much longer (e.g. changing recognition that there is a 'problem').

Social resilience is, therefore, about pre-emptive change which sees resilience as a *desirable state*, rather than simply a process to avoid disturbances. This is exemplified by Davidson's (2010, p. 1146) suggestion that

> rather than directing our attention primarily to identifying and prescribing conditions of sustainability, the [social] resilience framework directs our attention to information flows and cycles of change, exploring how our current institutions and connecting structures are likely to respond to disturbance, and how we can prepare for those outcomes.

The notion of social resilience is, thus, strongly focused on human *learning* pathways and how these may affect the resilience of communities. Resilience in this view is both an *outcome*, especially when linked to improved adaptive capacity of communities, and a *process* linked to dynamic changes over time associated with community learning and the willingness of communities to take responsibility and control of their development pathways (Chaskin, 2008). It is this importance of human agency which "defines an additional conceptual layer not present in ecological systems, and consequently not reflected in ecological theories of resilience ... Our agency distinguishes social systems from ecosystems" (Davidson, 2010, pp. 1142–1143). Indeed, "human agency is the most contentious wrinkle in the application of an ecological framework to social systems" (ibid., p. 1145). While the ecological resilience literature has focused more on the ability of systems to return to function after a disturbance, social resilience is, therefore, about seeing disturbances as an opportunity for *change* and *development*. Magis (2010, p. 404) thus argued that the focus on social resilience "shifts attention from controlling change in presumably stable community systems to managing the capacity of dynamic communities to cope with, adapt and shape change", and Hopkins (2010, p. 75) similarly suggested that

> addressing [social] resilience is not just about preserving systems as they are, and retaining their existing functions. Given human communities' ability to anticipate change, and given the inevitability of some of the changes facing humanity ... there is also a great opportunity for innovation.

Cutter *et al.* (2008) highlighted that the notion of social resilience is essentially about understanding a 'positive' quality of a community under investigation, not dissimilar to the notion of 'strong sustainability' (e.g. Ekins *et al.*, 2003). As a result, understanding social resilience is more closely associated with normative judgements about 'good resilience' and 'bad vulnerability' (Brand and Jax, 2007; Resilience Alliance, 2007). The close association of resilience with the ability of a human system to absorb impacts/disturbance and to re-organize into a fully functioning (but qualitatively different) system is, therefore, closely associated with the notion of 'positive' quality, while community vulnerability – usually used to describe exposure and sensitivity of a human system not able to cope with risks, hazards and slow or catastrophic change – is generally associated with 'negative' quality (Adger, 2000, 2006). Brand and Jax (2007, p. 10), therefore argued that "a broad concept of resilience includes normative dimensions". In contrast to ecological systems where resilience can be seen as an ideal linear end-point, some human systems such as 'resilient malign dictatorships' (i.e. a resilient system that maintains a malign dictator), or 'resilient malign ideologies' (where ideologies [e.g. Nazism] can be resilient to change), can be resilient in a 'negative' context for the well-being of communities/ societies (i.e. 'bad resilience') (Davidson, 2010). As Folke (2006) suggested, researchers involved with social resilience research increasingly, therefore, avoid the use of terms such as 'recovery' and prefer concepts of 'renewal', 'regeneration' and 'reorganization' following disturbance.

The latter point highlights that, from a social resilience perspective, resilience/vulnerability are, therefore, intricately linked to notions of 'good' or 'bad' community development pathways. Although several concepts of the interlinkages between resilience and vulnerability have been used (see Gallopin, 2006, or Cutter *et al.*, 2008, for good summaries), resilience/vulnerability can be expressed as a simple *spectrum* (Figure 2.1) (Smit and Wandel, 2006; Magis, 2010). Extreme ends of a spectrum are usually most easily conceptualized. For example, few would contest that the complete disappearance of a community due to destruction of the livelihood base (e.g. depletion of soils leading to desertification), or a malign dictatorship that has negative implications for the well-being of most of its citizens, can be seen as a 'bad' development pathway associated with extremely vulnerable communities (Oudenhoven *et al.*, 2010). This highlights that, ultimately, *normative moral judgements* based on our conceptualization of social resilience are generally rooted in measures of human survival – e.g. complete disappearance of a community means no resilience (Cumming *et al.*, 2005; Van Rheenen and Mengistu, 2009). However, as Gallopin (2006) emphasized, these normative assumptions become more blurred as we move along the spectrum shown in Figure 2.1. As Section 2.3 will discuss, it is more difficult to find a common understanding of 'good' development pathways associated with resilient communities. Indeed, as Pirsig (1974) argued, any notion of *quality* (such as resilience/vulnerability) is relational and, therefore, always subjective – in other words, different individuals and stakeholder groups will view quality in different ways. As the following will highlight, finding a commonly or cross-culturally acceptable definition of a strongly resilient community is, therefore, almost impossible.

2.2.2 Social resilience and economic, social and environmental capital

As various commentators have suggested, community resilience and vulnerability can best be conceptualized on the basis of how well different 'capitals' are developed in a community, in particular the three key arenas of economic, social and environmental capital ('social' including 'political' and 'cultural' capital; see Chapter 1) (see also Adger, 2000; Western *et al.*, 2005; Kinzig *et al.*, 2006; Magis, 2010). As Abel *et al.* (2006, p. 3) argued, "the concept of capital links resilience theory to economics, sociology, ecology, [and] broader discussions about sustainability". The Resilience Alliance (2007, p. 38) similarly suggested that "a useful way to envision [a] system's resilience and adaptability ... is to consider the levels of and changes in the 'pools' of various capitals", while Magis (2010, p. 406) argued that "capitals are community resources that are strategically invested in collective endeavours to address shared community objectives". This approach, therefore, does not conflict with the 'classical' resilience definitions highlighted above. Instead, it further complements existing approaches as it enables both a recognition of the importance of community-environmental interactions emphasized in work related to social-ecological

resilience   **vulnerability**

Figure 2.1 Resilience and vulnerability as opposite ends of a spectrum (source: author).

resilience issues (e.g. Gunderson and Holling, 2002; Resilience Alliance, 2007), as well as acknowledging key resilience drivers linked to economic, socio-political, psychological and, indeed, moral issues (Cumming *et al.*, 2005; Cutter *et al.*, 2008).

To conceptualize social resilience and vulnerability at the intersection of various capitals, it is useful to briefly interrogate Bourdieu's (1987) multifaceted theory of capital as a macro-analytical framework. Bourdieu argued that the focus on economic capital has been due largely to the unambiguous immediacy and transparency of economic exchanges, and that, consequently, this has meant that other forms of accumulated labour (in particular capital in an embodied state) have tended to be neglected. In an attempt to redefine capital, Bourdieu proposed the existence of capital in three fundamental guises: as economic capital (material property), social capital (networks of social connections and mutual obligations) and cultural capital (prestige). In this framework, individuals and groups are seen to acquire or lose social, cultural, symbolic and economic capital, whereby capital is used both as a metaphor and a description of actual processes (i.e. capital as 'embodied labour') and as a culturally sensitive under-standing of power (see also Harvey, 2006, who recognized the need to go beyond labour theory of value to understand the notion of 'capital'). Although these concepts of capital have been widely used in studies over the past decades, the notion of social capital has since been extended to include all *non-monetized* attributes of cultural capital, social networks, complex notions of power, the rel-ative inter-connectedness of people, and characteristics such as 'trust' and the cultural and institutional 'glue' that binds communities together (Putnam, 1993; Fine, 2001; Bodin and Crona, 2008). Bryant (2005, p. 33) thus argued that "social capital has become a kind of benchmark for the ills of modern society in that its perceived absence becomes an indicator of decline". *Bonding* and *bridg-ing* forms of social capital are seen as particularly important, with the former emphasizing the importance of the *strengthening* of community networks, and the latter highlighting the importance of the *widening* of community stakeholder interactions (Adger, 2000; Sarkissian *et al.*, 2010).

Other notions of capital including 'economic' and 'environmental' capital have, in turn, been used to conceptualize economic, environmental and resource-based attributes of societal interactions (e.g. Thampapillai and Uhlin, 1997; Harvey, 2006). Sociologists and geographers in particular have extended Bourdieu's notion of economic capital to include not only forms of mercantile transactions, but also all human attributes associated with the use and generation of monetary capital (e.g. the monetary value of the built environment in a com-munity). In this sense, social capital can also be converted into economic capital and vice versa. The notion of 'environmental capital' is a more recent addition to the family of capitals, and has been used largely by ecologists, biologists, human geographers and anthropologists to conceptualize attributes of human-environment interaction linked to the availability and sustainable use of natural resources for human consumption (e.g. soil or water quality, availability of forest resources for a community, etc.) (e.g. Costanza, 1992; Harte, 1995; Thampapillai and Uhlin, 1997; Forbes *et al.*, 2009). The conversion of environmental and economic capital into social capital is highly dependent on *power relations* within a community, in particular power as an inscribed capacity to control or direct the actions of others (power possessed by an individual or group within a community), and power as a resource mobilized to achieve desired objectives within a community (Allen, 1997, 2003; see also Section 5.3). Power is rarely symmetrical within a community, and specific stakeholder groups or individuals will almost always attempt to exert their specific views of community-level pathways over others through force, manipulation, persuasion and authority (Granovetter, 1985; Peterson, 2000).

As the critical literature emphasizes, economic, social and environmental capital can be seen as the 'glue' that holds society together. Building on the 'triple bottom line' of sustainability (economic, social and environmental) (e.g. Redclift, 1987; Adams, 1990), these *three pillars of resilience* are increasingly seen as fundamental for understanding community-level processes (e.g. Adger, 2000; Cutter *et al.*, 2008; Ostrom, 2009). As part of the normative approach associated with understanding community resilience used in this book, the notions of 'strongly' and 'weakly' developed capital will be used throughout discussion in this book to denote well or poorly developed capitals at community level.

First, *economic capital* is the key foundation of financial and economic well-being of a community (Adger, 2000). Bourdieu (1987) defined economic capital as monetary income and financial assets, while Magis (2010, pp. 406–407) argued that economic capital "refers to the financial resources available to be invested in the community for business development, civic and social enterprise, and wealth accumulation". Factors such as availability of funding, high levels of community or household income, well-developed community infrastructure or well-established trade flows, are usually associated with strong economic capital (Bardhan, 2006). Economic capital has been an important indicator for community well-being since the emergence of *Homo sapiens* (e.g. bartering, exchange of goods, availability of food stocks, etc.), but has arguably assumed ever greater importance since the spread of global capitalism in the nineteenth and twentieth century (Gray, 2002; Carrier, 2004). Indeed, economic capital has become so important in modern society that some critical commentators have argued that economic indicators have been overemphasized in assessments of community resilience (Read, 2004; Young *et al.*, 2006).

Second, the notion of *social capital* emerged in the 1980s as one of the key sociological foundations for community survival and generally describes how well social, political and cultural networks are developed in a community (Coleman, 1988; Western *et al.*, 2005). Bourdieu (1987) defined social capital as capital mobilized through social networks and relations, while Magis (2010, p. 407) argued that "social capital refers to the ability and willingness of community members to participate in actions directed to community objectives, and to processes of engagement". Indeed, many sociologists and geographers see well-developed social capital as the key ingredient for resilient communities, especially in the context of bonding (group cohesion), bridging (ties between groups), linking (vertical relationships), and capitals (e.g. Pretty and Ward, 2001; Magis, 2010). Strong social ties, well-established trust and participatory, inclusive and democratic processes, are generally seen as key ingredients for strong social capital without which it is difficult for communities to thrive (Beierle and Cayford, 2002). Political capital may be the most contentious issue here (see Chapters 5 and 6), as the choice of strong indicators of political capital depends on the political background of the author. In socialist or autocratic countries, for example, indicators linked to democratic processes, freedom of speech or participatory decision-making, will be seen as less important (or not important) than in democratic societies (Johnston, 1996).

Third, *environmental capital* is the most recent type of capital to enter the pantheon of capitals identified in the literature, although, as debates on sustainability have shown since the 1980s, it is self-evident that any community relies on a 'healthy' environment (however defined; see below) for survival (Thampapillai and Uhlin, 1997; Magis, 2010). Only since the threat of climate change has become globally prominent, and especially since research on complex interlinkages between social-ecological systems has highlighted that it is difficult to understand the resilience of human systems without acknowledging the importance of understanding environmental processes affecting such resilience, has the notion of environmental capital been generally accepted as one of the three pillars of social resilience (Adger, 2000; Chaskin, 2008). Folke (2006, p. 257), therefore, suggested that there is increasing recognition "that shifts between states in ecosystems are increasingly a consequence of human actions that cause erosion of resilience", while Magis (2010, p. 406) argued that environmental capital "is influenced by individual and collective human action, but also presents opportunities and constraints" for communities. While environmental capital is also frequently referred to as 'natural capital' or as 'biocapacity' that seeks to assess demand and supply of natural resources available to a community (Ekins *et al.*, 2003; Ostrom, 2009), in the context of this book environmental capital is seen to encompass both natural capital and biocapacity. As Sections 2.3 and 2.5 will discuss, it is particularly indicators for strong environmental capital that tend to find more general acceptance across cultural divides (in contrast to indicators for strong social capital, for example) as they often describe core variables linked to human survival needs (Maslow, 1943) such as healthy soils, water or resource availability or 'well managed' land and environmental resources (Gunderson and Holling, 2002; Folke, 2006) – indicators that tend to resonate positively in all cultural settings. However, examples discussed in this book will also highlight that different cultures, as well as individual stakeholder groups within a society, can hold very different views and opinions about 'ideal' environmental management pathways (see Box 4.5 about New Zealand pioneer settlers).

This book proposes that community resilience and vulnerability can best be conceptualized on the basis of how well the 'critical triangle' of economic, social and environmental capital are developed in a given community and how these capitals interact. The critical literature on sustainability has already highlighted the importance of economic, social and environmental processes as the three pillars of sustainability (e.g. Ekins *et al.*, 2003; Ostrom, 2009), and many authors have emphasized that only by understanding the complex relationships between individuals, society and nature can we begin to understand community resilience. Allen (1993, pp. 2–3), for example argued that communities do

> not exist and cannot function except at the intersection of society and nature … It is important to understand that we are working in a situation in which both nature and society have been developed, produced and reproduced by the ideas and activities of human beings.

Figure 2.2 shows a conceptual model of how this intertwining of economic, social and environmental capital creates different spaces of resilience and vulnerability, with the strongest resilience achieved when all three capitals are *equally* well developed – in other words, the strongest form of community resilience can be found at the *intersection* between strong economic, social and environmental capital. Communities where only two capitals are well developed can be characterized as only moderately resilient, or indeed as moderately vulnerable (conceptual issue of glass half-full or half-empty), while communities that have only one (or no) well-developed capital are generally characterized by weak resilience/high vulnerability. For example, communities that have focused almost entirely on developing economic capital, at the expense of social or

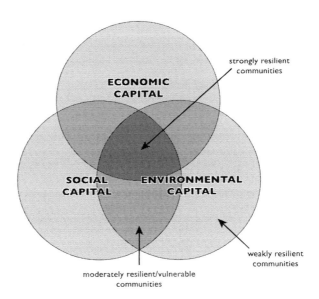

Figure 2.2 Community resilience, vulnerability, and economic, social and environmental capital (source: author; after Wilson, 2010).

environmental capital, will be vulnerable, despite the fact that some individuals within this community may benefit disproportionately in financial terms (see Chapters 3 and 5). Similarly, communities that have focused almost entirely on environmental capital (e.g. by reducing agricultural output and aiming at local self-sufficiency) at the expense of economic (and at times social) capital may be equally vulnerable (see Chapter 5). This emphasizes that the relationship among individual components of the three capitals matters more than the components themselves. The methodological attractiveness of this framework is that it can be applied to (almost) any community in the world and that it is relatively scale-independent (see Section 2.5).

Community resilience can, therefore, be seen as the *balance* between economic, environmental and social needs of communities – in other words, resilience is about communities being able to successfully weather the vicissitudes of endogenous and exogenous disturbances on the basis of well-developed economic, social (political/cultural) and environmental parameters (Rotmans *et al.*, 2002; Resilience Alliance, 2009). This resilience concept can be applied both with regard to the effects of *sudden and catastrophic disturbances* to communities (e.g. earthquakes) and to the effects of *slow-onset disturbances* such as the impact of globalization or climate change on communities (see Figure 1.1). Such resilience can be expressed through the robustness, the rapidity, the redundancy (extent of substitution) and resourcefulness of a community to find ways to address *internal* and *external* disturbances threatening community survival (Adger, 2000; Davidson, 2010). As Section 2.4 will discuss, such resilience can be scaled down from the community level to the household and individual level, and it is the totality of economic, social and environmental actions/responses of individuals and households within a community that shape a community's overall resilience. Chapter 7 will highlight that the maximization of such resilience should be at the heart of policy-makers' efforts to help communities in their struggles for survival.

2.3 Characteristics of resilient communities

How can the characteristics that make up resilient communities in the context of strong economic, social and environmental capital be identified? Table 2.1 suggests some of the components that may identify whether economic, social and environmental capital are well or poorly developed at community level. The aim of the table and of the discussion in this section is to establish a baseline against which community resilience can be assessed in any community.[1] However, the table is purposefully selective in the choice of variables, as different characteristics will be important in different locations and at different scales. Indeed, as highlighted above, notions of 'quality' in relation to economic, social and environmental capital will vary between cultural contexts. In addition, most indicators shown in Table 2.1 are based on the assumption that they can be quantified in one way or another (see Section 2.5). However, Cutter *et al.* (2008, p. 603) rightly warned that several criticisms of the quantitative indicator approach have been noted by researchers, including subjectivity regarding variable selection and weighting, lack of availability of certain variables, problems with aggregation to different scales, and difficulties validating the results ... However, the usefulness of quantitative indicators for reducing complexity, measuring progress, mapping, and setting priorities makes them an important tool for decision makers.

Despite these caveats, a suite of general characteristics of well or poorly developed capitals emerge that will find resonance almost anywhere on the globe. As Rigg (2006, p. 187) argued for the global South, "while the identification of general effects may be problematic, it is possible to identify some common forces propelling ... wide scale changes in the composition and trajectory of economic activity and livelihoods". In other words, the column in Table 2.1 showing strong economic, social and environmental capital shows characteristics that most communities strive to achieve, and that generally are consonant with conceptualizations of resilient communities highlighted in Figure 2.2.

'Economic well-being' of communities is a globally recognized trait of well-developed *economic capital* and a key component of resilience (Gahin *et al.*, 2003). Ultimately, it is the survival of communities that should be at the heart of assessments of the 'quality' of any human system, and poor quality communities are necessarily those that are unable to survive economically (Pretty, 2002; Oudenhoven *et al.*, 2010). As both Rigg (2006) and Chaskin (2008) highlighted, poverty is probably the most important constraint for community development and, therefore, a key component of vulnerable communities. Indeed, it is difficult for community members caught in the poverty trap to find ways to build up improved resilience, as most of their day-to-day activities will be almost entirely focused on raising sufficient income for survival (Maslow, 1943; Parnwell, 2007). However, economic well-being of communities does not necessarily rely on a large income, as recent studies about the relative 'happiness' of various societies have found (Pretty, 2007; Abdallah *et al.*, 2009). Communities with relatively moderate (in Northern terms) yearly household incomes of about US$10–15,000 tend to be 'happiest' with their lives, highlighting that community resilience may be best developed when communities have left the poverty trap and have sufficient economic well-being to satisfy all basic needs and *some* luxury needs (Anielski, 2007). As The Economist (2009, pp. 36–38) argued,

> wealth does not equal happiness. Rich countries are, by and large, happier than poorer ones; but among developed-world countries, there is only weak correlation between happiness and Gross Domestic Product [GDP]. And, although wealth has been soaring over the past half a century, happiness, measured by national surveys, has hardly budged.

In a similar vein, diversified income streams (e.g. a 'healthy' balance between primary, secondary and tertiary sectors) usually are seen as signs of well-developed economic capital and a key basis for resilient communities (see Kinsella *et al.*, 2000, for Ireland, and Oostindie *et al.*, 2006, for The Netherlands). On the other hand, overdependence on agricultural or primary production – as exemplified in some ephemeral mining communities that may only last as long as ores are being extracted, or in 'super-productivist' agricultural communities focusing almost entirely on industrial agricultural production – is often an expression of increasing vulnerability, as these pathways particularly expose communities to the vicissitudes of national/global markets (Pretty, 1995, 2007). While food and fibre production can be important for community resilience, as they are often the platform for well-developed economic capital, Rigg *et al.* (2008) rightly cautioned that a singular focus on agricultural pathways in the rural South (and in some communities of the North) is not necessarily the only solution for community development. Reviewing a global literature on rural change, Rigg (2006) highlighted the increasing disassociation between economic capital and agricultural pathways, as an increasing number of rural households in both North and South have no commitment to farming whatsoever (deagrarianization) and are increasingly aligning themselves with urban industrial or service-based economic pathways. Even subsistence farming communities, where agriculture and fisheries play a major role for community survival, often diversify their economic activities by outsourcing their labour for non-agricultural economic activities (Pretty, 1995).

In addition, many commentators would also agree that low dependency of communities on external funds (e.g. agricultural subsidies) is a good indicator of well-developed economic capital, as it increases the economic autonomy and resilience of rural communities (e.g. Goss and Burch, 2001). As Adger *et al.* (2002) highlighted, high dependency through remittances sent home by family members working abroad may be a sign of poorly developed economic capital, as it may indicate a lack of ability of communities to generate sufficient endogenous capital for community survival and suggests increased dependency and vulnerability if these funding sources 'dry out'. Anderies *et al.* (2006, p. 4) similarly argued that "excessive subsidization [e.g. through remittances] can reduce the capacity of a system to self-organize by generating perverse incentives". However, receipt of external remittances could also be seen as a sign of a more vibrant community in which certain members are willing to 'take a chance' and leave the economic confines of their home community environment (Aggarwal, 2006).

As both O'Riordan (2001) and Harvey (2006) highlighted, one of the most contentious characteristics of community resilience is whether integration of a community into the global capitalist system should be seen as a sign of well-developed economic capital (and, therefore, strong resilience), or whether it is an indicator of increasing dependency of a community on external forces outside of their control (see also Chapters 3 and 6). Debates intersect here with critical analyses of the impacts of globalization processes on constraints and opportunities for community development (e.g. Marsden, 2003; McCarthy, 2006), and will be highly space and scale dependent (Bardhan, 2006). While in some communities integration into the global capitalist system may indeed offer opportunities for the creation of new economic opportunities (e.g. by opening new markets for

Table 2.1 Community resilience and global indicators (selection) of strong and weak economic, social and environmental capital

Resilient/vulnerable communities	Strong capital	Weak capital
Economic capital	Economic well-being Diversified income streams (e.g. balance between primary, secondary and tertiary sectors) Low dependency on external funds (e.g. agricultural subsidies; community aid programmes) Diversified businesses Integration into global capitalist system (?) Happiness (?) etc.	Poverty/debt Overdependency on agricultural or primary production Poor infrastructure High dependency on external funding (e.g. subsidies; remittances from abroad) (?) Communities as net importers of food/goods etc.
Social capital	Close interaction between people (tight-knit communities, e.g. knowing neighbours) Ability to rely on neighbours at times of crisis Availability of skills training and education Good health and sanitation Availability of multiple services Low levels of corruption Good communication between stakeholder groups	Outmigration of young people (greying of rural communities) Service deserts Lack of leadership Mistrust of neighbours Lack of control over destiny of community High death rates and low life expectancy Poor communication between stakeholder groups

	Female empowerment/empowerment of ethnic/religious minorities Open-minded communities (ability to accept change) Good and transparent land ownership regulations (control over means of production) Stakeholders in control of development trajectories Strong governance structures at multiple geographical scales (democratic participation) etc.	High levels of corruption Female dependency/gender or ethnically/religiously based lack of self-determination Weak land ownership patterns (e.g. high levels of tenant/dependent farmers) General dissatisfaction with community pathways Poorly managed public spaces Weak governance etc.
Environmental capital	High levels of biodiversity Good water quality and availability Sustainable soil management Predictable agricultural yields Sustainable management of environmental resources in rural community Localized energy supplies Low carbon footprint Multifunctional environmental resources etc.	Soil degradation Desertification Salinization Poor water quality and availability Uncertainty over agricultural yields Peak oil and the inability of communities to source energy locally High carbon footprint etc.

Source: author; after Ekins *et al.*, 2003; Lebel *et al.*, 2006; Smit and Wandel, 2006; Parnwell, 2007; Chaskin, 2008; Cutter *et al.*, 2008; Ostrom, 2009; Magis, 2010; Oudenhoven *et al.*, 2010.

certain products), in others such integration may reduce economic (as well as social and environmental) capital, for example by creating new dependencies linked to new markets or new technologies, or by exacerbating the divide between 'winners' and 'losers' within a community (see Chakrabarti and Cullenberg, 2003, for India; Kaplinsky and Messner, 2008, for China). The latter is particularly true for rural communities where localized and locally/regionally well-networked agro-commodity chains are disrupted/destroyed through global economic reorientation of the community (Parnwell, 2007; Rigg *et al.*, 2008). The latter point highlights the importance of applying *situation-specific* methodologies that take into account the relative changes engendered by globalization processes in specific community settings (Wilson and Rigg, 2003; see also Section 2.5).

The situation is equally complex with regard to *social capital* as a driver for community development, although some common characteristics emerge that will find resonance as indicators for community resilience in most communities around the globe. Social capital is often described as the 'glue' that binds people in communities together based on strong local embeddedness (Coleman, 1988; Western *et al.*, 2005), self-regulating moral codes, or, as Chaskin (2008, p. 68) suggested, as "the nature of social ties and interaction ... and the context of trust and norms of reciprocity within which these relationships inhere". This suggests that close interaction between people through tight-knit communities, the ability to rely on neighbours in times of crisis and good communication between stake-holder groups, are generally seen as signs of well-developed social capital (e.g. Dorfman *et al.*, 2009), while the 'greying' of communities through outmigration of young people would usually be accepted as a sign of poorly developed (and further weakening) social capital (e.g. Zhao, 1999, and Ye and He, 2008, for China; Bell, 2004, for the USA; Rigg *et al.*, 2008, for Thailand; Forbes *et al.*, 2009, for arctic Russia). The latter is often closely associated with the (non-)provision of community services ('service deserts'), often linked to highly vulnerable community development pathways as they diminish opportunities for communities to perform multiple functions (Woods, 2005). Similarly, there is little debate about the importance of availability of skills training and educational opportunities for community members as an indicator of well-developed (or strengthening) social capital (Gahin *et al.*, 2003), or of the availability of good health and sanitation systems as positive indicators (Chaskin, 2008). Lack of leadership, weak governance structures, high levels of corruption (low moral and ethical standards, self-centredness), poorly managed public spaces (i.e. dirty, poorly maintained, 'nobody cares' attitude), or lack of control of a community over the destiny of future development pathways are also signs of poorly developed social capital (Smit and Wandel, 2006; Lebel *et al.*, 2006; see Box 2.1). Usually, transparent and clear land ownership regulations will also enhance resilience of communities as they increase community control over land and resources (Curry and Koczberski, 2009), while rural communities with high levels of tenant/dependent landholders may indicate poorly developed social capital and more vulnerable communities (but highly dependent on socio-cultural perceptions of the importance of freehold land) (Cumming *et al.*, 2005).

Box 2.1 Social and economic capital and the Haiti earthquake (January 2010)

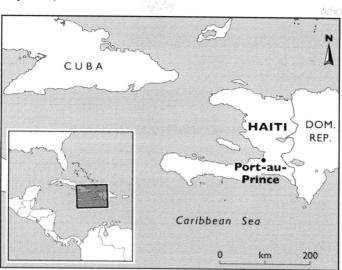

On 12 January 2010 an earthquake of magnitude 7.8 struck the island nation of Haiti in the Caribbean, with a shallow epicentre located near the capital Port-au-Prince (2 million inhabitants). Devastation of urban infrastructure in the capital was almost complete and the death toll exceeded 230,000 people. It became quickly evident that *social* and *economic capital* in Port-au-Prince were so poorly developed that the United Nations (UN) and the international community found it difficult to efficiently implement disaster relief programmes. Based on indicators shown in Table 2.1, news reports suggested that weakly developed social capital in Port-au-Prince was particularly associated with poor governance structures and lack of leadership (institutional support from within Haiti for relief organizations was almost non-existent) linked to weak political structures in the aftermath of the dictatorship of the dictatorial Duvalier clan (1971–1986), poor communication between affected stakeholder groups, and overall lack of control of individuals and stakeholder groups over community-level development trajectories before and after the earthquake (see also Diamond, 2006). These problems have been compounded by the fact that Haiti is the poorest country in Latin America and one of the poorest nations on Earth (per capita yearly GDP only US$380 in 2003), with weakly developed economic capital particularly evident in the absence of earthquake-proof buildings (the UN headquarters in Port-au-Prince itself collapsed, killing many UN officials), the absence of disaster management plans and early warning systems, and a lack of food storage facilities that would have helped alleviate the severe food shortages that became a major problem in the immediate aftermath of the earthquake. As a further result of the failure to substantially improve economic and social capital, in late 2010 a cholera epidemic killed over 1000 people due to continuing unsanitary conditions.

Gender relations and the status of ethnic minority groups are also key indicators for well or poorly developed social capital (Lebel *et al.*, 2006; Magis, 2010), although these may be some of the most culturally dependent indicators (Janssens, 2010). Most would agree that empowerment of women or ethnic minorities with regard to decision-making opportunities and land and resource ownership issues should be seen as a sign of well-developed social capital, leading to more inclusive and, therefore, more resilient communities (Cumming *et al.*, 2005; Chaskin, 2008). However, commentators from societies in which gender and ethnic roles are not (yet) widely open to debate (e.g. many Islamic states, but also some staunchly conservative former settler communities) may see empowerment of women and/or minority groups as a disruption to existing systems and, therefore, as a factor diminishing social capital (e.g. Reynolds, 2002, for the Dominican Republic). This latter point re-emphasizes both the importance of understanding power relationships within communities (see Section 5.3) and the cultural context in assessing characteristics of community resilience, as strong indicators for resilience for some may be seen as weak indicators for others.

Debates about well or poorly developed *environmental capital* of communities are less contentious, particularly as "the resilience of a community is inextricably linked to the condition of the environment and the treatment of its resources" (Cutter *et al.*, 2008, p. 601). This means that strong environmental capital is a crucial component for a resilient community, as the survival of communities is often predicated on 'healthy' environments (Ekins *et al.*, 2003; Smit and Wandel, 2006), or, as Folke (2006, p. 262) emphasized, "adaptability in a resilience framework does not only imply adaptive capacity to respond within the social domain, but also to respond to and shape ecosystem dynamics and change". Commentators have used the dichotomy between land degradation and sustainable environmental systems to describe strong or weak environmental capital, and have often linked environmental degradation issues (e.g. soil degradation, desertification, salinization or industrial pollution) to increasing vulnerability of communities (Blaikie and Brookfield, 1987; Adger, 2006). On the other hand, high biodiversity levels are usually seen as a key indicator for 'environmental health' and for communities that have reached a resilient 'balance' between exploitation and conservation of natural resources (Gunderson and Holling, 2002; Wilson, 2007) – exemplifying communities that may have the 'economic luxury' to set aside areas not directly linked to intensive production. However, as Section 2.4 will highlight, there are important scalar implications with regard to community-environment interactions. Thus, indirect availability of 'healthy' environments for communities that do not have the space to contain protected environments *within* the geographical boundaries of the community (e.g. densely urbanized communities) can nonetheless be a sign of relatively well-developed environmental capital through *access* and *rights of use* of these environments by community members (e.g. access to common grazing areas; access of urban communities to green spaces; etc.) (Bebbington and Perrault, 1999; Davidson, 2010).

In addition, debates on 'peak oil' (rapid decline of oil resources) and the need for communities to find ways to source energy locally (e.g. through local wind power generation or photovoltaics) have gained prominence in recent years (Deffeyes, 2001; WADE, 2003). As both Hopkins (2008) and Bailey *et al.* (2010) have highlighted, the key issue here is how resilient communities are in the case of severe shortages of energy supplies, and how easy it is for communities to disembed themselves from increasingly complex energy interlinkages at regional, national and even global scales. The dependency of UK and many other European communities from imports of gas from Middle Eastern countries or Russia is a typical case in point. Further, there is now much debate suggesting that communities with a low carbon footprint can be seen as more resilient than their high carbon footprint counterparts (Heinberg, 2004; Bailey and Wilson, 2009).

Although each community will have its own set of 'ideal' development pathways linked to economic, social and environmental capital, the discussion highlights that it is possible to identify some common global 'indicators' for the assessment of community resilience (see also Section 2.5). Some degree of *self-organization* within clusters of action for resilience (e.g. within the realm of social, economic or environmental capital) is, therefore, an attribute of any community system (Frigg, 2003). Figure 2.2 showed that only communities where most of these positive attributes are evident can be seen as resilient communities well armoured to face the challenges imposed by a rapidly globalizing world. As Adger (2000) emphasized, 'monofunctional' communities, meanwhile, with only one well-developed capital, may be the most vulnerable and are often those in need of urgent policy action (see Chapter 7). Often, factors defining resilient communities come clustered together (i.e. mutually reinforcing processes such as economic well-being leading to high levels of education, in turn leading to gender equality, etc.) (Oostindie *et al.*, 2006). However, the high degree of interdependence between the three capitals also means that any disruption in one capital causes a 'ripple effect' that affects other capitals, thereby reducing resilience (e.g. loss of productive capacity of soils impacts on economic survival of agricultural systems, etc.) (Kinzig *et al.*, 2006).

There will be few communities where *all* characteristics of economic, social and environmental capital are developed to the maximum, and equally few areas that are entirely monofunctional (see Chapter 3). This means that the strongest possible resilience can probably never be achieved in a community and that 'strong' resilience should be seen as an 'ideal state'. Many would agree that communities that are highly diversified (e.g. combining good service, skills and educational provision with environmentally sustainable use of local resources), that offer diverse opportunities for their residents in terms of agricultural and non-agricultural incomes (e.g. industry, manufacturing, tourism, educational sector), that have managed to maintain high environmental quality, and that are inclusive with regard to stakeholder involvement, democratic processes and education of its citizens, can be seen as strongly resilient. However, often such resilient communities also contain *some* characteristics of vulnerability (e.g. overdependency on one specific income stream; outmigration; unequal distribution of wealth generated within the community). Conversely, even the most vulnerable communities characterized, for example, by overdependency on agricultural production or poorly developed social capital, may have some resilient characteristics such as relatively well-developed economic capital (Wilson, 2008). Only in communities that have completely disappeared has the trajectory towards vulnerability been irreversible – in other words, such communities passed a 'vulnerability threshold' beyond which recovery was impossible (Diamond, 2006; Davidson, 2010; see Chapters 4–6).

A complex picture of social resilience characteristics within communities emerges, characterized by diverse, hybrid, non-linear and highly dynamic pathways of community change where a small change in one of the 'capitals' can propel a community towards strengthened or weakened resilience. Yet, the discussion has also highlighted that propelling forces influencing the 'quality' of economic, social and environmental capital are complex and highly dependent on cross-cultural interpretations of what is 'best' for communities and, indeed, whether – from a deep ecology and moral perspective – the survival of human communities (as opposed to the survival of natural systems, for example) should be a key goal at all (Smit and Wandel, 2006; Pretty, 2007). This suggests that researchers have to be careful not to *overromanticize* and *reify* certain community systems over others with regard to the interlinkages between economic, social and environmental capital and community resilience (DuPuis and Goodman, 2005). The discussion in Chapter 3 will emphasize that while many Western researchers would tend to emphasize the 'positive' attributes of seemingly resilient communities in the South (e.g. the frequent romantic emphasis on subsistence farming communities as an environmentally relatively benign system often characterized by strong social capital), researchers working in the South often argue that many stakeholders in these 'resilient' systems may be more than willing to abdicate some of their strongly developed social and environmental capital for improved economic capital (Wilson and Rigg, 2003; Parnwell, 2007; see also Chapter 7). While in the North monofunctional dependency of communities upon one economic sector alone (e.g. super-productivist farming communities in parts of the American Midwest) have become associated with perceptions of vulnerable communities (Bell, 2004), such development pathways, often characterized by strongly developed economic capital, may often be the goal of many poor rural communities in the South (Marsden, 2003; Rigg, 2006) or, for example, Mediterranean communities still in the process of agricultural 'modernization' (Caraveli, 2000; Wilson, 2001).

2.4 Community resilience and 'open' and 'closed' systems: geographical and socio-cultural boundaries of communities

The discussion in Section 2.3 has highlighted that although it is possible to conceptualize key characteristics of resilient communities, identifying what makes up a resilient community is nonetheless fraught with problems and is highly dependent on cultural interpretations of 'good' and 'bad' community development characteristics. As Chapter 1 highlighted, there has also been substantial debate about the meaning and constituents of the notion of 'community', about communities as 'open' and 'unbounded' systems rather than 'closed' easily identifiable geographical entities (such as a 'village community'), and about the fact that 'community' is largely an attitudinal construct that means different things to different people (Staeheli, 2008; Neal, 2009). This highlights that there are important issues of scale that need to be considered when discussing 'community resilience', especially as the notion of 'community' can be both scaled up and down.

As Figure 2.3 highlights, *downscaling* means taking into account that communities are not homogenous entities, but are comprised of *households, individuals* and *stakeholder groups* who all have their own resilience pathways that may be very different from those of the community within which they live (Granovetter, 1985; Smit and Wandel, 2006). What may be good for an individual or a household may not necessarily be good for the community as a whole (e.g. accumulation of wealth by an individual based on degradation of common community resources). Similarly, what may be good for a community may not necessarily be good for an individual, a household or a specific stakeholder group (e.g. religious, ethical, political or environmental norms and rules imposed

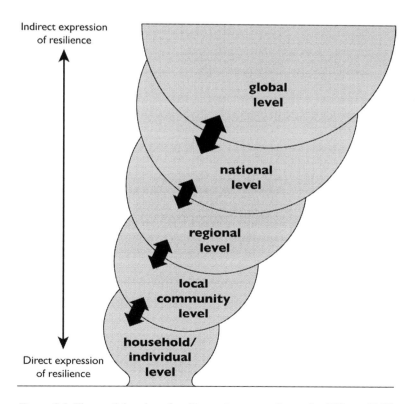

Figure 2.3 The spatial scales of resilience (source: author; after Wilson, 2009).

by community leaders). Although this book will refer to 'the community' in the following chapters, we need to acknowledge possible inequalities of resilience/ vulnerability at individual and household level. What is important is that the implementation of pathways of resilience can only find its most direct expression at the *level of the individual/household* and the *community*, as it is only at the most local level that outcomes of policies and decisions (often made higher up) are experienced with *tangible* effects 'on the ground' (Figure 2.3). In other words, any larger-scale process or action influencing environmental decision-making (e.g. regionally based norms, national policy, global drivers of change; see Chapters 6 and 7) is ultimately *mediated* by the individual/household within a community and turned into action with tangible effects in a given locality (e.g. decision to recycle; the cutting of a tree; the decision to use a highly polluting private car, etc.) (Kinzig *et al.*, 2006). The first level of aggregation of these individual actions is the *local community* level – the focal scale of analysis in this book.

Upscaling the notion of community resilience is equally complex. As Figure 2.3 highlights, local communities and individual decision-making pathways are embedded in *nested hierarchies* of scales, with close scalar interconnections between the community and the regional, national and global levels (see also Chapters 6 and 7) (Kinzig *et al.*, 2006; Resilience Alliance, 2007). At these levels, we find *indirect expressions of resilience* (e.g. policy and planning, societal ideological pathways) that inform and influence resilience action by individuals/households (Lebel *et al.*, 2006).

Communities can, therefore, be seen as both 'open' and 'closed' systems with regard to decisions up and down the scales affecting community resilience (Cumming *et al.*, 2006). Communities can be *geographically closed* when the geographical boundary of the community defines the parameters within which characteristics of resilience are situated. In these instances, the geography of the local community, with its residents, human processes (agriculture, manufacturing, services, etc.) and resources (soils, forests, water, air, etc.) is crucial for understanding community resilience parameters (Hopkins, 2008). Yet, there are few historical examples of such geographically closed communities. Classic examples include, in particular, Easter Island (in the south-east Pacific), where archaeological evidence suggests that initial contact with original island homes in the central Pacific was rapidly lost after initial settlement of the remote island between AD 1000 and 1200 (Flenley and Bahn, 2003; Diamond, 2006);[2] Norse settlements on Greenland's west coast AD 980–1450, possibly living in climatically induced complete isolation between 1380 and 1450 (Seaver, 1996); or Pitcairn Island (central/eastern Pacific) where Polynesian settlers survived from about AD 800 for several generations (probably without outside contact) until eventually disappearing, and where later the mutineers of the British ship *Bounty* and their descendants lived in self-enforced complete isolation between 1790 and 1814 (Diamond, 2006). Conceptually more controversial are examples of 'isolated communities' relating to hunter-gatherer tribes and subsistence farming communities in remote tropical forest areas. It is estimated that at the time of writing (2011) about 70 'uncontacted' tribes remained in remote tropical forest areas, of which about 50 were located in the Amazon rainforest. While the early to mid twentieth-century romanticized 'traditional' view often portrayed these tribes as self-contained communities living 'in harmony with nature' (see Chapter 4), more recent critical studies have highlighted that almost all hunter-gatherer tribes and subsistence farming communities were/are part of intricate social, cultural and economic networks that span large areas (e.g. large regions within the Amazon rainforest) leading to elaborate exchange of knowledge, skills, people and goods in relatively 'open' systems (Smith and Wishnie, 2000; Redford and Sanderson, 2000).

The latter highlights that boundaries between seemingly geographically 'closed' and 'open' communities are fuzzy and that it has been very rare in human history for communities to be completely isolated from other communities (Massey and Jess, 1995; Appadurai, 1996). Indeed, as in the case of Easter Island (see Box 4.3), Pitcairn Island or the Norse settlements on Greenland, isolation was *enforced* rather than *voluntary*, suggesting that community development, resilience and, ultimately, community survival are generally predicated on interactions of a community beyond its geographical boundaries (Diamond, 2006). Thus, with the exception of completely closed communities, *socio-cultural boundaries* of communities usually remain open, as new migrants bring with them social and cultural norms that will shape environmental pathways and transitions (Appadurai, 1996). We need to, therefore, distinguish between *geographically* open/closed and *socio-culturally* open/closed community systems, with the latter closely linked to 'social memory' and its important effects on environmental transitions at community level (e.g. Scarfetta and West, 2004; Ward and Styles, 2006) – an issue I will discuss in detail in Chapter 4.

Most communities on Earth are, therefore, part of 'open' systems (geographically and socio-culturally) that have inflows and outflows of people, goods, energy, skills and resources that permeate the boundaries of a community (Massey and Jess, 1995; Cumming *et al.*, 2006). At the regional level, these flows may include the migration of people in and out of the community (e.g. for work or education), the flow of agricultural and manufactured goods, or the use of services not available at community level (e.g. closure of many village shops and post offices in developed countries means that regional service centres are assuming increasing importance) (Gibbs, 2000; Lebel *et al.*, 2006). At the national level, these flows may include the effects of national policy implementation 'on the ground' (e.g. the impact of agricultural subsidies on land use patterns in a community; implications of policies for protected areas management in or near the community) or the in- and outflow of energy (e.g. electricity from the national grid). At global level, internet-based global information flows increasingly influence community processes and resilience[3] (Castells, 1996), as does the strength of community links to global markets or global energy flows (e.g. peak oil scenarios and their possible impacts on local communities; cf. Deffeyes, 2001; Hopkins, 2008). Overall, the larger the scale of investigation, the more difficult it is to assess resilience and the trajectories of environmental pathways.

The discussion in the following chapters will show that striking the right 'balance' between communities and their scalar interactions is key for maximizing community resilience: while too much isolation of a community may be bad in light of overdependency on local resources, skills and people (as the example of Easter Island in Box 4.3 illustrates), 'overglobalization', with possible loss of autonomy and identity, may be equally fraught with problems (see Chapter 3). In the past few decades, this 'opening up' of community boundaries (geographical, socio-cultural, political and economic) at various scales has been particularly accelerated by *globalization* processes that have affected even the most remote communities on the globe (Nederveen Pieterse, 2004; Young *et al.*, 2006), suggesting that completely geographically 'closed' communities are increasingly a thing of the past. Globalization, as well as climate change or the global 'energy crisis' can be seen as 'great levellers' that may lead to a harmonization of key challenges faced by most communities on Earth (i.e. most contemporary communities are faced by climate change in one way or another) (Adger, 2003; Read, 2004). This means that, inevitably, contemporary community resilience/vulnerability has to be understood in a context that goes well beyond the *physical* confines of a community. The characteristics discussed in Table 2.1, therefore, need to be understood in light of how resilience can be acquired/lost during *processes of exchange* between the community and the regional, national and global levels (see Figure 2.3). As highlighted above, community resilience can be enhanced, for example, through the inflow of remittances sent by relatives of community members living in other parts of the world (Adger *et al.*, 2002). Simultaneously, community resilience can be enhanced through the outflow of goods and services (enhancing economic and social capital, for example).

This raises the important question whether community resilience can be seen as a zero-sum-game where *all* communities around the globe can raise levels of resilience simultaneously, or whether increased resilience of one community necessarily means increased vulnerability of others (Wilson, 2009; see also Chapter 7). For example, a community relying on imports of tropical hardwoods for its manufacturing industry (thereby increasing community-level economic capital) may reduce resilience of hunter-gatherer or subsistence-based communities in tropical forests relying on sustainable use of these trees (Bryant and Bailey, 1997; Pretty, 2007). Japan's role as an 'ecopredator' is an interesting example in this respect, as critical environmental literature has argued that many Japanese communities have managed to maintain substantial areas of forest (Japan has over 60 per cent forest cover) based on overexploitation of forest resources elsewhere in the world (Turner *et al.*, 1990). Similarly, the import of foodstuffs from irrigated agricultural areas in the developing world to the developed world may lead to loss of environmental capital at source, and possible reduction in community resilience in areas characterized by water scarcity (Aggarwal, 2006; Earle *et al.*, 2010). I will return to issues of community resilience and the notion of 'zero-sum-game' in Chapter 7 when discussing in more detail the impact of policy-related transitional corridors on community resilience.

2.5 How can we measure the resilience of communities? Some methodological considerations

A framework for understanding community resilience also needs to consider 'practical' issues associated with questions related to how resilience can be assessed at community level. What methodological steps should be taken to address the complex issues raised above? This section will outline how the resilience of communities can be assessed based on a framework of economic, social and environmental capital. The following discussion of methodological issues is based on the case study of the EU-funded LEDDRA Project (2010–2014) which investigates interlinkages between community resilience and land degradation (especially forest mismanagement, overgrazing and loss of productive capacity of soils) in 15 case study communities located in Spain, Italy, Greece, Morocco and China (LEDDRA, 2011). The aim of this section is to illustrate that complex interlinkages between the three capitals and community resilience can only be understood through a *multi-method approach* that uses both qualitative and quantitative approaches. As Forbes *et al.* (2009, p. 22042) highlighted, any in-depth study of community resilience requires "a multidisciplinary surrogate approach to understand the relevant ecological and social drivers and the interplay between them". However, the Resilience Alliance (2007, p. 39) rightly argued that "we are in an exploratory mode at this stage without an established methodology", while Cumming *et al.* (2005, p. 976) suggested that "the abstract, multidimensional nature of the concept of resilience makes it difficult to operationalize. It is by no means obvious what leads to resilience in a complex system, or which variables should be measured in a given study of resilience." As a result, several methodological steps that enabled cross-checking and iterative validation were used in the LEDDRA Project to assess community resilience.

First, the structure of the project was based on two types of research teams collecting and interpreting data. *Local teams* 'on the ground' had knowledge of individual case study communities, local languages and land degradation challenges facing communities. The latter addresses Cumming *et al.*'s (2005, p. 978) cautionary note that "if resilience is to be assessed operationally, it must be in relation to a potential and specific change in the system" – i.e. land degradation issues threatening community resilience in the case of the LEDDRA Project. Based on their local knowledge, these local teams were in charge of selecting specific case-study communities (defined for the purpose of the study as villages with 100–500 inhabitants) and the collection of most of the data within these communities. They also helped with the wider interpretation of the data. A *coordinating team* working at supranational level was in charge of formulating a list of key questions (see below) to be asked in all case study communities, helping local expert teams with problems associated with data collection, interpretation of the data (with help from the local teams) and final comparative analysis of the data across the 15 case study communities.

Second, a key concern was that local teams varied in their expertise with regard to economic, social and environmental capital. For example, some teams were comprised largely of ecologists who had the skills to collect data related to environmental capital, but had little social science background to assess economic and especially complex social capital data. As a result, based on Cumming *et al.* (2005), the second methodological step involved an *iterative methodological approach* which was aimed at generating maximum high quality data for each case study community based on proxy indicators, all the while acknowledging that a 'complete' data set would be almost impossible to achieve. In other words, it was recognized from the outset that data collection would inevitably be uneven between the case study communities and depended largely on the expert knowledge of local teams, time spent 'in the field' by local and coordinating teams, and on issues related to the accuracy of interview translations and culturally related differential interpretations of research results.

Third, due to issues highlighted above, a further research step involved a joint visit of case study communities by *both* local teams and coordinating teams. The purpose of these visits was for all researchers to acquaint themselves with the case study communities (mainly through informal interaction with community residents and observational methodologies), and to gain an initial understanding of land degradation issues affecting community resilience. This enabled the coordinating team to better contextualize and understand the more detailed data provided later by local teams, and to provide meaningful cross-community and cross-cultural comparisons of community resilience pathways.

A list of questions (both proxy indicators and indicators directly linked to measuring resilience) sent to local teams addressing economic, social and environmental capital formed the fourth methodological step. These questions were loosely based on key themes highlighted in Table 2.1 and were associated with the specific hypotheses linked to community resilience/vulnerability discussed above. Although the questions were specifically framed towards opportunities for resilience, specific community resilience actions and land degradation issues (including assessment of changes over the past 50 years), most of the questions should be applicable in any research context assessing community resilience and vulnerability (see also Resilience Alliance, 2007). After piloting and extensive discussions between coordinating teams and local teams, 43 questions were used to investigate economic capital, 83 to explore social capital and 28 to assess environmental capital (Table 2.2). The focus was on variables that helped identify key resilience issues of continuity, sources of innovation, threats and opportunities. Although for other studies the required type and number of questions will vary depending on research questions, types of disturbances, specific resilience issues under investigation and the complexity of community structures, the number of questions in the LEDDRA Project highlights that investigating social capital is likely to be the most difficult and that several blocks of questions are needed to gain understanding of 'how a community works' (Cumming *et al.*, 2005; Masten and Obradovic, 2008). Environmental capital-related questions, meanwhile, emerge as those that need to be tailored most carefully towards a specific case study community, while questions about social and economic capital shown in Table 2.2 tend to be more generic and should be applicable in diverse case study contexts. The local teams involved in the LEDDRA Project had most problems with questions associated with social capital (see also Resilience Alliance, 2007), with some of the researchers struggling particularly with the perceived 'fuzziness' of questions attempting to unravel complex socio-psychological issues and processes (e.g. questions linked to the 'happiness' of community residents, questions about trust or questions related to power structures or corruption; see Table 2.2).

Fifth, building on Forbes *et al.* (2009), for each question local teams were asked to use *the most appropriate methodologies* to collect data, ranging from statistical information (e.g. economic data on GDP or poverty), interviews with key community representatives (e.g. to understand how environmental resources are used and by whom), in-depth interviews (e.g. to understand complex issues of community cohesiveness, corruption or community-based learning processes), participant observation (e.g. to better understand stakeholder interactions; to assess general appearance of the community), roundtable discussions (e.g. to discuss how the community's adaptive capacity could be strengthened) or focus groups (e.g. to discuss how community environmental resources can be better managed). In some cases, Masters or PhD students were used by local teams to research one or several blocks of questions as part of their dissertations/theses. A key problem was linked to the *representativeness* of individuals/stakeholder groups interviewed, and issues related to power networks (powerful actors more likely to be heard) had to be considered throughout. Triangulation with other methodological steps (e.g. participant observation; use of local and coordinating research teams; workshops) ensured some cross-checking of the representativeness of views, but it was acknowledged throughout that 'complete' information could never be gathered, even in relatively small communities. Overall, about two years were allocated to the data collection process, which enabled an iterative process of in-depth communication and feedback between the coordinating team and local teams about questions where problems had been encountered.

Sixth, a combination of quantitative and qualitative approaches was used to interpret the data. As a first step, data were used to establish a 'storyline' for each community, which focused on community-specific histories, environmental transitions, idiosyncrasies and stakeholder and power networks. Based on Cumming *et al.* (2005), a series of workshops were held to cross-check and discuss indicators with local residents and experts with knowledge of the area, which enabled community resilience to be assessed in relation to the properties of interest to local stakeholders. A third step then involved the quantification of resilience for each indicator for each community based on a subjective ranking score from 0 (indicator of high vulnerability) to 10 (indicator of strong resilience) (see Gahin *et al.*, 2003, Western *et al.*, 2005, Thomalla and Klocker Larsen, 2010 and Nurul Islam *et al.*, 2011, for similar approaches). For example, if the question 'have regional policies or actions been introduced in the last 50 years as a response to land degradation problems in the region?' was answered 'none', then a score of '0–1' (indicator of high environmental vulnerability) was allocated. Conversely, if the question 'does everyone have equal access to the natural resources in the community?' was answered 'yes, almost everybody in the community has equal access' a score of '7–9' was given (indicator of strong

Table 2.2 Resilience issues and indicators examined in the EU-funded LEDDRA Project

Economic capital

Resilience issue	Specific resilience indicator at community level
Gross Domestic Product (GDP)	GDP per capita Average household income
Employment levels	Percentage unemployed Percentage in full-time employment Percentage in part-time employment
Poverty	Poverty levels (% of households < 50% of country average GDP) Household debt levels
Dependency on external income streams	Does the community receive agricultural subsidies? If yes, how important are they to the community? What percentage of the community's income is derived from state/welfare support? Is the community successful in attracting funds from external sources? Is access to external funds open to all stakeholder groups? Are there any key needs in the community which are not met because of a lack of funds (if yes, what are they)? Is the community dependent on earnings sent by relatives living and working outside the community (if yes, % or rough estimate)?
Economic sectors	How stable are existing economic sectors? Have there been significant changes in the main employment sector in the last 50 years? What percentage of the community is employed in agriculture and related industries (and has that changed significantly over past 50 years)? What percentage of the community is employed in manufacturing and related industries (and has that changed significantly over past 50 years)? What percentage of the community is employed in tertiary/service industries (and has that changed significantly over past 50 years)? What percentage of the community is employed in tourism-related industries (and has that changed significantly over past 50 years)?

Economic development over time	What are the prospects for future/ongoing economic development? What are the main threats to economic stability?
Sources of income	Do households have more than one source of income? Have households needed to develop multiple sources of income? If yes, why?
Development of new income streams	Are there opportunities for new businesses to be developed (if yes, please give an example of an opportunity that has been established)? Are there opportunities for women to develop new income streams? Are there business support networks and services available to help new businesses to establish (if yes, what help do they provide)?
Connectivity	Quality of road infrastructure Quality of public transport Is electricity available to everyone? Does everyone have access to internet and computer networks if they want them? If yes, percentage of households with internet access? Does the local infrastructure constrain income generation?
Housing	What is the quality of the local housing stock? What is the percentage of empty properties in the community (and has that changed significantly over the past 50 years)? What is the percentage of property owned by those outside of the community (i.e. second homes)?
Community goals and economic decision-making	Who makes decisions at the regional level about economic development? What are the community priorities for economic development? Who makes the decisions within the community about economic activities? Is the local government structure effective at dealing with abuse of local economic resources? Are locally produced goods sold locally?
Value added for local products	Have people developed new local products in any sector (diversification)? Can producers sell directly to consumers (if no, why not)? Do consumers actually sell directly to consumers (if no, why not)? Do prices for local products fluctuate much (if yes, what are the reasons for these fluctuations)?

continued

Table 2.2 continued

Social capital	
Resilience issue	Specific resilience indicator at community level
Community identity	What stakeholder groups are present (list all key groups)?
	What stakeholder networks (linkages between stakeholder groups) are present?
	Are those networks important to the stakeholder groups?
	What is the general appearance of the community and its immediate environment (e.g. dilapidated, dirty, well kept)?
	What is the average length of residence in the community?
	What community-owned resources are there (e.g. buildings, environmental resources, etc.) which are owned collectively?
	What is the average level of health in the community?
	Do people have pride in their community?
	Are the majority of buildings owned by the occupants or are they mostly rented?
Community cohesiveness and trust	Do stakeholders trust fellow stakeholders/groups within the community?
	Do stakeholders trust other stakeholders outside of the community (such as regional policy-makers, NGOs, absent landlords)?
	What (if anything) undermines the community?
Relationships	Do neighbours trust each other?
	Do neighbours provide support for each other in times of need?
	Does the community network with other communities elsewhere in the region?
	Does the community network with other local communities?
Contentment with life	Is the community happy?
	Do community members see themselves staying in their community long-term?
Conflicts	Is there any significant conflict between key individuals within the community?
	Are there conflicts between stakeholder groups?
	How is such conflict managed (if at all)?

Communication between stakeholder groups	Do stakeholder groups within the community communicate with each other (if yes, has that always been the case)?
	Are certain groups or individuals left out?
	Do stakeholder groups support each other by sharing knowledge?
	Do stakeholder groups support each other by sharing tangible resources (e.g. equipment, buildings, money)?
	Do community leaders facilitate interaction and collaboration between groups?
	Are community leaders well networked with external organizations (public bodies, private and voluntary sector organizations)?
Power	Do community members feel empowered to act?
	Are community members satisfied with the way that decision-making is assigned?
	Do community members have an opportunity to choose leaders?
	Is corruption a problem?
	Do community members/stakeholders trust those in power?
	Are there informal power structures/networks of power/powerful individuals?
	What is the basis of their power (land, money, family/party connections)?
	Do religious leaders hold positions of power?
Political structures	How well is the community integrated with regional institutional structures (e.g. policies, directives, decisions)?
Engagement of young people	Do young people get involved in working in the community?
	Do young people get involved in developing new opportunities or projects in the community?
	Do young people get involved in community decision-making (if yes, why)?
	Do young people think differently or have different ideas to older people?
	What role do local schools play in responses to land degradation?
Responses to and opportunities for influencing change	Do people prefer to keep things the same way?
	Do people try new ways of doing things?
	Do people believe that they can influence things and make changes happen?
	Do people take part in making change happen?
	Can the community successfully adapt to change (if yes, has this changed over time)?

continued

Table 2.2 continued

Social capital

Learning and knowledge	Average level of education for community members
	Is training in relevant skills and knowledge available to community members (if not, what are the barriers to access)?
	Are local knowledge or skills passed on from the older to the younger generation?
	Are knowledge and skills passed back from the younger to the older generation?
	Is there communication and support between generations in the community?
Knowledge utility and transfer	Is 'expert' knowledge (scientific, technical) available to support local decision-making?
	Is local knowledge available to decision-making?
	Is such knowledge available in a useable form?
	Are there any key gaps in knowledge?
	Is local knowledge useful in addressing land degradation problems?
	Does the older generation contribute their knowledge to responses to land degradation?
	Is knowledge from the older generation valued?
	Is community/local knowledge available for use by regional policy-makers in the environmental planning process?
	Is all relevant knowledge used by regional policy-makers in the environmental planning process?
Learning from experience	What (if anything) has worked in the past when dealing with land degradation problems?
	Why did it work?
	What helped make it work?
	Was there anything that would have prevented if from working?
	What (if anything) has not worked?
	Why did it not work?
	Was there anything that would have made it work?
Participation in decision-making	Which stakeholder groups are involved in local decision-making?
	Do they have access to the information and expertise that they need to make decisions?
	Are they aware of all relevant local issues?
	Do all those who could participate actually participate in decision-making? If not, why not?
	Can those who have opposing viewpoints participate in decision-making?
	Is there a discussion if different viewpoints are raised?
	Are there any groups or individuals who do not participate in decision-making (e.g. women, young people, etc.)?

Engagement of community resources	Is the community governance structure effective at dealing with the problems facing the community?
	Do stakeholders comply with regulations and decisions?
	Do community projects exist (if so, please give an example of an active community project)?
	How important are community groups for contributing leaders/leadership and volunteers for these community projects?
	How much opportunity is there to get together with other community members and generate/exchange ideas to cope with problems in the community?
Stakeholder agency	Can individual members of the community affect the community's well-being?
	Are many community members involved in groups or organizations (political, economic, social, environmental)? If yes, does this affect the community as a whole?
	How self-reliant is the community in dealing with its problems?
Environmental capital	
Resilience issue	Specific resilience indicator at community level
Access to environmental resources	Does everyone have equal access to natural resources in the community?
	Does everyone get involved in planning the use of those resources?
Resource limitations	Does the environment pose limitations on the community? Is so, what are they?
	How could/does the community get around these limitations?
Land and resource use	Percentage of land use for cultivation within community boundaries?
	History of land use and main changes over past 50 years
	What do stakeholders see as the main land use issues?
	What is the quality of terraces, barns, drainage channels, etc.?
	Are these maintained? If not, why not?
	What is the main type of land tenure (owner or rented)?
	What is the environmental quality of the main land use system?

continued

Table 2.2 continued

Environmental capital	
Sustainability of resource use (water)	Are water resources of good quality? Are water resources sufficient for local needs? Are water resources distributed fairly? Are water resources managed sustainably? Do all water users have a say in how water resources are managed?
Sustainability of resource use (soils)	Are soils of good quality? Is local land sufficient for local needs? Is access to good quality land distributed fairly? Are soil resources managed sustainably? Do all soil users have a say in how soil resources are managed? Are local soils/lands eroded/degraded? Extent of soil erosion/land degradation (percentage)
Responses to environmental degradation	Have national/regional policies or actions been introduced in the last 50 years as a response to land degradation problems in the region? Have local policies or actions been introduced in the last 50 years as a response to land degradation problems in the community? Do these policies or actions work (if not, why not)?
Decision-making	Who are the main decision-makers in terms of environmental management? Are there important traditions, taboos or rites which influence the management of community resources?

Source: LEDDRA, 2011; after Cumming *et al.*, 2005; Geddes *et al.*, 2007; Resilience Alliance, 2007; Bodin and Crona, 2008; Derkzen *et al.*, 2008; Masten and Obradovic, 2008; Shortall, 2009; Ostrom, 2009; Magis, 2010; Oudenhoven *et al.*, 2010

Note
The list of questions started with a brief description of the community, especially location, size, community boundaries, and main disturbances threatening the community (in the case of the LEDDRA Project focusing on land degradation issues).

environmental capital, but not optimum level as only 'almost everybody' has access). Further, if the question 'does the local infrastructure constrain income generation?' was answered with 'yes (plus explanation)' then a score of 0–2 was allocated (weakly developed economic capital). On the other hand, if the question 'is access to external funds open to all stakeholder groups?' was answered 'yes, for most stakeholder groups' a score of 7–9 was given (strongly developed economic capital, but not optimum level). Similarly, if the question 'do stakeholders trust fellow stakeholders/groups within the community?' was answered 'yes, very much so' a score of 9–10 was allocated (indicator of strong social capital), while answers to the question 'do people have pride in the community?' such as 'not really, although some stakeholders have more pride than others' were allocated a score of 3–5 (moderately developed social capital).

As a seventh step, a specific average score could then be calculated for each of the three capitals in each community, and an overall average for the three capitals could be established, enabling quantitative comparison across diverse socio-cultural boundaries. The advantage of the LEDDRA methodology is that there is no prescription about how many questions are needed to assess each of the three capitals. This *cumulative methodology* means that the larger the number of questions used to assess the intricacies of individual capitals, the more 'accurate' the assessment of resilience will be (see also Resilience Alliance, 2007). However, it also needs to be acknowledged that the 'full' assessment of resilience or vulnerability will remain a hypothetical goal as, inevitably, answers to the questions will be incomplete or will not be always fully answerable (see also below). Assuming that a numerical average can be calculated within and across the capitals for each community, Figure 2.4 shows a hypothetical example of two case study communities. Community A is characterized by relatively well-developed economic

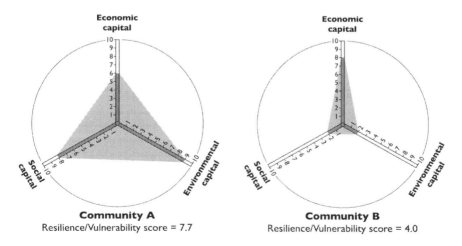

Community A
Resilience/Vulnerability score = 7.7

Community B
Resilience/Vulnerability score = 4.0

Figure 2.4 Hypothetical example of two case study communities with high and low resilience scores based on quantification of social, economic and environmental capital (source: LEDDRA, 2011).

(average score = 6), social (= 8) and environmental (= 9) capital, overall averaging 7.7 across the three capitals. Community B, on the other hand, has well-developed economic capital (= 8), but only weakly developed social (= 2) and environmental (= 2) capital, with an overall average of only 4.0. Connecting the numerical scores on the three axes creates a *resilience triangle* whose shape and size is characteristic of strong or weak resilience. The larger the area of the triangle, the more resilient a community is likely to be. Both the numerical averages and the size of the resilience triangle suggest that Community B is more vulnerable to disturbances than Community A. Such information can be used to specifically target policy or action aimed at enhancing resilience and adaptive capacity (see Chapter 7).

Eighth, inevitably there are practical and philosophical problems associated with the quantification of resilience (Gahin *et al.*, 2003; Thomalla and Klocker Larsen, 2010), especially as "if we define a priori the variables that lead to system resilience, then our conclusions will be largely driven by our initial selection of variables" (Cumming *et al.*, 2005, p. 976). Further, it may be relatively easy to allocate scores to some indicators where there is likely to be little cultural difference in interpretations of 'good' or 'bad' resilience scores (e.g. happiness of a community would be universally seen as a high scoring indicator for social capital; cf. Abdallah *et al.*, 2009). However, with many indicators the distinction between 'good' and 'bad' resilience indicators is not straightforward. For example, as highlighted above it will be highly context-dependent whether several sources of income for each household (economic capital, block of questions about 'sources of income') are a good or a bad thing for the development of community-level economic capital and, ultimately, resilience. Similarly, as Chapter 6 will discuss in detail, whether a community is well integrated with regional institutional structures (social capital, block of questions on 'political structure') may be an indicator of either poorly or well-developed social capital, depending on local, regional and national socio-political contexts. In addition, it was one thing for stakeholders to talk about resilience and another to assess resilience *actions* (i.e. had talk been converted into action?). Again, cross-checking with other methods (e.g. analysis of specific resilience actions such as flood defences, terracing or establishment of community groups to tackle disturbance) enabled some triangulation of results (with adjustment of scores where necessary).

In addition, the above methodology assumes that all indicators assessed in the list of questions shown in Table 2.2 have 'equal' value and are directly comparable in their achieved scores. This is, of course, highly questionable, although the cumulative nature of the methodology (i.e. as many questions can be added as necessary for each of the capitals) means that the larger the number of questions, the more 'accurate' the final average score for each capital is likely to be. As the LEDDRA Project highlighted, missing data (i.e. local teams not being able to obtain data on certain questions or even blocks of questions) further exacerbates the problem. In addition, the above quantitative approach is also based on the assumption that the three capitals themselves are 'equal', although they are likely to be based on different sets and numbers of questions and may operate on different temporal and spatial scales. Further, it also needs to be acknowledged that the list of questions only provides a snapshot in time to assess resilience issues, and although some questions enquired about processes over the past 50 years, results could only be interpreted in a wider context of local expert knowledges about past and present pathways of change in the case study communities.

These problems highlight that quantitative resilience scores are always context- and locality-specific (Resilience Alliance, 2007). Some indicators are more problematic to assess and, as Cumming *et al.* (2005) convincingly highlighted, issues of subjectivity and cultural positionality are almost impossible to avoid (depending to some extent on the scale of the research question and which case studies are selected). Indeed, "given the impossibility of studying all aspects of any real-world system, some level of subjectivity in determining which system properties to study seems inevitable in any applied study of resilience" (Cumming *et al.*, 2005, p. 978). Issues of positionality highlighted in Section 1.2 are, therefore, particularly important to recognize and acknowledge. As a result, as alluring as the quantified results shown in Figure 2.4 may be due to their simplicity and ease of interpretation for decision-makers, quantitative assessments of community resilience should never be used in isolation and should *always* be supported by (where possible) field visits, researcher embeddedness, qualitative data, focus groups or the establishment of community-specific storylines, that help cross-check and contextualize quantitative research findings. The LEDDRA approach, with its observational methodologies and establishment of qualitatively based storylines for each community, ensured that the quantitative community resilience scores could be interpreted within a wider context that, at times, also enabled the questioning, and adjustment, of subjective quantitative scores.

2.6 Conclusions

This chapter suggested an analytical framework for assessing community resilience and environmental transitions based on notions of economic, social and environmental capital and how these may help conceptualize resilience at community level. Different characteristics of community resilience and vulnerability were discussed and the complexity of interactions of different characteristics that make up a resilient community were highlighted. In particular, the complex interlinkages between economic, social and environmental characteristics were discussed as a basis for understanding environmental transitions over time. The chapter also discussed scalar issues for understanding community resilience, in particular with regard to communities as partly 'open' systems that can obtain skills, services and resources from 'outside' the confines of the physical community boundary. The chapter concluded with a critical discussion of possible methodologies to assess community resilience, highlighting that multi-method approaches that combine quantitative and qualitative approaches are probably best.

The following chapter will use this model of community resilience as a yardstick, and will use transition theory to argue that, globally, we have witnessed a spatially heterogeneous lowering/strengthening of community resilience based on a variety of endogenous and exogenous propelling forces.

3 Transition theory
Pathways of change and resilient communities

3.1 Introduction

Transition theory will be used in this book to understand how environmental pathways at community level evolve, and how resilience and vulnerability of communities change over time. The chapter will first introduce transition theory and will explain why it is an important approach for understanding the link between pathways of change and resilient communities (Section 3.2). Specific focus will be placed on how transition theory can help better understand community transition issues related to social memory, path dependency and transitional corridors. In Section 3.3 a transitional model will be presented which suggests that, over time, many communities around the world have lost resilience based on both increased embeddedness into a globalized world and the global capitalist system, and due to increasing global environmental challenges such as climate change. The section then discusses the contemporary bifurcation and hybridization of community development pathways, resilience 'thresholds' and 'tipping points' associated with community transitional pathways, and debates on the impact of globalization on community resilience. Concluding remarks are provided in Section 3.4.

3.2 Transition theory and community pathways

This section will explain what transition theory is and how it can be used as an approach for understanding the link between social and environmental transitions and community resilience and vulnerability. Specific focus will be placed on how transition theory can help better understand community transition issues related to social memory, path dependency and transitional corridors.

3.2.1 Theorizing transition

Transition theory is a general theory at the heart of which lie general principles, patterns and processes applicable across different fields (Pickles and Smith, 1998; Martens and Rotmans, 2002). From a social science perspective, transition theory can be seen as a theoretical framework that attempts to understand and unravel socio-economic, political, cultural and environmental complexities of societal transitions (or sub-systems of society …) from one state of organization to another … Transition theory suggests that, at times, coherent phases of societal organization can be identified … while at other times complex and even chaotic transitional characteristics may dominate, leading eventually to a new set of 'structured coherences'.

(Wilson, 2007, p. 14)

The increasing importance of transition theory in the social sciences is linked to recent radical changes in conceptualizations of societal change associated with the 'cultural turn'. As Pickles and Unwin (2004, p. 14) argued, the cultural turn has meant that "scholars are now more interested in the contingencies of transitions and the ways in which local people and ways of life shape the specific outcomes of transition in particular places". As a result, Chakrabarti and Cullenberg (2003, p. 5) suggested that 'transition theory' now forms one of the key analytical components in the social sciences, as concerns over community trajectories "have multiplied in recent years given the amount of literature on transition and development as well as the media coverage on the transition process". Theorizing transition has also received added impetus through emergent literature on complexity theory in which the complex nature of transitional processes (e.g. path dependency; see below) is becoming increasingly evident (O'Sullivan, 2004). However, in a recent book that used transition theory to understand the notion of 'multifunctional agriculture' I argued that transition theory has not yet gelled into a coherent theoretical framework (Wilson, 2007), although some overarching concepts and ideas for theorizing transition have been applied across disciplinary and philosophical divides (e.g. Frigg, 2003, on self-organized criticality). In this sense, transition theory shares common ground with other newly emerging 'theories', such as complexity theory, seen by some as 'quasi-theories' rather than fully fledged theories on their own (Thrift, 1999; Rotmans *et al.*, 2002).

Nevertheless, there are sufficient indications that the concept of transitions is an attractive and helpful aid for figuring out social complexity and coherence. There is now a wide variety of literature on transition, from both social and natural science perspectives, which identifies specific patterns and types of transitions. A transition in this context can be defined as "a gradual, continuous process of societal change where the structural character of society (or a complex sub-system of society) transforms" (Rotmans *et al.*, 2002, p. 3). Transition theory, therefore, assumes that there are key stages or periods in societal transition (but never 'end points'; cf. Davies, 1995), and that any of these stages may, in turn, become the starting point for the next transition – an assumption that will be critically examined throughout this book with regard to social/environmental transitions and community resilience.

Transition theory has been strongly embedded within regulation theory (e.g. Dunford, 1998; Smith and Swain, 1998), as both transition and regulation theory share the conception that societal transition phases, i.e. the structuring and restructuring of everyday life, occur "within complex articulations of local, regional, national and globalizing contexts. Histories, political economies, discursive formations, and institutional assemblages and practices each comprise complex articulations of *universalizing* and *particularizing* processes" (Pavlinek and Pickles, 2000, p. 22, emphases added). As economic theorist Lipietz (1987) argued, these articulations can be seen as structuring moments which *normalize* and *regulate* social, economic and political life. Lipietz (1992) further referred to 'development models' that characterize particular economic and political organizational forms adopted (or imposed by external forces) during different stages of societal transitions. Transition theory also draws from academic traditions like new institutionalism to stress the importance of social memory, path dependency and transitional corridors created by ideological commitments, and political, institutional and social legacies which filter learning and choice-making options (Bailey and Wilson, 2009). As a result, transition theory has been used as a key theoretical approach to understand societal change in diverse fields such as the transition from socialism to post-socialism (e.g. Stiglitz, 2002), policy change (e.g. Martens and Rotmans, 2002), rural transitions (e.g. Wilson, 2007, 2008), and general shifts from 'isms' to 'post-isms' such as the Fordist transition (e.g. Lipietz, 1992; Hudson, 2000), the transition towards post-modernism (e.g. Latour, 1993; Macnaughten and Urry, 1998) or to post-colonialism (e.g. Abdel-Fadil, 1989; Childs and Williams, 1997).

There are important differences between the application of transition theory in the social and natural sciences. In the natural sciences transition processes are usually *non-anticipatory*, where a system under investigation (e.g. natural landscape change) cannot forecast and adjust for a change in output (Thornes and Brunsden, 1977). Human systems, meanwhile, such as a local community, are usually *anticipatory* (Davidson, 2010). In the latter, therefore, *social memory* is crucial and may lead to a *learning* and *adjustment* phase based on past experience. Social memory, thus, implies that knowledge, experience and accumulated wisdom are passed on from generation to generation and from actor to actor within a community (and beyond) (see Chapter 4). These 'learning pathways', in turn, often streamline transitional processes characterized by *path dependency* – transitional pathways within a community that can be very difficult to alter (see Chapter 5). Such pathways are further influenced by human institutions and forms of governance (frequently at national/supra-national level) that can actively shape transitional processes, often in the shape of relatively narrowly defined *transitional corridors* (Chapter 6). The role of policy and other institutional interventions is particularly important in defining, shaping and, at times, distorting, the direction and pace of these corridors (Chapter 7). Analysing transitions in human systems, therefore, means that there is no objective way of observing and understanding transition, and – as Chapter 2 illustrated – transition theorists always need to be aware of their positionality and subjectivity in making suggestions (e.g. through policy) for shaping and changing transitional pathways.

3.2.2 Transitional models and community resilience

Walker and Salt (2006, p. 9) offer a succinct definition of resilience by arguing that "at the heart of resilience thinking is a very simple notion – things change – and to ignore or resist this change is to increase our vulnerability and forego emerging opportunities". Addressing change is, therefore, a key element of resilience, and highlights why it is important to understand societal transitions (Resilience Alliance, 2007). There has been much debate about the specific shape that societal transitions can take. Chapter 2 argued that transitions at community level can be conceptualized along a spectrum of resilience and vulnerability (see Figure 2.1) which can be used to define the 'y'-axis in transitory models with bounded spaces defined by the most resilient and the most vulnerable pathways within which human environmental decision-making takes place. Using the framework of economic, social and environmental capital to define resilience (see Chapter 2), community transitions can be seen to consist of 'bundles' of economic, social and environmental pathways (themselves comprised of several transitional bundles) which, in their overlapping totality, define the transitional pathway of a community within 'pathways of the possible'. Figure 3.1 shows a hypothetical model of these transitional bundles at local community level, with pathways of the possible bounded by the extremes of individual decision-making pathways (in this case centred broadly around moderate resilience and vulnerability).[1] Further, transition theorists conceptualize transitions as a series of evolutionary decision points ('nodes of decision-making' in Figure 3.1), each of which becomes the starting point for future decisions and transitional stages along hybrid pathways (Marten and Rotmans, 2002; Wilson, 2007). Each of these nodes can lead to either an increase, stagnation or reduction of a specific capital in question (e.g. the first node shown in Figure 3.1 could be linked to a decision that has led to a weakening of environmental capital). If the totality of

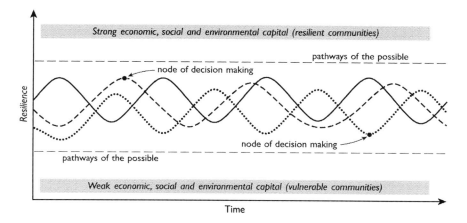

Figure 3.1 Economic, social and environmental capital and pathways of the possible (source: author).

transitional pathways goes beyond the boundary of 'weak economic, social and environmental capital' (i.e. if the lowest vulnerability threshold is surpassed), then complete or partially irreversible destruction of the community may be the outcome (see Section 3.3) (Adger, 2006).

Models of transitional pathways include *linear transitions* involving a steady movement from one transitional point to another (points 'a' and 'b' in Figure 3.2). Linear transitions are rare in human systems, and their specific shape and direction depend on the temporal and geographical scale of analysis. Over large scales, individual economic, social and environmental transitional pathways may cluster together to suggest linear evolutionary pathways, especially when observed over long time periods. However, when human transitional processes are scrutinized at larger scales, more complex non-linear processes become apparent (O'Sullivan, 2004; Resilience Alliance, 2007). *Failed transitions*, meanwhile, are characterized by trajectories where the quality of the transitional process under investigation is the same at the end point as it was at the starting point ('a' and 'b' in Figure 3.3), i.e. where transitional processes occur but ultimately lead back to the transitional quality characteristic for the starting point (e.g. abandonment of specific policies, community projects or programmes).

Stepped transitions are another common transitional model which may involve *transitional ruptures* (sudden usually 'downward' breaks in transitional pathways) involving more abrupt paradigm changes but also intra-paradigmatic experimentation with novel policies or instruments (Figure 3.4). Such ruptures (or 'regime shifts'; cf. Kinzig *et al.*, 2006) would most usually be linked to exogenous forces outside the community including environmental catastrophes such as tsunamis (e.g. Indonesian or Japanese communities after the 2004 and 2011 mega-tsunami events; e.g. Rigg *et al.*, 2005), earthquakes or volcanic eruptions (leading to a temporary or permanent weakening of economic, social and environmental capital and partial loss of social memory at community level; Paton *et al.*, 2001; Donovan, 2010) or sudden political upheavals (e.g. revolutions or

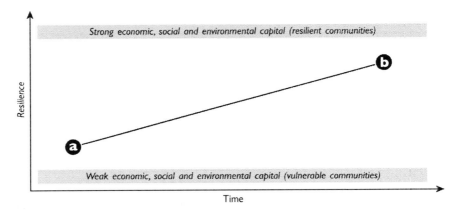

Figure 3.2 Linear community transitions (source: author).

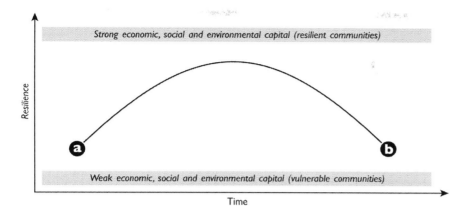

Figure 3.3 Failed transitions at community level (source: author).

uprisings that may lead to the complete breakdown of 'dissident' communities; the 'forced' transition to post-socialism in Eastern European countries; cf. Stiglitz, 2002) (see Chapters 5 and 6). As Anderies *et al.* (2006) and Kinzig *et al.* (2006) highlighted, transitional ruptures are not necessarily triggered by a single event affecting resilience, but may be the result of a series of smaller events leading to a 'cascading' regime shift (e.g. post-socialist transition; economic recessions). If a community is able to (at least partially) recover from the trauma of a transitional rupture, transitional models suggest that communities go through a 'period of readjustment' (which may be characterized by chaotic and random transitional pathways in the early stages) and a (possibly more linear) 'period of recovery' which may enable the community to 'rediscover' the more

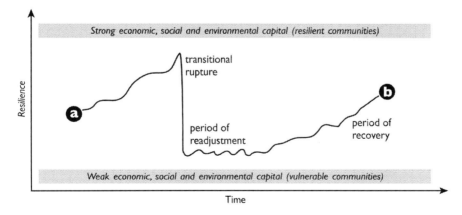

Figure 3.4 Transitional ruptures, readjustment and recovery in community transitions (source: author).

resilient pathways it had adopted before the catastrophe (i.e. points 'a' and 'b' in Figure 3.4). Folke (2006, p. 259), therefore, argued that "the dynamics after a disturbance or even a regime shift is crucially dependent on the self-organizing capacity of the complex adaptive system".

However, it is important to recognize that points 'a' and 'b' in Figure 3.4 need not be qualitatively similar. As Chapter 4 will discuss, where communities are able to survive disturbances and use their adaptive capacity to 'bounce back' during the period of readjustment, processes of social learning often mean that the community will gain a different 'type' or 'quality' of resilience to the one it had before the disturbance (Cumming *et al.*, 2005; Hopkins, 2010). Folke (2006, p. 258) rightly argued that "disturbance is part of development, and ... periods of gradual change and periods of rapid transition coexist and complement one another". Similarly, the Resilience Alliance (2007, p. 49) argued for "using disturbances to generate transformations" within communities. For example, perceptions of risks associated with experiences of disturbances survived by a community (e.g. a hurricane) inevitably will change post-disturbance adaptive capacity and may lead to better preparation of the community for the next disturbance (Homer-Dixon, 2008; Clerveaux, 2010). In other words, it will often be impossible for a community to recreate resilience attributes it may have had before the onset of the disturbance, especially as post-disturbance processes of learning, changing actor networks and changing socio-economic and environmental parameters, all mean that the past can never be reinvented.

It is evident that all these transitional patterns are *not* mutually exclusive, that certain transitional pathways can turn into others (e.g. a stepped transition with multiple transitional ruptures can lead to a failed transition in the short or long term) and that multiple transitional processes may be the most common form of transition encountered at any scale in human systems due to the complexity of actor interactions (Adger, 2000). Such a *multiple transitions perspective* is closely associated with social science debates on 'co-evolution' that argue for increasingly complex interlinkages and pathways of space, place and human territoriality (Norgaard, 1994; Graham, 1998), with Harvey's (1996, pp. 260–261) notion of 'cogredience' as "the way in which multiple processes flow together to construct a single consistent, coherent, though multi-faceted time-space system", and with Amin's (1990) notion of multiple development pathways in an increasingly 'polycentric' world. This model also intersects with debates in transition theory about the issue of 'oscillation' versus 'trend' in transitional pathways, and highlights the importance of investigating long-term changes which enable the identification of trends.

The multiple transitions model, therefore, argues that it is impossible to identify *one* transitional pathway for individual communities. Instead, we find a multiplicity of possible transitional pathways, all occurring simultaneously (see Figure 3.1 above) where different actors or actor groups within a community adopt different transitional pathways (e.g. in non-homogenous communities or in communities where multiple political actors are vying for power). Figure 3.5 shows a hypothetical example of transitions related to social capital and how different stakeholder groups may choose multiple pathways ranging from strong

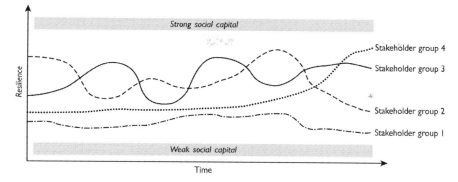

Figure 3.5 Transitions, stakeholder groups and social capital at community level (source: author).

to weak social capital. For example, while Stakeholder Group 1 is characterized by a pathway of social capital that remains close to the weak end of the spectrum (increasing community vulnerability or at least the vulnerability of their own stakeholder group), Stakeholder Group 4 has adopted strategies that have gradually raised the quality of social capital (increasing community resilience). For each capital, the sum total of these stakeholder pathways (at individual, household or stakeholder group level) defines the transitional pathway of a local community which can be described as 'pathways of the possible' (Chapter 5) within which human community-level action can take place.

It is evident, however, that the totality of individual stakeholder pathways in a community is not necessarily a zero-sum-game (Wilson, 2008) and that stakeholder groups or individuals who may choose pathways of weak economic, social or environmental capital may be able to do so precisely because other stakeholder groups have chosen pathways leading to stronger resilience of the community as a whole (Granovetter, 1985; see also Chapter 7). The sum total of community pathways is, therefore, often characterized by how power (economic or political) is exerted by some actor groups over others (Bryant and Bailey, 1997; Allen, 2003). As the following chapters will show, it will be rare to find communities where *all* stakeholder groups strive for the same pathways of resilience, especially if the choice of more resilient pathways is associated with potential loss of economic and/or political power (Peterson, 2000; Haxeltine and Seyfang, 2009). The more complex a community in terms of stakeholder groups and/or population size, the more likely it will be that multiple pathways of resilience exist. Some authors, therefore, argue that transition should not only be conceptualized as a directional movement from one point to another, but that a transition itself can act as a trigger for specific action *within* and *across* a multi-stakeholder community, akin to a development with a life of its own (Wilson, 2007). As discussed in the remainder of this book, this assumption suggests that, once embarked on a pathway, the outcome of a transition is often indefinable and that any of the multiple pathways shown in Figure 3.5 may ultimately lead to the 'final outcome' for the community as a whole. Yet, individual pathways should not necessarily be seen as closed systems, as *complementarities* may exist between different (and closely related) trajectories within a community (e.g. through processes of learning or political power; see Chapters 4 and 5). What the model of multiple simultaneous transitions, therefore, usefully highlights is that understanding transition should be based on different and multiple vantage points, and that individual pathways may be interpreted differently depending on who does the interpretation (see also Section 2.5, especially the discussion on positionality related to methodologies for assessing community resilience). It is evident that we will have to bear this multiple transition model in mind when discussing community pathways with seemingly *specific* outcomes in subsequent chapters of this book. Throughout I will, therefore, emphasize that community transitions are often characterized by multiple simultaneous trajectories, even if a community is, at times, described as a 'coherent unit'.

The attractiveness of the transition theory framework for understanding community resilience and vulnerability is, thus, manifold. First, it appeals through its focus on the 'contingencies of transition' (Pickles and Unwin, 2004) by understanding interactions between local, regional, national and global actors and contexts – in other words, the scale-independence of transition theory (both in terms of geographical and time scales) is one of its major theoretical and methodological assets (see also Chapter 2). Second, transition theory allows us to both forecast into the future based on existing pathways of change and to look back at the past because of incremental transitional evidence that enables us to 'test' the robustness of our transitional models.[2] Third, transition theory allows us to unravel the complex power relations in politics, ideology, culture and behaviour that contribute towards resilience or vulnerability of local communities through its focus on understanding the continuation, stability or disruption of particular transitional processes (e.g. ideologies, attitudes, policies) and their effects in creating predictable (but never deterministic) transitional behaviours. Fourth, it provides insight into the bounded nature of short- and long-term transitional opportunities and the way successive choices can progressively alter boundaries of community evolution through incremental progression or more significant ruptures. Finally, and arguably most importantly, transition theory allows us to draw attention to the often overlapping nature of processes of change at community level that *often lie submerged* beneath stylized portrayals of polarized pathways, especially by deciphering these through its emphasis on how decision nodes create and alter trajectories between community resilience and vulnerability.

3.3 Environmental transitions at community level: from subsistence communities to relocalized pathways

This section will use transition theory to analyse environmental transitions at community level, both over space and time. A conceptual model will be presented that suggests that many communities around the world have lost resilience over time while others have the potential to strengthen resilience. The section will also discuss conceptual issues related to establishing 'thresholds' and 'tipping points' with regard to loss of community resilience. The section pays specific attention to key drivers affecting community resilience, in particular globalization and the increasing embeddedness of many communities into the global capitalist system – processes that remain highly controversial with regard to their impact on community resilience.

3.3.1 Conceptualizing community resilience over space and time

Building on the above discussion, Figure 3.6 shows a conceptualization of changing community resilience and vulnerability over time. The figure shows highly stylized transitional processes which should be seen as thought experiments, where the necessary and contingent implications of transitional assumptions can be examined, without making claims about precision or predictive capacity (see O'Sullivan, 2004). The position of individual communities in the figure is comprised of multiple indicators (see Figure 3.1), the totality of which defines the position on the spectrum, and single-factor explanations will rarely be sufficient to explain the position of a community on the resilience spectrum. The figure builds on several associated studies that have attempted to establish spectra of human decision-making, in particular the UN Human Development Index (largely based on quantitative indicators) (UNDP, annual), the multifunctionality spectrum (Wilson, 2007, 2008) which uses normative notions of weak and strong transitional pathways linked to agricultural pathways of change, Diamond's (2006) analysis of the 'failure' of communities in different

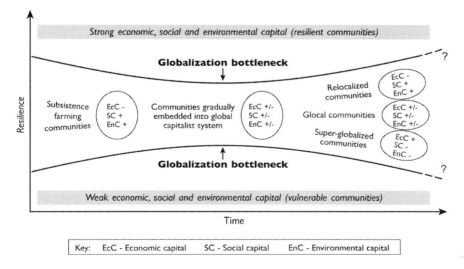

Figure 3.6 Types of communities and changing community resilience over time (source: author).

environmental and historical contexts, and Martens and Rotmans' (2002) assessment of transitions in a globalizing world. All these studies have highlighted that
it is possible to provide conceptualizations of changing human/societal trajectories over space and time, but, at the same time, they have also warned about the
subjectivity and problematic issues associated with the 'boxing in' and 'drawing
boundaries' around human decision-making entities that may, ultimately, not be
entirely possible. Key drivers of change include in particular globalization, especially the interlinkages between globalization and the integration of communities
into the global capitalist system (discussed separately in Section 3.3.3), but also
drivers such as climate change, changing dietary needs in countries such as
China and India, population change (through natural change and migration) and
cultural change (e.g. Adger, 2000; Kelkar *et al.*, 2008).

Several key features of the figure are apparent. First, the figure shows the
'quality' of resilience as a spectrum ranging from strong resilience where economic, social and environmental capital are all well developed, to weak resilience (vulnerability) where economic, social and environmental capital are
poorly developed. The figure is based on the assumption that resilience and vulnerability are oppositional and mutually exclusive (see Chapter 2). This spectrum of decision-making should be understood as a complex system in which a
myriad of actors and pathways intertwine in complex ways to assert their views
and actions of resilience over others. At community level, these transitional
pathways can be understood as the sum total of individual, household or group
actions associated with economic, social and environmental capital that define
the position of a community (or indeed a household within a community) on the
spectrum of weak/strong resilience. As Chapter 2 highlighted, it is, of course,
not possible to write of 'resilient communities' unproblematically, as the unit of
analysis within a community is in itself highly complex, and within single communities various levels of resilience/vulnerability are likely to coexist. The *sum
total* of individual, household or group actions means that we need to conceive
of community resilience evolving in diverse and often uneven ways within
apparently 'singular' contexts, and as rather diffuse and diverse sets of transformations which apply variously across spaces and population groups within communities. Building on Chaskin (2008) and Cutter *et al.* (2008), vulnerable
households/individuals can, through the sum total of actions at community level,
be sustained and, at times, helped to embark on more resilient pathways. In other
words, various levels of household vulnerability may be embedded in a community where resilience arises from the ways in which *collective* action helps negate
individual vulnerability (or vice versa).

Second, as both Martens and Rotmans (2002) and Wilson (2008) argued, we
can conceive of environmental change at community level as a 'transitional corridor' which shows the space where decision-making for resilience is most likely
to take place (see also Chapters 6 and 7). This space is bounded by pathways of
the 'possible' that tend towards strong resilience closer to the 'top' of the figure
and that, closer to the 'bottom', tend towards vulnerable communities. The transitional corridor should not be seen as an absolute boundary for decision-making

opportunities, as 'outliers' will always exist. Instead, the corridor should be seen as the centre of a bell-shaped curve distribution of the most likely resilience trajectories or, in Shucksmith's (1993) words, 'pathways of the possible'. Within this corridor some decisions taken at the community level are likely to reduce resilience (e.g. outmigration of young people), while others are likely to raise quality (e.g. soil conservation measures).

Third, Figure 3.6 shows the temporality of environmental transitions at community level. Building on previous work that has suggested that, historically, communities may have both lost and gained multifunctional quality (McMichael, 1995; Pretty, 2002, 2007), the figure suggests a temporal transition shaped like a *horizontal hourglass*. This suggests both a reduction and increase in resilience over time, albeit with pronounced geographical variation (see below). This argument is underpinned by the fact that in many communities indicators of strong community resilience have both weakened (e.g. loss of environmental capital through destruction/degradation of the environment, weakening social capital through outmigration, etc.) while in other communities resilience has been strengthened (e.g. through improved access to education, skills, markets, etc.) (e.g. Pretty, 1995; Parnwell, 2007).

These studies highlight that a variety of interlinked factors are contributing towards loss and rise of community resilience. Negative factors, for example, are often associated with disturbances to communities related to climate change (loss of productive capacity in many areas)[3] (Kelkar *et al.*, 2008; Mestre-Sanchis and Feijoo-Bello, 2009); changing food consumption patterns towards wheat- and meat-based nutrition in high-population transition economies such as China and India, reinforcing neo-productivist food production practices and often reducing environmental (and social) capital in rural communities (Davis, 2000; Veek and Veek, 2000); rapid expansion of both biocrops (e.g. oil palm plantations) and genetically modified crops, often replacing 'traditional' food crops and increasing the economic dependency of communities on volatile external markets while simultaneously affecting environmental capital (Curry and Koczberski, 2009; Steinberg and Taylor, 2009); or outmigration from rural areas and associated rapid (and often uncontrolled) urbanization with associated loss of social and economic capital at local community level (Rigg, 2006; Cutter *et al.*, 2008). Loss of community resilience, therefore, often emerges as a highly dynamic process akin to a 'slow-onset hazard' (rather than catastrophic change) over longer time spans and often typified by what Marsden (2003) termed a highly problematic 'race to the bottom' for many communities. Indeed, as Chapter 6 will discuss, declining resilience is a dynamic process dependent on antecedent conditions and influences from outside forces often beyond the control of local communities (Wilson, 2008).

Positive factors that lead to a strengthening of resilience are often associated with modernization, technological change and globalization although, as discussed in detail below, these can also contribute towards community vulnerability. Based on the discussion of indicators of resilience in Table 2.1, modernization, globalization, technological change and gradual embeddedness of communities into the global capitalist system may empower communities, or specific stakeholder groups such as women, to take more control over their own destinies (e.g. Rogers, 1995; Martens and Rotmans, 2002). The opening up of new markets for local produce, the mechanization of agricultural practices or improvements in children's and women's education, are only some of the many factors that may improve resilient capacity at community level (Pretty, 1995; Janssens, 2010). In particular, democratization processes that can accompany the gradual embeddedness of communities through processes of globalization (e.g. in many communities in India or Brazil since the 1950s) help empower communities in terms of electoral power, endogenous decision-making and effective policy implementation (Wilson and Bryant, 1997; see Chapter 6).

Fourth, Figure 3.6 positions different examples of local communities within a temporal evolution from relatively 'simple' to more 'complex' communities, and shows how economic, social and environmental capital tend to be developed within these communities.[4] At the left, we find rural *communities characterized by subsistence farming* (including subsistence fishing communities), which can be seen as the 'oldest' type of local community system, but still comprising hundreds of millions of farm households in today's world. As Oudenhoven *et al.* (2010) emphasized, these will often be characterized by a relatively wide decision-making corridor that contains both strongly resilient pathways based on relatively well-developed social and environmental capital, as well as vulnerable communities in which some capitals (especially economic capital) may be poorly developed (see Box 2.1 with the example of Haiti). While most of the indicators in Table 2.1 would resonate well with some subsistence farming systems, most will also show vulnerabilities, especially with regard to their ability to cope with natural hazards or with factors outside of their control such as insecurity over property rights (Adger, 2000; Prändl-Zika, 2008). Most importantly, most subsistence farming systems will rely almost entirely on agricultural production as the mainstay of their economies, and may, therefore, be overdependent on a monofunctional economic base. While social and environmental capital are usually well developed, economic capital usually is not (Pretty, 1995; Bardhan, 2006). As a result, and based on our discussion in Chapter 2, Figure 3.6 situates subsistence farming systems within a wide decision-making corridor, with some communities close to the upper boundary of strong(est) resilience and others closer to the weaker end of the resilience spectrum.

Communities gradually embedded into the global capitalist system are situated in the middle of the transitional corridor. These systems, often characterized by low technological and external inputs and as rural or urban communities with strong social capital, may be particularly vulnerable to capitalist forces that threaten to weaken strongly resilient characteristics (Macleod, 2002; Parnwell, 2007). Although such systems are still largely predicated on agricultural production as the basis for economic capital (in both the global North and South), such communities have been gradually embedded into the global capitalist system (Rigg *et al.*, 2008). This often means that communities may be forced/encouraged to intensify agricultural production and/or to seek alternative means of income generation – a process referred to by Rigg (2006) as a 'squeeze of decision-making opportunities' in the global South, or as a shift from self-sufficiency to *interconnected dependency* on the capitalist market, often associated with rapid urbanization (Van Rheenen and Mengistu, 2009). Although in itself this may not necessarily lead to a reduction of resilience, it is likely that some of the indicators of well-developed social and environmental capital are weakened in the process (e.g. Cumming *et al.*, 2005, for remote communities in Amazonia; Aggarwal, 2006, for communities in semi-arid savannah ecosystems; or Abidi-Habib and Lawrence, 2007, for northern Pakistan). This may be particularly true for social capital where outmigration of young people may lead to a disintegration of formerly close-knit communities (Bryceson, 2002), where a gradual loss of control over the destiny of the community may lead to a disintegration of local leadership (Bell, 2004; Folke, 2006), and where formerly strong locally based 'horizontal' governance structures are increasingly replaced by weaker 'vertically' oriented governance patterns (e.g. through increasing dependency of the community on externally controlled businesses) (Macleod, 2002; Wilson and Rigg, 2003). The increasing embeddedness of many communities into the global capitalist system is, therefore, often associated with the loss of endogenous power and control of communities over internal decision-making structures (Dicken, 1998; Rofe, 2009). Parnwell (2007, p. 1004), therefore, argued that through globalization "formerly cohesive and mutually supportive communities have become much more differentiated, competitive, and commercially oriented … Social capital has been depleted, less visible, less effective, and to some extent less necessary than it was in the past." In addition, global embeddedness may also lead to a reduction in environmental capital through land use change (especially intensification), in the most extreme cases threatening the livelihood base of local communities (Aggarwal, 2006). However, as highlighted above, globalization may also offer opportunities for *raising* resilient quality through, for example, improved infrastructure, reduced dependency on external funding, improved education or better information about how to tackle environmental degradation (Bardhan, 2006). Cumming *et al.* (2005, p. 979), therefore, argued that "resilience may be highest at intermediate levels of connectivity that break social isolation, without imposing outside interests on local groups". As a result, Figure 3.6 shows a transitional corridor characterized by a relative narrowing of decision-making opportunities – 'the capitalist straightjacket' – but that can also raise the quality of resilience for some communities with hitherto weakly developed economic (and at times socio-political) capital. This simultaneous squeezing and raising of resilience opportunities for communities gradually embedded into the global capitalist system is referred to as the *globalization bottleneck* in Figure 3.6.

To the right of the figure the situation becomes increasingly complex as we witness a *bifurcation* of community transitions that has been particularly pronounced in modern society. On the one hand, we find *glocal communities*[5] where agriculture no longer plays a major role and where new service-oriented functions are becoming increasingly important (Robertson, 1995; Noe *et al.*, 2008).

Until recently, such communities were almost entirely restricted to developed countries where the gradual loss of agriculture's position and importance in society has been particularly pronounced since the 1950s (Sheingate, 2000). However, increasingly, rural communities in the South are also characterized by processes of rapid deagrarianization (Bryceson, 2002; Rigg, 2006). Although deagrarianization can be a mixed blessing for rural communities (as witnessed by major upheavals in Western European rural communities that lost their agricultural base since the 1950s), it may also lead to improved community resilience. As Table 2.1 highlighted, overdependence on agriculture can be an indicator of community vulnerability, and the diversification of former *agricultural* communities into *rural* communities – with a wide variety of stakeholders from second home owners, to professional people working from their rural homes, to new non-rural businesses – can often raise community resilience (Woods, 2005). However, *counter-urbanization* and the dramatic changes associated with this process in many rural communities of both the global North and South also highlight the complexity of issues linked to the conceptualization of 'community' as a heterogeneous and complex construct in which power relations (e.g. between long-standing residents and newcomers) often define which community stakeholder groups benefit disproportionately from increased resilience (Massey and Jess, 1995; Allen, 2003). Diversification is the key issue for these communities, and in areas where multiple pathways of economic development have become possible and accessible for various stakeholder groups in a community, evidence suggests that resilience has increased (Meert *et al.*, 2005).

The right side of Figure 3.6 also highlights the emergence of *super-globalized community pathways*. Such communities have become particularly pronounced since the onset of wider globalization from the 1970s onwards and particularly after the breakdown of the Soviet Union in 1990 and the opening of most communities to the forces of the global capitalist market.[6] Super-globalized communities transcend the boundaries between the urban and the rural. In rural areas, these are characterized by communities embarked on super-productivist pathways predicated almost exclusively on the maximum production of food and fibre for profit (closely associated with global agri-businesses) (Wilson, 2007). In urban areas, super-globalized communities are usually part of larger conurbations or mega-cities where the geographical boundaries of the 'community' become increasingly blurred (Knox and Pinch, 2006). Indeed, super-globalized communities also include 'virtual communities' – communities no longer defined by geographical space but by internet-based global interconnections (Castells, 1996). Although, as Chapter 1 suggested, these virtual communities form an increasingly important part of global society,[7] I will restrict myself here to discussion of geographically bounded super-globalized communities (e.g. an 'urban' or 'rural community' with which residents can still more or less identify through the existence of a community centre with locality-specific services). Super-globalized communities are usually closely associated with a profit-maximizing strategy of dominant stakeholder groups (e.g. banks, global businesses, 'global citizens') and are often associated with Promethean and ecological modernization views of the world, characterized by a belief in human ingenuity, technocentric views of environmental problems and the assumption that economic development can be associated with environmental conservation on the basis of a win-win scenario (Bailey and Wilson, 2009). Figure 3.6 suggests that these systems can cover a large temporal span in the transitional corridor (e.g. in the developed world since the 1950s or earlier; in developing countries since the 1970s), and that they are likely to dominate community futures for some time to come, as they are largely driven by accelerating globalization processes and the spread of the global capitalist system (Johnston, 1996; Gray, 2002).

The coexistence of super-globalized and glocal communities emphasizes the complexity and spatial and temporal heterogeneity of contemporary community systems (Harvey, 1989; Knox and Pinch, 2006). Many commentators have suggested that the emergence of super-globalized communities since the 1950s has been largely responsible for a rapid reduction in community resilience. While economic capital is usually well developed, social and environmental capitals tend to be weak precisely because these communities – in the global North and increasingly in the South – are predicated on trajectories of profit maximization. Recent critical urban sociology literature suggests that although these communities cover a wide spectrum of decision-making that also contains elements of resilience based on usually well-developed economic capital, social and environmental capital are often severely threatened (Harvey, 1989; Bulkeley, 2006). While some adaptive capacity is present through the availability of money and mobility of community members, resilience may only be increased for individuals and not for the community as a whole (Granovetter, 1985). In other words, some stakeholder groups that are 'vertically' well integrated into the global capitalist system may be able to develop more resilient pathways than their less integrated neighbours, often leading to further disintegration of the last remnants of social networks in super-globalized communities – referred to as 'lost urban communities' by Knox and Pinch (2006). Writers from the political left, in particular, refer to these communities as 'morally bankrupt' spaces where greed and short-term thinking overshadow other human aspirations (e.g. Harvey, 1989; Robertson, 1992). Such *monofunctional* trajectories (see Figure 2.2) are often characterized by pronounced path dependency with often little option to revert back to less globalized community structures (Knox and Pinch, 2006).

In most developed countries and increasingly also in the developing world, the last few decades have also witnessed a process whereby communities continue to be based on more extensive and locally based production strategies – referred to as *relocalized communities* (Hines, 2000; Goodman, 2004).[8] Often, such processes have been aided by policies such as EU agri-environmental schemes that aim to enhance environmental quality in rural communities or by local initiatives in urban areas (Marsden and Smith, 2005; Hopkins, 2008). In many ways 'old' meets 'new' in these systems, as these communities attempt to rediscover low-intensity traditional production methods (food, fibre and other goods) that were present in subsistence farming systems for thousands of years

(Bohnet *et al.*, 2003). Relocalization has also occurred out of necessity during times of hardship, for example during the devastation caused by the bubonic plague in Europe in the fourteenth century, or during World War Two (WW2) in Europe which saw many communities (e.g. in the UK) being forced to relocalize food (the allotment movement) or energy production (reduced dependency on external energy supplies) (see Section 6.4).

The most prominent example of relocalized communities[9] is associated with the *Transition Town Movement* which incorporates about 1000 small towns and rural communities around the world (Hopkins, 2008). This involves small-scale relocalization pathways of individual communities aiming to disengage from the global capitalist system and exogenous energy dependency (see Box 4.6). Relocalization is thereby defined as the ability of communities

> to diversify their economies so as to provide for as many of their needs as possible from relatively close to home ... This does not mean elimination of trade altogether ... It is about finding a more secure and sustainable balance between trade and local production
>
> (Norberg-Hodge, 2003, p. 24).

From a more structuralist perspective, Hines (2000, p. 4) suggested that "localization is not a return to overpowering state control, merely government's provision of a policy and economic framework which allows people, community groups and businesses to rediversify their own local economies". Bailey *et al.* (2010) suggested that these relocalized communities are often associated with environmental attitudes linked to green romanticism and survivalism, and that they can be interpreted as a counter-reaction to capitalist globalization, neo-liberalism and the increasing economic dominance of super-globalized communities. The focus in these communities is on implementing radical ecocentric solutions, often associated with an attempt to reduce carbon-based energy dependency and on transforming social values and behaviour.

At the time of writing (2011), relocalized communities have tended to remain niche resistance movements and have been criticized for finding little acceptance in mainstream society (e.g. Pielke, 2006; Dahle, 2007; see Chapter 6). Even within relocalized communities the radical ecocentric approach sits uneasily with currently perceived global realities and personal lifestyle preferences (Bailey *et al.*, 2010). Winter (2003) also warned about romanticizing and reifying 'the local', as it is often associated with 'defensive localism' that may be closely associated with parochialism and nationalism. Yet, there is strong consensus among commentators (mostly from the political left) that these relocalized communities show characteristics of well-developed social and environmental capital, although they often lack well-developed economic capital (Hines, 2000; Bailey *et al.*, 2010). Relocalized systems indicate that the general decline of community resilience suggested in Figure 3.6 is not necessarily irreversible, and that the social, cultural and institutional memory that remains can provide the basis for the *resuscitation* of strongly resilient characteristics (see

Chapter 4). As a result, relocalized communities often have both the potential for the conversion of economic into social capital and for strong resilience. However, corridors of decision-making are wide and may also include characteristics of community vulnerability (e.g. lack of food self-sufficiency).[10] Nonetheless, some commentators argue that relocalized low-intensity systems are beginning to form an important counter-weight to super-globalized communities predicated on capitalist profit-making and that, as a result, they may help guide modern communities out of the 'globalization bottleneck' shown in Figure 3.6 (e.g. Hopkins, 2008).

3.3.2 Thresholds and tipping points for community resilience

One aim of this book is to discuss transitional community *thresholds* linked to both anthropogenic and natural disturbances that may have internal or external causes and that may be sudden and catastrophic or slow-onset disturbances. Resilience thresholds and tipping points linked to any form of disturbance will be associated with an inability of a community to recreate the original state before the transitional rupture, with the possible inability to implement a period of readjustment and recovery. Cutter *et al.* (2008) argued that a community's resilience threshold can be exceeded if the disturbance is so large that it overwhelms local capacity (e.g. a sudden volcanic eruption), or if existing coping responses are insufficient to handle the impact. The outcome for these communities may be a complete disintegration of the last remaining social support networks, outmigration of a large proportion of the community and possible complete reconstitution of community boundaries and spaces of community ownership (Cumming *et al.*, 2005).

Figure 3.6 (above) suggests that although many communities are losing resilience, not one system is either totally resilient or totally vulnerable, and elements of both will almost always be present within any community. The complexity of disturbances affecting communities shown in Figure 1.1 already suggested that communities are never 'stable', but that they are continuously and simultaneously affected by slow-onset and sudden disturbances. It would, therefore, seem almost impossible for any community to have 'maximum quality' with regard to all indicators of strong resilience discussed in Table 2.1 – at least for longer periods of time (Resilience Alliance, 2007). This means that communities can only strive towards the highest level of resilience achievable within their specific contexts of continuous disturbances (approximations of strong resilience). Historical evidence suggests that communities can disappear or be destroyed when one or several disturbances overpower communities' capacity to adapt. Wars, for example, usually negatively affect economic, social and environmental capital simultaneously, while natural catastrophes can lead to the destruction of environmental and economic capital and, as the example of the 2010 Haiti earthquake shows, often result in the concurrent weakening of social capital (Diamond, 2006; see Box 2.1). Building on Gladwell's (2000) theoretical discussion of *tipping points* and 'how little things can make a big difference', the following will investigate in more detail conceptual notions of 'resilience thresholds' and 'tipping points' and how these can be assessed for community-level transitions.

As Chapters 1 and 2 argued, any assessment of community resilience is linked to normative assumptions and the positionality of commentators. Any notion of community transition cannot be value-free, and when a specific transition is *interpreted* it inevitably becomes *value-laden* and *directional* (Davidson, 2010). We are, therefore, likely to witness increasing polarization of opinions in multi-faceted globalized societies, and finding consensus about the 'right' or 'wrong' community pathways is becoming increasingly difficult (Resilience Alliance, 2007). Indeed, notions of thresholds depend very much on cultural factors (e.g. different perceptions of risk and the importance of different 'capitals'), and labels such as 'vibrant', 'stagnant' or 'dying communities' associated with processes shown in Figure 3.6 need to be interpreted with different cultural and socio-economic interpretations of the terms in mind (see below). As Davidson (2010, p. 1146) argued, "our ability to identify with any objective confidence critical conditions or thresholds precipitating societal collapse is elusive". In addition, different *temporal scales* also make it difficult to exactly pinpoint thresholds and tipping points (Gunderson and Holling, 2002). Indeed, a community may be deemed resilient to short-term disturbances (e.g. a flood event) due to mitigation measures that have raised resilience for that specific threat, but may nonetheless remain vulnerable to longer-term disturbances such as climate change (Adger, 2003; Kelkar *et al.*, 2008).

Yet, while it may be more difficult to find general agreement on what makes up 'good' community pathways and 'strong' resilience (see Chapter 2), we can probably more easily identify 'bad' community trajectories, especially those associated with *complete annihilation* of communities. As Figure 1.1 highlighted, it is important to distinguish between community destruction linked to sudden natural hazards (e.g. tsunamis, earthquakes or volcanic eruptions) over which humans have no influence, and community destruction linked to human factors which are usually 'slow-onset hazards'. Although the latter may include 'sudden' hazards such as wars, human processes of change usually occur over longer time periods to which local communities may be able to adjust and adapt, including in particular globalization processes, the embeddedness of communities into the global capitalist system, changing human behaviours (e.g. dietary change, technological transitions) or human-induced climate change (Diamond, 2006; Davidson, 2010). 'Bad' community trajectories in this context refer to specific decisions made at specific nodal points in community transition processes linked to economic, social or environmental capital shown in Figure 3.1 (above). The key question is whether these bad decisions may eventually lead to the destruction of the community (Adger, 2000; Cumming *et al.*, 2005). This may involve a combination of poor economic decisions (e.g. poor investments, wrong prioritization of community funds, loss of economic assets), poor social decisions (e.g. poor policies or non-implementation of policies, decisions leading to the undermining of social networks, negative shifts in stakeholder power balances, a move away from inclusive governance structures) or poor management of community-based natural resources (e.g. clearfelling of forest leading to soil erosion, poor soil management practices, poor water management) (see also Chapter 5). While such changes may seem linear over certain time periods (see Figure 3.2), most often transitions will take the shape of a transitional rupture (i.e. a sudden loss in resilience characteristic) (see Figure 3.4). Tipping points and thresholds for community vulnerability, therefore, are related to the notion of 'catastrophic bifurcations' where, once a tipping point has been passed, a series of negative feedbacks drive the community into an often irreversible downward spiral (Gladwell, 2000).

Figure 3.6 suggests that local communities can potentially lose resilience, especially if there is a *transformation* from subsistence farming to communities gradually embedded into the global capitalist system to super-globalized communities. At which point could these communities be seen to have become so vulnerable through a loss of either economic, social or environmental capital (or of all three capitals simultaneously) that a 'move back' towards stronger resilience becomes impossible? The key question is whether communities that have fallen below a 'resilience threshold' after a transitional rupture linked to poor human decision-making can bounce back and survive? This will depend both on levels of *adaptive capacity* at community level and whether remnants of economic, social and environmental capital can be harnessed to enable a period of readjustment and recovery (Diamond, 2006; Folke, 2006). As Figure 3.6 shows, the 'rediscovery' of resilience may be easier for communities where economic, social or environmental capital were relatively well developed *before* the onset of the transitional rupture. Let us, therefore, investigate in the following the importance of resilience thresholds for different types of communities discussed in Figure 3.6.

While subsistence farming communities, for example, usually have poorly developed economic capital, they often have strongly developed social and environmental capital which may aid them to weather transitional ruptures. This may help some subsistence communities tackle external disruptions with more ease than many other communities through strong social networks and well-developed inclusive community-level governance structures. However, as Figure 3.6 suggests, subsistence farming communities also face immense challenges to their resilience, as extreme poverty often means that some challenges facing these communities may remain insurmountable (Rigg, 2006; Parnwell, 2007) – the reason why in Figure 3.6 many of these communities are located towards the weaker end of the resilience spectrum. While these communities may be able to successfully tackle short-term environmental or economic challenges (e.g. droughts, floods, temporary breakdown of trade), the lack of financial capital can pose a severe barrier for addressing problems linked to long-term global pressures such as climate change (Adger, 2003; Kelkar *et al.*, 2008; Box 3.1). It is estimated that there are already about 50 million 'climate refugees' globally (complete loss of environmental and economic capital), and most of these will be among the world's poorest subsistence farming communities (Pretty, 2007).

Most are located towards the lower resilience end of the transitional corridor shown in Figure 3.6 and may, ultimately, fall beyond resilience thresholds marked by their complete disappearance.

Box 3.1 Sea-level rise and resilience thresholds for low-lying farming/ fishing communities

For low-lying subsistence farming/fishing communities in the Pacific and Indian Oceans or in the Caribbean, sea-level rise linked to global warming induced by anthropogenic carbon emissions may lead to one of the most extreme forms of loss of resilience, i.e. when the land base upon which communities rely for survival (for settlement, food) disappears completely (Hastrup, 2009; Madaleno, 2010). In this case, external factors beyond the control of the community can exacerbate endogenous drivers, especially as the irreversible loss of environmental capital itself often creates a 'ripple effect' of loss of economic and social capital (Briguglio, 1995; Kinzig *et al.*, 2006). 'Irreversibility', 'thresholds' and 'tipping points' in this case refer to the inability of the community to recreate or reinstall its land base and associated lost environmental resources. With the current global rise in sea levels of several millimetres/year due to melting ice and thermal expansion of the oceans, many coastal communities in countries such as Kiribati, Tuvalu or Bangladesh are projected to disappear by 2050 (Diamond, 2006). For example, the extremely low-lying Carteret Islands (off Papua) may be completely flooded as early as 2020, with plans to evacuate all the 2500 inhabitants to the island of Bougainville (Papua) as soon as possible. In Bangladesh, every year several hundreds of thousands of people have to flee from rising waters, in Tuvalu 12,000 people are threatened by rising water, and in Kiribati 110,000 inhabitants may leave their islands over the next few decades to settle permanently in New Zealand and Australia. In the Maldives, as the lowest-lying country in the world (highest point only 2.4 m), a recent government meeting was held under water as a form of protest against climate change-induced sea-level rise, and plans are already underway to purchase land for resettlement of communities in India, Sri Lanka and Australia.

As Figure 3.6 suggests, relocalized communities share some of the attributes of subsistence farming communities, although they have usually 'gone through' pathways of globalization and integration into the global capitalist system with possible loss of social and environmental capital in the past. However, relocalized communities are a *response* to the loss of resilience in globalized community systems, and may highlight how *adaptive capacity* can be harnessed to rediscover more strongly developed resilience pathways. By advocating local food and energy production (based on local foodsheds for example; see Figure 5.2), relocalized communities such as the Transition Towns Movement are attempting to reduce dependency from external drivers such as food imports or fickle energy supplies (Marsden and Smith, 2005; Pinkerton and Hopkins, 2009; see Chapters 5 and 6). Indeed, they aim at embarking on pathways that take their communities away from perceived resilience thresholds (with more or less success; see Hopkins, 2008; Bailey *et al.*, 2010). Relocalized communities in the developed world have the advantage that although economic capital can be negatively affected by the adoption of relocalization pathways that partly disconnect them from the global capitalist system (with huge variations; see North, 2010), these communities remain nonetheless relatively wealthy (in a global context), enabling them to tackle global drivers such as climate change in a different (and arguably more technologically focused) way than would be possible for poor subsistence farming communities. Due to the recency of the relocalization movement, there is as yet little tangible evidence whether relocalized communities can effectively *fully* disengage from global capitalist profit-oriented transitional pathways and whether levels of resilience are indeed *substantially* improving (see also Chapter 6).

Communities gradually embedded into the global capitalist system or glocal communities, meanwhile, face different resilience thresholds. As highlighted in Figure 3.6, these communities are often characterized by both a weakening/strengthening of social and environmental capital and moderately developed economic capital (with large geographical variations). For these communities resilience thresholds may be less associated with immediate threats linked to disturbances such as climate change, as existing economic capital may allow these communities to respond in the short to medium term through technological solutions, but are likely to be associated with increasing erosion of social and environmental capital. The latter may in some cases undermine the ability of these communities to successfully implement adaptive strategies, and may jeopardize the successful implementation of processes of adjustment and recovery after exposure to anthropogenic or natural disturbances. Resilience thresholds in these communities will, therefore, be less tangible and immediate, as the rise in economic capital may help cushion negative external influences more easily, but ultimately the relative loss of social and environmental capital may outweigh other positive gains (Pretty, 2007). As a result, communities gradually embedded into the global capitalist system are often characterized by a 'squeeze' of decision-making opportunities (the 'globalization bottleneck' in Figure 3.6).

Super-globalized communities characterized by strong economic capital, but with usually weak social and environmental capital, meanwhile, may be the most vulnerable to transitional ruptures and closest to 'resilience thresholds' and 'tipping points' beyond which readjustment of community strategies may no longer be possible. The evident erosion of social capital in particular means that notions of 'community' (in a geographically defined sense) are no longer clear. Resilience thresholds in these cases are linked more to the needs and aspirations of *individuals* in a community than to the physical/geographical community as a whole within which these 'centres' are embedded, often resulting in 'communities' in which 'the heart has been ripped out', where there is no feeling of neighbourhood and trust, and where, at worst, moral bankruptcy may be most evident (Granovetter, 1985; Pretty and Ward, 2001). Resilience strategies of individuals in these communities are, therefore, often linked to short-term profit maximization overshadowing community-level strategies (Gray, 2002; Bardhan, 2006), possibly best exemplified with reference to super-globalized communities in some of the world's financial centres such as London, New York or Dubai, especially in the wake of the global economic crisis of 2008–2011. Although strong economic capital is usually existent in these 'communities', this capital is often global in nature and no longer necessarily linked to the locality within which the capital is being produced. This is best exemplified by multinational organizations which, although embedded within communities in some form or another, rarely pass on the profits of their transactions to the locality (Korten, 1995; Bardhan, 2006). Although globalized communities can contain some elements of strong (individual and largely economic) resilience, the sum total of transitional pathways linked to different forms of capital (see Figure 3.1) suggests that globalized communities are often situated closer to the bottom of the community resilience threshold.

3.3.3 Globalization and the loss of community resilience

The previous discussion has highlighted that globalization can be both a positive and negative driver for community resilience. Figure 3.6 is based on a variety of assumptions, most important of which is the argument that globalization, and the associated embeddedness of local communities into the global capitalist system, can lead to both a loss of resilience for some communities and an increase of resilience for others. In the past few decades, this 'opening up' of community boundaries (geographical, socio-cultural, political and economic) at various scales has been particularly accelerated by globalization processes that have affected even the remotest communities on the globe (Wilson and Bryant, 1997; Young *et al.*, 2006), suggesting that completely geographically 'closed' communities are increasingly a thing of the past. Globalization in this context is characterized by *time-space compression* and the *acceleration of worldwide social relations* which are transforming the structure and scale of human relationships as economic, social and environmental processes operate at a global rather than regional/local scale (Giddens, 1990; Gray, 2002). Globalization is particularly associated with global harmonization and uniformity of human processes, especially with regard to tastes and cultures increasingly satisfied through the provision of standardized global products made by global corporations that have lost their allegiance to place or community, trade liberalization, changing consumer preferences, and virtual networks linked to the internet (Castells, 1996; Van Rheenen and Mengistu, 2009).

Broadly speaking, two opposing views about the impact of globalization on community resilience can be identified. One school of thought (the 'pro-globalization school') argues that local communities increasingly brought into the 'orbit' of the capitalist world may benefit from positive 'spin-off' effects for *increasing* community resilience, in particular by providing better access to financial capital and trade through neo-liberal free market-oriented policies and processes, and better access to education, technology and global services such as the internet (Held *et al.*, 1999; Rofe, 2009). This school of thought also argues that globalization reduces the economic, social and environmental isolation of communities, thereby providing more opportunities for increased resilience, while the increasing embeddedness of even the remotest communities into the global system also helps to avert total community collapse at times of extreme crisis (e.g. food aid can be brought into globalized communities more quickly; Brunk, 2002; Clapp, 2005). While in the past many communities were 'left to fend for themselves' in the face of severe disturbances, globalization means that many of these communities are now more embedded in wider global economic and social networks which help 'buffer' negative effects of disturbances. Associated with this is the argument that these improved interlinkages and the emergence of the 'global village', in turn, may help increase social capital at community level and, in some instances, may also help improve environmental capital (Featherstone, 1995; Pretty and Ward, 2001). There is a close link here with those advocating that neo-liberal market reform may help local communities partake in capitalist modes of accumulation (Langhorne, 2001; Bhagwati, 2004).

A second school of thought – mainly from the political left, from a neo-Marxist perspective, and from the 'alternative' political scene – can be broadly described as 'anti-globalization' and 'anti-neo-liberal'. This school views globalization as malign with regard to community resilience, and foregrounds its negative aspects with regard to the loss of community integrity and social capital through increasingly globally integrated stakeholder interaction (e.g. Mander and Goldsmith, 2000; Stiglitz, 2002; Gray, 2002). In this view, 'horizontal' interactions at local level, that in the past led to the formation of strong trust and bonds between members of a community, are replaced with 'vertical' interactions in which stakeholders 'scale up' their connections with the wider world, thereby often neglecting the local community level (Harvey, 2006; Jackson, 2009). Davidson (2010, p. 1142) thus argued that "key sources of connectivity in contemporary globalized society may … produce 'deviation-amplifying mechanisms' that condition future transformations in a manner that reinforces maladaptive behaviour", while Hastrup (2009, p. 25) suggested that globalization means that "age-old certainties and patterns of resilience are melting away, thereby effectively blocking out people's visions of a local future, and certainly shrinking the space of certainty within which they may act". Associated with these processes, anti-globalization commentators argue that individuals or stakeholder groups are 'losing touch' with the local level, leading to possible disintegration of social and environmental capital (Lang, 1999; Mander and Goldsmith, 2000). Rotmans *et al.* (2002, p. 2), therefore, argued that "there are justified fears that [globalization] may be exacerbating the gap between rich and poor, and creating new threats to human security in terms of financial volatility, political and cultural insecurity and environmental degradation". For rural communities in the global South, meanwhile, freer trade associated with neo-liberal processes is seen as playing into the hands of the rich North, permitting multinational corporations to further dominate markets of the South, rather than empowering local communities (Goodman and Watts, 1997; Harvey, 2005). In these globalized communities, 'community interaction' is, therefore, increasingly disembedded from the geographical community (e.g. a village or urban community) and replaced with non-place-based 'virtual' communities characterized by global 'business communities', virtual 'internet communities' or geographically dispersed actor networks (Castells, 1996; Gray, 2002). Most importantly, critics argue, globalization can be seen as a cancer-like growth resulting from uncontrollable market forces (Jones, 1997), inexorable and unstoppable, which can only be accommodated and not effectively resisted (Leichenko and O'Brien, 2008; Jackson, 2009).

Arguments of the 'pro-globalization' school are shown in Figure 3.6 for communities that start with low levels of resilience and that experience *gradually rising* resilience with increasing embeddedness into the global capitalist system, while arguments from the 'anti-globalization' school are shown through the gradual loss of resilience for communities that started with strongly resilient characteristics. This partly echoes cautionary notes that reification of the 'local' can be problematic, as it may reinforce an optimistic view of an overly simplistic opposition between disembedded global capitalist actors and their embedded local counterparts (Agrawal and Gibson, 1999; DuPuis and Goodman, 2005). While the pro-globalization proponents are probably correct in arguing that increasing economic capital does indeed open up new opportunities for increasing resilience, the anti-globalization school is also correct in pointing out the frequent disintegration of social capital in globalizing communities (Hastrup, 2009). As a result, Adger (2000, p. 353) argued that "the resilience of ... communities can therefore be affected in both positive and negative ways by market integration", while Bardhan (2006, p. 1393) suggested that

> globalization can not only cause many hardships ... but it can also open up some opportunities which some countries can utilize and others do not ... and the net outcome is often quite complex and almost always context dependent, belying the glib pronouncements for or against globalization made in the opposing camps.

Despite these more 'neutral' voices, loss of environmental capital has been identified as a particular problem associated with the spread of global capitalism (Porritt, 2007; Leichenko and O'Brien, 2008). The Millennium Ecosystem Assessment (2005) has been particularly critical and has documented for various types of landscapes, ecosystems and communities around the world how environmental degradation has accelerated over recent decades linked to globalization pressures. It highlights that mean species abundance between 1970 and 2050 is likely to decline from 78 per cent to 60 per cent, mostly due to increases in crop and pasture areas and for infrastructure development, with a rising component linked to climate change. Globally, €14 trillion/year are linked to losses of land-based environmental capital (especially biodiversity and ecosystem functions) or 7 per cent of gross world product by 2050 (Costanza *et al.*, 1997; Pretty, 2007). While in some communities integration into the global capitalist system may indeed offer opportunities for the creation of new economic opportunities (e.g. by opening new markets for certain products), in others such integration may reduce economic (as well as social) capital, for example by creating new dependencies linked to new markets or new technologies or by exacerbating the divide between 'winners' and 'losers' within a community (see Chakrabarti and Cullenberg, 2003, for India; Kaplinsky and Messner, 2008, for China). The latter is particularly true for rural communities where localized and locally/regionally well-networked agro-commodity chains are disrupted/destroyed through global economic reorientation of the community (Parnwell, 2007; Rigg *et al.*, 2008).

As is evident from Figure 3.6, many non-globalized communities facing extreme pressures linked to external drivers such as climate change may not be in a position to raise resilience without financial (and other) help from the more globalized rest of the world (see examples of low-lying island communities in Box 3.1) (Adger, 2003; Kelkar *et al.*, 2008). As Robinson (2004, p. 146) argued,

> within the ongoing arguments over the limits to the future extent of ... globalization are different views over who will benefit. In examining the experience of globalization to date, there have been strong contentions that benefits are highly confined to those at the hub of the process or to those retaining particular connections to it. Elsewhere the overwhelming mass of humanity has either not experienced any significant benefits or are actually being impoverished.

As Chapter 2 highlighted, striking the right 'balance' between communities and their scalar interactions with the global level is, therefore, key for maximization of community resilience: while too much isolation of a community may be bad in light of overdependency on local resources, skills and people (as the example of Easter Island and the destruction of environmental capital illustrates; see Box 4.3), 'overglobalization', with possible loss of autonomy and identity, may be equally fraught with problems.

If we accept, then, that globalization does play a role in influencing community resilience, at what point on the time axis in Figure 3.6 did globalization begin to influence transitional trajectories at local community level? Much critical literature has highlighted the importance of historical globalization and colonial processes on the widening of decision-making opportunities for local communities in the past. Michie and Grieve Smith (1995), for example, argued that in quantitative terms the world was perhaps at least as open economically in the nineteenth century as it is today, and Hirst and Thompson (1996) also questioned whether current globalization trends and their effects on community development were different from those of the colonial era in terms of direct effects on livelihoods of economically marginal communities. However, there is general consensus that the nature of global integration during the colonial era was *qualitatively* different and that eighteenth- and nineteenth-century global processes were characterized by *internationalization* (extension of global economic activities across national boundaries) rather than *globalization* (functional integration of remote communities into the global economy) (Goodman and

Watts, 1997). In other words, while the pre-1914 world economy was an increasingly internationalizing economy, the nature of integration was more 'shallow' based primarily on arm's-length trade in goods and services, while today's globalized communities are characterized by a deeper degree of community integration based upon interconnected configurations of production (Waters, 1995; Gray, 2002). What could be argued, therefore, is that the current coexistence of super-globalized and relocalized communities shown in Figure 3.6 suggests that decision-making opportunities are again *widening* in both the global North and South, and that the decision-making corridor for community resilience may be currently one of the widest since the emergence of the first subsistence farming communities 12,000 years ago. As Bardhan (2006) emphasized, this widening transitional corridor for community resilience suggests both an environmentally and socio-culturally problematic deepening of more vulnerable pathways in some super-globalized communities, as well as new opportunities for the 'rediscovery' of strong resilience in relocalized communities.

3.4 Conclusions

This chapter suggested that transition theory forms a useful theoretical framework for understanding how environmental pathways at community level evolve, and how resilience and vulnerability of communities change over time. Different transitional models were discussed, highlighting the complex nature of community transitions and the spatial and temporal heterogeneity associated with transitional pathways. Based on an approach situated conceptually between 'sustainable development' and 'green romanticism/survivalism', I have adopted an argument critical of globalization and the global capitalist system. As a result, the main argument was predicated on the assumption that, over time, many local communities around the world have lost resilience based on both increased embeddedness into a globalized world and the global capitalist system, and because of increasing global environmental challenges such as climate change. This has meant that many communities have adopted transitional pathways that take them close to, or indeed beyond, resilience thresholds and tipping points, and that in some cases community-based adaptive capacity to recover may be insufficiently well developed due to loss of social and environmental capital. I also argued that more recently we witness a bifurcation and hybridization of community development pathways, with super-globalized communities with often low levels of resilience on the one hand, and relocalized communities attempting to re-engage with environmental practices that may raise community resilience (with more or less success) on the other.

These debates form the basis for understanding some of the key transitional processes that shape community resilience and how communities cope with environmental and social change at the local level: social memory, path dependency and transitional corridors. These key transitional issues will provide the focus for discussion in Chapters 4–7.

4 Social memory

Community learning, tradition,
stakeholder networks and community
resilience

4.1 Introduction

In the previous chapters it was argued that we can conceptualize community
resilience by paying specific attention to how well economic, social and environmental capital are developed within a community. I also argued that transition
theory provides a particularly suitable lens through which we can understand
environmental transitions at local community level. We have also seen that different types of communities have different levels of resilience to environmental
change, and that such resilience can also change over space and time.

Building on the discussion of transition theory in Chapter 3, this chapter will
argue that a local community can be understood as a social system exposed to
manifold endogenous and exogenous drivers (e.g. climate change). Such a
system will have specific inherent qualities that will be shaped by the 'memory'
contained within the system – a memory linked to individuals (individual life
histories) and stakeholder groups (acquired memory, communal memory). It is
this notion of *social memory* that will be the focus of this chapter, and that will
form the basis for better understanding the importance of the interlinkages of
path dependency and local community resilience (Chapter 5), transitional corridors (Chapter 6) and policies and resilience (Chapter 7). Section 4.2 will, first,
discuss what social memory means and how it is interlinked with learning processes, tradition and historical networks at community level. Using examples
from around the world, Section 4.3 will then discuss how social memory can act
both as a malign and benign force in shaping social and environmental transitions at local community level, how 'exported' social memory can shape socio-
environmental pathways at community level, and how lost social memory can be
'rediscovered' to increase the resilience of communities. Conclusions are provided in Section 4.4.

4.2 Social memory at local community level

This section will focus on four interlinked themes: understanding social memory
(Section 4.2.1), exploring the interlinkages between social memory and
community learning (Section 4.2.2), analysing the role of tradition in local

community transitions (Section 4.2.3) and an investigation of historical stake-holder networks and social memory (Section 4.2.4).

4.2.1 Understanding social memory

The notion of 'social memory' was popularized by Von Bertalanffy (1968) who highlighted that any system – whether human or natural – is imbued with a 'memory' that relates the system to events and processes that occurred in the past. The importance of memory in the shaping and understanding of landscapes shaped by human action was further highlighted by Schama (1995) in his seminal book *Landscape and Memory*, in particular with regard to how memory can shape environmental management strategies at community level (see also Olick and Robbins, 1998; Folke, 2006). There is a clear link to transition theory (see Chapter 3), as the notion of social memory is predicated on the assumption that the position of a system in any transitional process is directly linked to events in the past, i.e. that transitional pathways do not occur in a vacuum but that they are embedded in often complex antecedent histories (Brierley, 2010). As Tudge (2005, p. 301) argued,

> history marches on an infinity of timescales simultaneously. Every living creature or the ancestors that gave rise to it has been influenced by events that happened yesterday, decades ago, thousands of years ago or hundreds of millions of years ago and by the same token, everything that happens in any one moment affects the next second, the next year, and so on into the indefinite future.

Social memory leads to a *learning* and *adjustment* phase based on past experience (see also Figure 3.4) (Resilience Alliance, 2007; Stump, 2010). Social memory thus implies that knowledge, experience and accumulated wisdom are passed on from generation to generation and from actor to actor within a community (and beyond) (Rival, 2009; Oudenhoven *et al.*, 2010). Any community system will be at its specific starting point in a transition precisely because of the history of decision-making trajectories *preceding* that starting point. In other words, a system carries with it the memory – or, in a more negative sense, the 'baggage' – of previous decision-making trajectories (O'Sullivan, 2004). Chapter 3 high-lighted that there is an important distinction to be made here between natural and human systems. Although natural systems are imbued with system memory (e.g. the way a river has carved out a river valley over millennia), natural systems are usually *non-anticipatory* as the system (e.g. natural landscape change) cannot forecast and adjust for a change in output (Thornes and Brunsden, 1977; Brierley, 2010). Human systems, on the other hand, are *anticipatory*. In these systems, social memory is a crucial transitional element and may lead to a *learning* and *adjustment* phase based on past experience that streamlines transition pathways (Dudley *et al.*, 2009) (see Figures 3.4 and 3.6). Transitions in social systems are, therefore, *non-deterministic* (Wilson, 2007).

There is a close link between social memory and path dependency (discussed in Chapter 5), especially as transition theorists with roots in evolutionary political economy point to the importance of path dependency that shapes the nature and pace of societal transitions (Stark, 1992; Grabher and Stark, 1997). In these debates, the emphasis is largely on how social memory of human systems (e.g. a local community) is shaped by, and in turn shapes, institutionalized forms of learning and institutional thickness (Olick and Robbins, 1998) and on the fact that personal choices can be *self-reinforcing* and, therefore, often self-fulfilling (Davidson, 2010). In other words, means may become ends and alternative pathways may not even be considered. This means that social memory can be both a *good* and *bad* thing as, on the one hand, it may 'lock-in' local communities on pathways that may be more resilient, but, on the other hand, may also propel local communities down transitional pathways that may, ultimately, lead to the complete erosion of economic, social and environmental capital (Diamond, 2006). Social memory thus implies that once a transitional pathway has been chosen it may be very difficult to leave this pathway due to various cultural, socio-economic, political and institutional factors (O'Sullivan, 2004). Yet, Rotmans *et al.* (2002, p. 3) argued that "a transition process is not set in advance, because during a process of change, humans are able to adapt to, learn from and anticipate new situations". However, Hudson (2000, p. 301; emphasis added) rightly cautioned that

> it remains an open question as to whether a revolutionary shift from one path to another can be achieved through *incremental change* and evolutionary reformist modifications to the existing developmental trajectory or whether it requires a *rapid quantum leap* from one trajectory to a qualitatively different one.

For human systems, this means that forecasting the effect of transition may be even more complex than it is for natural systems, as the direction of change is influenced by both the passing of time and often unpredictable human adjustment strategies (Diamond, 1998, 2006; Gunderson and Holling, 2002). In addition, and as Chapters 6–7 will show, the direction and pace of transitional pathways can be specifically influenced by policy and other institutional interventions.

The critical literature on social memory suggests that there are three human processes most closely associated with social memory: community learning, tradition and historical stakeholder networks. It is to each of these that the following discussion will turn.

4.2.2 Social memory and community learning

Chapter 3 argued that community-level resilience thresholds and tipping points associated with human factors of change will particularly be linked to the inability of a community to recreate the original state before a transitional rupture, with an associated inability to implement a period of readjustment and recovery. A community's resilience threshold can be exceeded either if the disturbance is so large that it overwhelms local capacity, or if existing coping responses are insufficient to handle the impact, with the possible complete disintegration of a community (Dudley *et al.*, 2009; Davidson, 2010). A community's adaptive capacity will largely depend on past and present *learning processes* – often referred to as 'social learning' (Keen *et al.*, 2005; Osborne *et al.*, 2007). Adger *et al.* (2005b, p. 1038) defined social learning as "the diversity of adaptations, and the promotion of strong local social cohesion and mechanisms for collective action".

As Jazeel and McFarlane (2010) emphasized, learning is a complex process that involves individual and community interpretations of information, reflections on previous experience (social memory), group discussion and established practices (rites). Davidson (2010) added the importance of human imagination and anticipation as crucial aspects of community-level learning processes. Learning is often non-linear, uncertain and unpredictable and depends on community-specific space-times and histories. New knowledge gained through the adaptive resilience process (e.g. learning from having experienced a past hurricane) can both influence antecedent conditions and enhance the potential for resilience in the future through the implementation of new resilience strategies (Homer-Dixon, 2008; Magis, 2010). In this sense, both mitigation processes and preparedness of a community to future disturbance will be enhanced, for example through measures to strengthen environmental capital such as planting new mangroves for better protection of vulnerable coastal areas from storm surge impacts (e.g. Adger, 2000, for Vietnam; Dudley *et al.*, 2009, for Hawaii). Social learning at community level is closely linked to issues of learning quality, scale, learning processes (i.e. how is learning passed on?), attachment to place and the associated desire to preserve pre-disturbance cultural and environmental norms, and to power structures within communities (who is learning and who benefits most from learning processes?) (Keen *et al.*, 2005; Osborne *et al.*, 2007).

First, understanding the *quality* of community-level learning processes is crucial for understanding adaptive capacity and, ultimately, community resilience. Cutter *et al.* (2008) highlighted that it is important to distinguish between positive learning in the context of the adaptive resilience process and 'lessons learned' from the past (i.e. learning from mistakes). While the former can be seen as a proactive learning quality in which communities may learn to anticipate disturbance based on improved risk awareness and associated preparedness (e.g. floods, political change), the latter is reactive in that the learning process occurs *after* a disturbance has already taken place. One key advantage of human systems over natural systems is that the quality of learning can be enhanced in human systems as communities can *benefit from hindsight* about environmental pathways that have 'gone wrong' (Davidson, 2010; Stump, 2010). Yet, as Homer-Dixon (2008) highlighted, learning quality associated with 'lessons learned' can only be turned into a positive learning experience if the community survives the disturbance. Provided the community has not been destroyed through poor decision-making in the past, a community may be able to enhance resilience by implementing improved high quality learning pathways building on previous mistakes (Diamond, 2006; Pretty, 2007). Positive learning quality, therefore, also has to be associated with learning processes that occur before a disturbance takes place and is closely associated with levels of education (formal and informal) in a community and how information about the possible effects of disturbances is communicated to, and within, the community. Yet, human systems rarely (if ever) follow linear pathways of change as shown in Figure 3.2, but, instead, are usually characterized by multiple complex pathways that may occur in unpredictable ways. This means that learning processes need to constantly adjust to new challenges, such as finding the best possible ways to pass on information to the next generation which may, in turn, challenge how things were done in the 'olden days'. Critical literature on learning theory, therefore, argues that only 'partial learning' may be possible between the generations and that each generation has to experience similar challenges and disturbances to previous generations (e.g. wars) before being able to successfully implement lessons learned (Keen *et al.*, 2005; Osborne *et al.*, 2007). As a result, social learning can be either *incremental, episodic* or *transformational*, with only the latter having the potential to lead to strengthened adaptive capacity as "the key to transformational learning is to know what to keep in terms of memory, experience, and wisdom and what to discard" (Anderies *et al.*, 2006, p. 3).

Second, issues of *scale* are equally important in social learning at community level and are closely associated with power relations within communities and beyond (Peterson, 2000; Allen, 2003). Although it may be possible for all members in small communities to be involved in preparing for disturbances, in most communities a scale-dependent *compartmentalization of social learning* is likely to take place (Gale, 1996). This will usually be based on the expertise and the individual social memory of stakeholders, and how this expertise can be best put into practice in the case of a disturbance. In particular, scale-dependant compartmentalization of social learning is evident when disturbance or disaster management is delegated to specialist actors outside the community, for example to regional experts in building and managing flood defences. This can lead to loss of endogenous adaptive capacity and overreliance on external knowledge and actions (Anderies *et al.*, 2006; Lebel *et al.*, 2006). Individual community members and their own specific expertise how to tackle disturbances will, nonetheless, be important in most disturbance scenarios. For example, in small farming communities, the farmers themselves will usually be the best actors to implement farm-level adjustment strategies to cope with droughts, floods or socio-political disturbances (Wilson, 2007). Many studies highlight, however, that the most successful social learning takes place when the entire community is given the opportunity to take part in a joint learning effort about how to best tackle disturbances to the community (Gale, 1996).

Third, how *learning processes* function and how knowledge about how to tackle disturbances is passed on to individuals in a community is another crucial step in social learning. Some argue that social learning is most successful when beneficial actions linked to environmental management at community level are put into formal or non-formal (e.g. oral tradition) policy for handling future events (Dorfman *et al.*, 2009; see also Abidi-Habib and Lawrence, 2007, for a good example of resilience learning processes in remote communities in northern Pakistan). It is this 'encoding' of learning that is seen to be particularly important by sociologists, as individual memory can be subject to decay over time (Dudley *et al.*, 2009; Stump, 2010). The most successful learning processes are, therefore, those that successfully encode knowledge so that it is available to members of the community over several generations (Keen *et al.*, 2005; Oudenhoven *et al.*, 2010). A classic example relates to how information is passed on within contemporary communities situated at the slopes of dormant volcanoes about impacts of past eruptions on the community (Paton *et al.*, 2001; Donovan, 2010). Although individual-level oral tradition still plays an important part in most communities in developing countries and is still important in many communities of the developed world, some commentators argue that oral history is more likely to distort the severity of past disturbances. Historical distance to disturbance events, in particular, may skew risk perceptions (e.g. volcanic hazards) towards the more beneficial aspects of living in danger areas (e.g. benefiting from rich volcanic soils) (Donovan, 2010). Individual 'encoding' of knowledge is, therefore, often selective and may lead to ruptures in social memory, for example through the outmigration or death of a knowledgeable community member. Successful encoding, therefore, is often associated with the enshrining of risk knowledge and successful adaptive community responses from the past into more communal and long-term processes, such as communal traditions or subconscious rites and 'taboos' linked to historically harmful activities (see below) (Lambek, 1992; Berkes, 1999).

Fourth, *attachment to place* and the *desire to preserve pre-disturbance cultural and environmental norms* are important aspects of both social learning and social memory (Merrett, 2001; Devine-Wright, 2009). Attachment to place is often dependent on the embeddedness of actors to 'their' community. Sociological literature suggests that the longer an individual or a family has been living in the same community, the stronger attachment to place is developed, and the more social learning processes will be shaped by this long-term interaction (Keen *et al.*, 2005; Pretty, 2007). This is probably best highlighted in subsistence farming communities not yet touched by globalization (e.g. central Amazon, Papua) where hundreds of generations of a family may have lived within the same area and adopting similar environmental management strategies over centuries. In these cases, the likelihood that preservation of pre-disturbance cultural and environmental norms will be paramount is high, and adjustments to new qualitatively different transitional pathways (see Figure 3.4) may be particularly difficult. Attachment to place may, therefore, be most closely associated with social memory at community level, as strong development of both is predicated on long-term residence in, and embeddedness of, a community (Scarfetta and West, 2004; Ward and Styles, 2006). As the next section will discuss in more detail, attachment to place is also closely interlinked with the development of traditions which may find either benign or malign expression in community-level environmental management strategies.

Finally, social learning is shaped by *power structures* at community level. Who is learning to cope with disturbances and who benefits most? In almost any community, power is unevenly distributed, with some actors or stakeholder groups having disproportionate access to information and communication about possible impacts of disturbances (Allen, 2003; Whatmore, 2009). As a result, disturbances to a community do not affect all stakeholders equally. For example, those stakeholders with access to finance and technology may be in a better position than others to implement adaptive capacities needed to cope with natural catastrophes (e.g. they may have houses that are less prone to flooding or better protected as evidenced in some Japanese coastal communities affected by the March 2011 mega-tsunami). Certain stakeholder groups will also be better placed to cope with social disturbances affecting their communities due to better embeddedness in networks of power and knowledge (Keen *et al.*, 2005). In some cases, certain stakeholder groups may even benefit from disturbances, i.e. powerful elites may be able to capitalize on disturbances/catastrophes through the weakening of their political or economic opponents (Johnston, 1996). This suggests that the period of readjustment and recovery shown in Figure 3.4 may not benefit all stakeholders in a community equally, and that the 'new' transitional trajectory after a transitional rupture is almost always *qualitatively different* from preceding community structures with regard to shifts in power structures and networks of decision-making.

4.2.3 Tradition and local community transitions

'Tradition' is closely interlinked with social memory at community level. It is associated with environmental beliefs and customs usually handed down orally from generation to generation within a community (Berkes, 1999; Donovan, 2010). Tradition is predicated on strong embeddedness and attachment to place of actors within a community, and can often be found in communities where a core group of stakeholders have lived in one place over several generations. As examples discussed in Section 4.3 will illustrate, tradition as part of social memory can also be transferred from one place to another, for example through migration of individuals, families or groups of stakeholders to new places. The latter has been particularly evident in 'settler societies' (e.g. from Europe to the United States of America (USA), Australia or New Zealand) where mass migration has often led to the reinstatement of 'traditional' living structures and environmental practices in settler communities.

Tradition is closely interlinked with specific conscious or subconscious environmental management practices that can be either benign or malign for the environment (Devine-Wright, 2009; Stump, 2010; see Section 4.3). As a result, environmental customs, rites or 'taboos' are often closely associated with traditional beliefs and can be seen as orally encoded sets of practices about 'how things have been done for generations' (environmental customs), or as restrictions on certain environmental decision-making behaviours (taboos) (Lambek, 1992; Berkes, 1999). From an environmental transitions perspective, therefore, most communities or individual stakeholders attempt to encode (consciously or subconsciously) successful past environmental management or disturbance avoidance strategies into tradition (Aggarwal, 2006; Donovan, 2010). Taboos are a particularly interesting way with which many communities around the world have attempted to regulate their human-environment interaction (Wilson and Bryant, 1997). The word 'taboo' originally comes from Polynesian (*tabu, tapu*) and was used in traditional Polynesian society to denote actions forbidden to general use or to a particular group of stakeholders. It has since been globalized as a term and has been appropriated into many languages beyond Polynesia. There is still much debate as to whether taboos in pre-modern societies were a means of conscious encoding of forbidden environmental practices (akin to an oral 'policy' framework; cf. Lambek, 1992; Wilson and Bryant, 1997), or whether taboos and associated environmental management practices are an expression of subconscious attempts at preserving specific environmental resources (Smith and Wishnie, 2000). The latter may be given credence through the fact that many taboos restrict the use of specific resources or places (e.g. game animals, special places such as water holes or forest groves) either temporarily or permanently and are, therefore, a powerful means through which over-exploitation of community-level environmental capital can be prevented. Taboos are, therefore, often an important aspect of 'epiphenomenal conservation' (subconscious environmental conservation) in traditional societies (Lambek, 1992; Smith and Wishnie, 2000).

The passing on of a tradition through customs and taboos takes on many different forms in communities. The longest record of community-level traditions is usually related to hunter-gathering societies such as the Australian Aborigines or the !Kung bushmen of the Kalahari desert (Africa) that have stayed within a specific area for hundreds of generations (Simmons, 1996; Gammage, 2008). In Aboriginal communities, for example, social memory has been particularly important, as these communities show(ed) strong levels of encoding of spiritual beliefs (e.g. linked to the ancestral 'dreamtime', the creation myth of Aboriginal society) with specific customs and taboos linked to sacred places and environmental resources (Head, 1989, 1993; Forbes *et al.*, 2009). As Wilson and Bryant (1997, p. 45) highlighted, the Aboriginal notion of 'dreamtime' – which specifies how the world was created as a manifestation of spirituality and which locates human existence within this spiritually conceived environment – "can be construed as an attempt, in part, to ensure the protection of some elements of the landscape from over-exploitation". Specific places near Aboriginal communities were seen to be embedded in the dreamtime, such as waterholes or forest groves, where the hunting of animals was constrained either temporarily or permanently. Ultimately, some researchers believe, this led to the preservation of important game species (e.g. marsupials) for millennia, and may explain why Aboriginal hunter-gatherer lifestyles survived for over 50,000 years in very harsh environments (Gammage, 2008). The passing on of tradition is also important in 'modern' communities and not necessarily restricted to 'traditional' societies. Most farming families around the world pass on traditions, customs and even taboos (e.g. preventing certain farming actions such as sowing or harvesting before specific dates) to their successors, with the ultimate aim of ensuring a viable and sustainable farm for the future (Rival, 2009; Stump, 2010).

Complexity is added in modern communities increasingly comprised of a varied mix of ethnic groups. In the UK, for example, it is estimated that by 2020 about 20 per cent of the population could be ethnic minorities. Many of these ethnic groups maintain some of their traditions for several generations (e.g. Indian or Pakistani communities in the UK), which means that for many (largely urban) communities multiple and parallel pathways of traditions and traditional values will be evident (Ward and Styles, 2006). Although there is little or no research on the topic so far, the implications for community resilience are likely to be complex, as ethnic minorities may bring with them (or pass on through the generations) skills that could be useful for raising community resilience (Magis, 2010). Sheller and Urry (2006, p. 211), for example, argued that "in leaving a place migrants often carry parts of it with them which are reassembled in the material form of souvenirs, textures, foods, colours, scents, and sounds – reconfiguring the place of arrival both figuratively and imaginatively". As Section 4.3.3 (below) will discuss in more detail, several authors (e.g. Scarfetta and West, 2004; Ward and Styles, 2006) have highlighted that certain traditions (e.g. a strong inclination towards recycling materials among Bangladeshi immigrants to the UK) remain prominent for several generations and may, at times, help raise community resilience.

4.2.4 Historical stakeholder networks and social memory

Beyond social learning and tradition, social memory is also closely associated with *historical* stakeholder networks within a community. As highlighted above, social memory will be at its most effective when it is implemented by the majority of a community, rather than just specific individuals. As Lebel *et al.* (2006) emphasized, understanding community networks, and associated power relations, is, therefore, crucial for understanding how social memory may affect environmental and social transitions at community level. Stakeholder networks in a community can take several forms, most important of which will be embedded (well interlinked) and disembedded actors (marginalized actors). Although marginalized actors can still shape community pathways if they wield a lot of power, power within a community usually stems from the fact that individuals or stakeholder groups are well connected and command the respect of other members (Allen, 2003; Whatmore, 2009). Often, it is the social memory of these powerful actors that tends to shape environmental pathways for the community as a whole through the implementation of traditions, customs and rites linked to specific environmental management practices.

There are several ways in which such historical stakeholder networks can be disrupted. First, they can be changed over time through shifting power structures within a community. Such power can be affected by various endogenous and exogenous processes, including in particular exogenous political change (changing political balances within a community), market upheaval (questioning existing customs and norms regarding community-level generation of economic capital) or endogenous changes such as the death of a community leader who steered the community 'into a certain direction' (Allen, 2003; see Bodin and Crona, 2008, for shifts in stakeholder networks in a Kenyan fishing community). Although this may not necessarily affect social memory of the community as a whole (especially if there is strong consistency in traditions accepted by the community as a whole), changes in power balances within communities often go hand-in-hand with changes or adjustments to existing environmental management practices (Peterson, 2000). 'Preferences' of the new stakeholder group in power may change (e.g. with regard to water management and allocation), emphases may shift (e.g. more focus on forest protection rather than exploitation) or traditions and customs may be 'interpreted' in slightly different ways (e.g. relaxation of taboos or other environmental protection mechanisms).

Second, historical stakeholder networks can be severely disrupted through inmigration of newcomers or outmigration of existing community members (Massey and Jess, 1995; Paagman *et al.*, 2010). Inmigration may be linked to wider social changes in society, such as counter-urbanization associated with increased mobility, which can bring people from urban areas into formerly close-knit village communities (Savage *et al.*, 2005). For example, there is much empirical evidence of the impacts of counter-urbanization on rural communities in Europe. While studies are ambiguous as to whether counter-urbanization necessarily negatively affects economic, social and environmental capital of communities, most studies agree that immigrants – usually from urban areas – contribute towards changes of the social fabric of communities and, most importantly, may shift long-established power balances within communities (Massey and Jess, 1995; Woods, 2005). Counter-urbanites often come with greater wealth and better education, and are, therefore, often in a position to assert themselves politically and economically more vociferously than long-standing residents. Social memory will, inevitably be disrupted, although newcomers may also inject vital new skills, information and knowledge that may, ultimately, raise community resilience (Halfacree, 1999; Savage *et al.*, 2005). Conversely, counter-urbanites may also lead to the erosion of long-standing community structures and networks and may, therefore, gradually undermine social capital of a community. Similarly, the influx of large numbers of foreign workers (e.g. into communities in the United Arab Emirates), often with low educational skills, may disrupt community-level social memory as immigrants lack space-based empirical knowledge and connection to stakeholder networks in their new communities (Locke *et al.*, 2000). Salamanca (2010) highlighted how, in the aftermath of a large hurricane in the Turks and Caicos Islands (Caribbean), this lack of social memory and local embeddedness of immigrants led to post-disturbance looting and other disruptions considerably slowing the process of recovery.

Outmigration of community members or entire stakeholder groups also affects social memory of a community, as these outmigrants 'take with them' long-acquired local knowledge, disrupt existing power structures (often it is younger people who leave the community) and may also reduce economic capital of the community (e.g. Hwang *et al.*, 2007, for China; Forbes *et al.*, 2009, for arctic Russia). Although human history has seen a permanent in- and outflow of people into and from communities, the most pronounced changes to local communities have occurred during distinct phases of societal evolution, in particular during industrialization in the modern era and mass outmigration to the New World (Pretty, 2007). In developed countries, the main impacts on local (rural) communities through outmigration of young people of working age occurred between 1750 and 1950 with immense repercussions for social and economic capital in the home communities, and associated potential loss of environmental capital through lack of personpower (Wilson, 2007). Since the 1950s, similar processes have occurred in the developing world. In China, for example, it is estimated that as many as 400 million people have left, or are planning to leave, rural areas to find work in the wealthier cities. Inevitably, this changes the structure and composition of stakeholder networks in their home villages (for better or worse) (Cartier, 2001; Ye and He, 2008).

The impacts for communities receiving new migrants are equally complex, especially if entire stakeholder groups or communities 'resettle' in a new area. One of the most interesting questions regarding environmental transitions at community level concerns the potential impacts that European settlers had on environments in the New World, especially as they brought with them both 'good' and 'bad' social memory and 'cultural baggage' that has affected how these settler societies managed the new environments they found in countries such as the USA, Canada, Australia or New Zealand. It is to specific examples of the impact of such 'good' or 'bad' social memory on community resilience that the next section now turns.

4.3 Social memory and community resilience

Building on above discussion of interlinkages between social memory and social learning, tradition and historical stakeholder networks, this section will address four key themes associated with social memory and community resilience. Section 4.3.1 will, first, analyse how social memory can be positive for community resilience. However, social memory can also be associated with negative environmental trajectories at community level, and Section 4.3.2 will analyse, through examples, both why this is the case and how it is affecting community resilience. Section 4.3.3 then focuses specifically on the issue of 'exported' social memory in settler societies and what impacts this has had on environmental pathways at community level. How lost positive social memory can be rediscovered in communities is then addressed in Section 4.3.4.

Social memory can work both ways with regard to the resilience of communities: as a good thing related to social learning and traditions associated with environmentally beneficial and benign practices, and as a bad thing closely related to traditions that may encourage environmentally harmful and malign practices. Here, it may be worth briefly reconsidering the notion of 'resilience thresholds' explored in Section 3.3.2. Environmentally benign social memory will usually be associated with communities that have managed to 'stay afloat' or even thrive and that have survived the many disturbances affecting them over centuries/millennia. Environmentally malign social memory, on the other hand, can be associated with the complete disappearance of communities which may have forced outmigration in the first place. Let us investigate first examples where social memory has acted as a positive process.

4.3.1 Social memory as a positive process for community resilience

Most communities will have built up long-term positive memories associated with sustainable environmental management practices. Key examples include implementation of soil conservation strategies, such as using organic fertilizers, contour ploughing to avoid surface erosion, traditional grazing land management techniques (Box 4.1), or various practices associated with fallow periods to enable soil nutrients to regenerate (Pretty, 1995; Rival, 2009). Sustainable water management practices have also been particularly important in communities in arid and semi-arid environments, and often rely on intricate communally managed irrigation systems that can be hundreds or even thousands of years old (Simmons, 1996). As the sustainable management of these irrigation systems relies on close cooperation between community members, honesty (e.g. regarding water allocations to individual fields) and good communication (especially in times of water shortages), the successful functioning of these systems often suggests that social capital is well developed at community level (Pretty, 2007). Indeed, many historical examples highlight (e.g. some South American and Middle Eastern civilizations) how the lack of resilient capacity of communities linked to poor or disturbed social capital often led to a dismantling of irrigation systems and, consequently, the disappearance of communities (Diamond, 2006). Many communities also rely on sustainable forest management practices for survival, especially if forests used by the community are used for food and timber. Again, the sustainable management of complex forest ecosystems (especially in the tropics) relies on social learning processes and traditions passed on through the generations often based on trial and error with regard to how much human disturbance a forest can tolerate without leading to irreversible environmental degradation (Wilson and Bryant, 1997; Smith and Wishnie, 2000).

Box 4.1 Social memory and sustainable mountain grazing systems in the southern Pyrenees, Spain

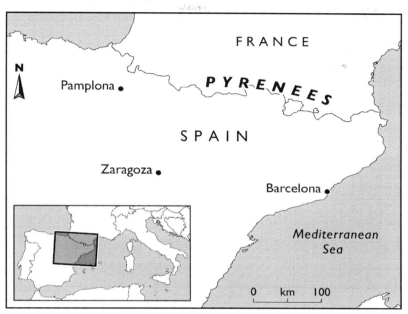

Small communities in remote valleys in the southern Pyrenees (Spain) are characterized by complex transhumant farming systems that have been in place since the Arab invasion of the Iberian Peninsula in the eighth century AD. Positive social memory is particularly linked to knowledge among shepherds passed on through the generations about the most appropriate seasonal use of ecologically fragile high alpine meadows (2500–3000 m) in often relatively inaccessible terrain – knowledge necessary for the survival of these communities. This knowledge has been positive for community resilience, as it has enabled farmers to maximize the use of both upland and lowland meadows over centuries without degrading the environment (LEDDRA, 2011). However, since the 1970s this social memory has been gradually lost due to outmigration of young people, and the fact that shepherds can no longer find successors from within the communities. Although new shepherds have been brought into the remote valley communities, they have come from outside the area (mainly from Romania and central Africa) and lack the social memory and knowledge necessary to sustainably use mountain pastures. The result has been the almost complete abandonment of complex alpine transhumance in the southern Pyrenees, with resultant loss of biodiversity (e.g. shrub and forest regrowth into less biodiverse ecosystems) (LEDDRA, 2011).

Gaillard *et al.* (2008) highlighted how 'positive' social memory about the impacts of past natural catastrophes such as tsunamis can help survival of affected communities. This was demonstrated through the self-evacuation of 78,000 residents of Simeulue Island (150 km off the west coast of Sumatra, Indonesia) during the 2004 Indian Ocean tsunami (see also Rigg *et al.*, 2005, for Thailand). Gaillard *et al.* argued that less than 1 per cent of the island population died during the tsunami, because the community was able to use oral history linked to a past tsunami event (in the nineteenth century) that had killed 70 per cent of the population leading to loss of community resilience for more than a generation. This example highlights that if certain practices prove successful and sustainable over longer time periods, they then often become encoded into more 'formal' social learning processes such as rites, taboos (e.g. the preventing of house building in tsunami-prone coastal zones) and 'traditions' that ensure that knowledge about 'best practice' and how it can be implemented is retained within a community (e.g. how to read the signs of a forthcoming tsunami). In modern communities, this encoding of social learning processes is also helped through technologies such as the internet which enables communities to quickly access knowledge and information about how to tackle disturbances at any time – best evidenced through rapid digital information dissemination warning Japanese residents of the March 2011 mega-tsunami (with more or less success).

Such encoded social learning is often also associated with long-term social processes such as religious beliefs and rites. As both White (1967) and Passmore (1980) argued, religious beliefs and practices are often closely intertwined with both positive and negative environmental transitions, and are an intrinsic aspect of social memory. Wade (2009) even suggested that, from a Darwinian perspective, human propensity for religion has some adaptive function, i.e. that it may contribute towards more resilient communities by encoding certain aspects of positive social memory and by enshrining religious moral codes that may enhance community resilience (see also Dennett, 2006). While there is much debate about the benign or malign nature of religion for sustainable environmental management practices (e.g. Black, 1970; Greeley, 1993; see also Section 4.3.2), some authors have suggested that certain religions such as Buddhism are often associated with sustainable environmental transitions at community level (e.g. Callicot and Ames, 1989; Bruun and Kalland, 1994). Box 4.2 highlights, for example, how Buddhism and strong community resilience have been closely interlinked in the remote Himalayan country of Bhutan.

The most prominent examples of positive social memory are usually associated with long-term social-ecological systems, where 'trial and error' approaches over millennia and the constant need for harnessing adaptive capacity (e.g. during slow climate change or to address population increase) have led to intricate environmental management systems. For centuries, *paddy rice cultivation* in East Asian countries, for example, has led to high food security among rural and urban communities (Oudenhoven *et al.*, 2010). Van Rheenen and Mengistu (2009, p. 330), therefore, suggested that the paddy rice system is important for strengthening social capital, as it carries "tremendous historical and cultural

Box 4.2 Buddhist religion and strong environmental and social capital in Bhutan (eastern Himalayas)

Bhutan is a small remote and mountainous kingdom east of Nepal with less than 700,000 inhabitants and with Tibetan Buddhism (Lamaism) as the predominant religion (70 per cent of population). Bhutan can be characterized as one of the least globalized countries in the world (e.g. strict limits set on tourist visitors per year to *c.*5000) in which religious practices and rites largely dictate day-to-day social and environmental management activities. Bhutan has been variously described as a country with relatively strong social capital, possibly best highlighted by the fact that it has developed the concept of 'Gross National Happiness' where all new development projects are scrutinized for their impacts not only on community well-being but also whether they may influence people's happiness. It also prides itself for a relatively self-sufficient subsistence-based lifestyle with strong environmental capital predicated on the preservation of large tracts of forest where erosion is less pronounced than in comparable high altitude environments. The Buddhist lifestyle of the Bhutanese (and that of many other Buddhist countries) has been associated with more benign environmental pathways in which conservation has tended to predominate over exploitation and where intricate myths and rites related to human-environment interactions encode the regulation of community-level environmental management pathways (Callicot and Ames, 1989; Bruun and Kalland, 1994). This positive social memory is particularly based on Buddhist philosophies and traditions linked to notions of equality of all beings on Earth, the relative absence of greed and notions of 'profit', and beliefs in 'karma' and reincarnation closely associated with sustainable environmental management (Jazeel and McFarlane, 2010; Oudenhoven *et al.*, 2010). This places great emphasis on the importance of socially close-knit communities and the prevention of destruction of environmental resources for future reincarnations, highlighted in Bhutan through the community-level conservation of forest groves, animals and other environmental resources.

value in that it [is] considered as the basis of the social order, and occupies a major place in Asian religions and customs". The timing of forest-based *shifting cultivation cycles* is another case in point, where communities have to learn the most appropriate length of these cycles based on traditional knowledge passed on through the generations. A slight change in the cycle (especially shortening) can have disastrous consequences and may lead to the loss of food security for the community (Smith and Wishnie, 2000; Oudenhoven *et al.*, 2010).

Some of the most interesting examples of positive social memory relate to examples of communities living in extremely challenging environments where resilience thresholds are particularly precarious and where one small error linked to environmental mismanagement can tip the balance towards community destruction (Kinzig *et al.*, 2006; Rival, 2009). An often cited example in the literature relates to the management of avalanche protection forests by local communities in the European Alps. In these harsh environments, where communities live up to altitudes of 2400 m and where the risk of avalanches is ever-present in winter, most communities have found the right 'balance' between forest use for timber (and in the past for the feeding of animals) and forest protection (e.g. Teich and Bebi, 2009, for the Swiss Alps). Here, social memory is related to processes of 'positive forest management traditions' being passed on through the generations, where it has been imperative that sufficient forest is left standing (with sufficient regeneration) to protect the communities from avalanches (Grêt-Regamey *et al.*, 2008). Recent catastrophes in the Alps (e.g. in the village of Galtür in Austria in the 1990s) show that globalization processes through the rapid expansion of skiing and the felling of forest for the establishment of new ski runs has, at times, led to transitional ruptures in social memory, with a foregrounding of economic over environmental capital (see also below) (Teich and Bebi, 2009).

The survival of Australian Aboriginal or arctic communities in some of the harshest environments on Earth are further examples of positive social memory. Especially in the arid and semi-arid territories of Australian Aboriginal communities, only the most assiduous application of very specific environmental management practices guaranteed the long-term survival of communities (Wilson and Bryant, 1997; Abel *et al.*, 2006). Indeed, those Aboriginal communities present at the time of European colonization of Australia in the eighteenth century were the 'successful' communities, whose positive social memory enabled their survival, while many other Aboriginal communities had disappeared long ago (Gammage, 2008). As highlighted above, in Aboriginal society encoding of spiritual beliefs linked to the ancestral 'dreamtime' was particularly associated with specific customs and taboos linked to 'sacred' places and environmental resources. In many communities, this is believed to have protected environmental resources from overexploitation over thousands of years through subconscious protection through spiritually sanctioned temporary hunting bans and taboos (Head, 1989, 1993). Similarly, arctic herder communities traditionally lived in equally challenging environments, where the balance between survival and community destruction was always precarious. Positive social memory among the Nenets of the Yamal Peninsula (Russia), for example, was particularly evident in traditional knowledge passed on through the generations about sustainable management of fragile reindeer pastures necessary for community survival (Forbes *et al.*, 2009; see also Ford and Smit, 2004, for communities in the Canadian Arctic).

Yet, social memory is not always associated with positive community trajectories. The following will discuss examples where social memory has acted as a negative process for community resilience.

4.3.2 Social memory as a negative process for community resilience

Just as community-level transitional pathways need to be understood as a multitude of resilient and vulnerable pathways occurring simultaneously in complex ways (see Chapter 3), so transitional pathways can be seen as comprised of a multitude of *positive and negative social memories* affecting resilience. 'Bad' social memory can survive in communities and be passed on through the generations if it is at least in part counterbalanced by positive social memory that has enabled the community (or parts thereof) to survive. It is only when encoded traditions are beginning to tip a community over the resilience thresholds (see Section 3.3.2) that such negative memories may die out or disappear – or, as the next section will discuss, that such negative memories may be 'exported' to other places through migration of entire communities.

Negative social memory can affect all forms of capital in a community, for example by reducing the nature and scope of economic capital, by damaging or changing social networks and cohesion, or by leading to degradation of community-level environmental resources (Bodin and Crona, 2008). The sociological and psychological literature highlights that explanations why negative social memory survives in communities (and in entire societies) are complex and culture-dependent (e.g. Bonnano, 2004; Vitaliano, 2007). Often, negative social memory has gradually emerged from previously positive social memory that has been changed and distorted over time due to specific path dependencies (see Chapter 5) (Bellaigue, 1999). Recent examples relate to the continuation of environmentally malign traditions, despite the knowledge that such traditions may be harmful to people's health and the environment. For example, in the town of Linfen (province Shanxi, north-east China) a 1000-year old tradition survives linked to the burning of coal pyramids for Chinese New Year where every stakeholder group in the community is vying for the tallest pyramid. Hotels burn piles of a few metres of coal, while the local coal-fired power stations build pyramids of over 30 tons. This produces large-scale pollution in an already heavily polluted urban environment, contributing to Shanxi's position in the top ten of the most polluted places on Earth. Beit-Hallahmi and Argyle (1997) argued that such spiritual or religious rites and beliefs are often behind the most environmentally 'irrational' practices associated with negative social memory, although socio-political factors can also explain the perseverance of certain practices that would normally be questioned by the community. The latter is particularly evident in communities with pronounced power imbalances, for example where disproportionate decision-making powers rest with one or a few individuals (malign dictatorships) who have specific views about economic, social and environmental processes affecting their community.

Religion is often closely interlinked with debates about both 'good' and 'bad' social memory. Critics of environmental decision-making processes affected by religious beliefs have argued that some religious beliefs do not help in human adaptive processes and that they, instead, may lead to a reduction in community resilience (e.g. Greeley, 1993; Dawkins, 2006). Wade (2009), in particular, argued that religion is often closely associated with pragmatic politics where the advent of agriculture some 10,000 years ago led to a new division of labour in which priestly castes attempted to monopolize access to the 'divine' with increasing control over myths and religious rites. One of the most poignant examples of negative social memory associated with religious cult and the eventual demise of an entire community relates to the example of Easter Island in the south-eastern Pacific. As Box 4.3 highlights, loss of environmental capital through complete deforestation of the island, linked to an ever more demanding ancestral religious cult by a dominating cast of priests, eventually led to complete loss of economic and social capital and the ultimate demise of the community.

Such examples are, however, not restricted to geographically isolated communities. Chester *et al.* (2008), for example, described religious reactions to volcanic eruptions in Italy, highlighting how communities threatened by lava flows (Vesuvius 1944; Etna 1971) paraded images and bones of local saints to halt the advance of lava flows. In this case, social memory related to long-standing religious rites appears to have replaced more 'common sense' adaptive capacity linked to the short- and mid-term evacuation of threatened settlements. A similar case is described by Donovan (2010) in Indonesia – one of the most volcanically active regions in the world – where many communities have complex traditional and animistic beliefs related to volcanic hazards. In 1963, for example, 2100 people were killed during an eruption of Mt Agung, the most sacred volcano on the island of Bali. Thought to be the dwelling place of holy and evil deities by local communities, hundreds were killed while processing towards the lava flows, believing that these hazards represented their gods descending from the volcano. Similarly, Madaleno (2010) argued that inhabitants of low-lying islands in Tuvalu (Western Pacific) threatened by sea-level rise frequently invoke 'divine providence' as the possible solution to their loss of environmental capital, suggesting that no contingencies exist with regard to purchase of land elsewhere to escape the flooded islands – a further example where fervent religious beliefs may stifle the discovery of new resilience pathways.

Negative social memory is also often associated with communities with power imbalances, especially with 'malign dictatorships' where disproportionate decision-making powers rest with one or a few individuals. Here, specific norms, traditions and rites that may lead to a reduction in environmental capital are 'imposed' onto the community with negative consequences. Although this may

Box 4.3 Negative social memory linked to religious cult and loss of environmental capital on Easter Island (South East Pacific)

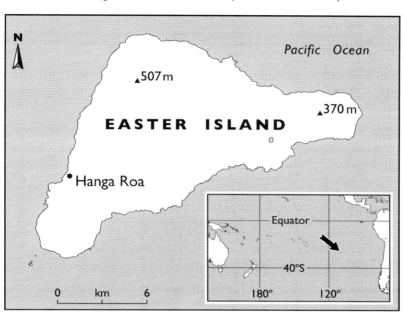

The history of Easter Island is one of the most intriguing examples of human-environment interaction, and one of the most poignant examples of how negative social memory linked to religious cult can lead to wholesale destruction of environmental capital. Located in the remote south-east Pacific at 27 degrees south and over 1000 km from the nearest neighbouring island, Easter Island was first settled by Polynesians around AD 1000 from islands in the central Pacific. Archaeological evidence suggests that contact with original island homes in the central Pacific was lost after initial settlement (Flenley and Bahn, 2003). Easter Island, therefore, is one of the few examples of *enforced isolation* where a geographically 'closed society' evolved over centuries without external influence – an ideal laboratory for analysing factors that influence community resilience (see also Section 2.4). Easter Island is best known for the remains of over 400 large stone statues (moai) carved out of local volcanic rock. These statues were associated with a *religious cult* that gradually evolved on the island out of existing Polynesian traditions linked to the veneration of high-ranking ancestors (Diamond, 2006). Archaeological evidence suggests that the moai cult grew more elaborate between AD 1100–1600, with ever larger statues erected on large stone platforms (marae). It is now scientifically accepted that the transporting of these statues over long distances required the use of large amounts of timber, as logs were used both as rollers (Polynesians did not have the wheel) and for elaborate ramps used to place statues into their final vertical positions. In addition, up to 500 workers had to be fed over months during the carving, transport and placing of each statue, leading to an unsustainable intensification of agriculture beyond normal community needs. At the time of human settlement, Easter Island was covered in subtropical forest comprised of about 20 different tree species, including a formerly abundant palm tree with an over two-metre trunk diameter which provided the main timber for the building of the statues (Flenley and Bahn, 2003). By the time of European discovery of Easter Island in 1722, all forests had been destroyed, together with many other plant and animal species. Most of the large trees had been felled by around AD 1450 (including about 16 million giant palm trees) and grass and herb pollen increased dramatically after AD 1600. Diamond (2006, p. 107), therefore, suggested that "the overall picture for Easter [Island] is the most extreme example of forest destruction in the Pacific, and among the most extreme in the world". Immediate consequences for the islanders were almost complete loss of environmental capital (especially raw materials, wild-caught foods, inability to build wooden boats for open ocean fishing, increased erosion and decreased crop yields) and associated loss of economic and, ultimately, social capital – all fuelled by a religious cult that at first glance does not appear to have served any 'practical' or 'evolutionary' purposes (cf. Dawkins, 2006; Wade, 2009). Cannibalism is thought to have become widespread in the century before European discovery, and only about 4000 islanders had survived by 1722 down from 10,000–20,000 during the peak of Eastern Island civilization centuries earlier.

mean that, ultimately, the power base of the ruling elite will be gradually undermined through loss of environmental capital, in the medium term their power can also be enhanced through these unequal relationships by increasing the economic dependency of large parts of the community on the ruling elite. In many ways, politics and religion can be closely associated in such systems, as religious rites may be used by such powerful elites to regulate environmental decision-making at community level (Greeley, 1993; Wade, 2009). Easter Island, where a powerful caste of priests appears to have had undue control over environmental pathways, is one of the most poignant examples (see Box 4.3 above), but evidence also comes from contemporary sociological, anthropological and geographical studies (e.g. Heggelund, 2006, for China; Kelkar *et al.*, 2008, for India).

Key examples of powerful elites within communities controlling negative social memory that has led to loss of environmental capital can, for example, be found in many communities around the world at risk of desertification, where striking the right balance between sustainable environmental management and maximum exploitation of the soils is particularly critical (Briassoulis, 2005). Indeed, evidence from various research projects on desertification in Mediterranean communities highlights several key patterns and processes. First, desertification issues tend to be worst in communities where powerful agricultural elites, or powerful groups linked to the commercial forestry sector, are in control of productivist agricultural production pathways aimed at maximization of economic profit (Wilson, 2007). Box 4.4 illustrates the example of the Italian region of Basilicata where the dominance of productivist agricultural pathways has led to severe erosion problems on farmland owned by large agri-businesses. Similar examples can be found in many other communities increasingly embedded within the global capitalist system around the world (e.g. Mertz *et al.*, 2005). Second, desertification in Mediterranean communities is often exacerbated by the fact that certain stakeholder groups impose their views about the meaning of 'desertification' over weaker stakeholder groups. Wilson and Juntti (2005) suggested that powerful actors within rural communities in Portugal, Spain, Italy and Greece often tended to promote views of desertification linked to factors external to the communities involved – in particular climate change – rather than to environmentally unsustainable actions by community members themselves (e.g. failure to use contour ploughing to prevent destructive run-off, failure to practice crop rotation, planting of crops with high water demand). Community-level social memory about the threat of desertification was, therefore, manipulated – and to some extent distorted – by powerful stakeholder groups to suit their own short-term profit-maximizing goals.

Box 4.4 Powerful elites and negative social memory: dominant productivist agricultural pathways and desertification in Basilicata, Italy

As part of an EU-funded project on Mediterranean desertification, Povellato and Ferraretto (2005) highlighted how negative social memory can be imposed by powerful agricultural elites within rural communities, leading to a reduction in environmental capital (desertification). In rural communities in the region of Basilicata (southern Italy), desertification linked to overintensive use of agricultural land has been a problem for over one hundred years, leading to increased soil erosion and, ultimately, loss of agricultural productive capacity and associated loss of economic capital. Yet, despite the knowledge among village communities that less extensive agricultural production will lead to soil protection in the long term, powerful local agricultural elites linked to the lucrative production of high-intensity durum wheat (used in many Italian pastas exported around the world) have been able to implement productivist agricultural pathways leading to rapid loss of soil productive capacity through erosion, to a further reduction in the availability of scarce water resources, and to a further depletion of local biodiversity relying on traditional less intensive mixed farming systems. Although critical voices are heard from within the communities, Povellato and Ferraretto highlighted how these voices are often silenced by the complex and unequal power structures that exist within southern Italian communities. Over the past few decades, it is particularly community-level actors with close links to large multinational agri-business corporations that have been able to impose their views of desertification as an *externally* driven climate change-related issue, rather than allowing voices to be heard that emphasize environmentally destructive *endogenous* community-level processes linked to productivist agriculture. In this sense, the social memory of the community related to the best way forward for tackling desertification has been hijacked by a powerful elite which has been able to impose its 'negative' social memory upon the entire rural community – with disastrous effects for long-term environmental capital.

These examples highlight that social memory is a crucial factor in shaping community resilience. What happens, however, to acquired social memory when communities emigrate to other parts of the world (exported social memory), and what implications does this have for community resilience in their country of destination? What shape do community-level learning processes take in communities marked by high levels of immigrants? It is to these questions that the next section will turn.

4.3.3 'Exported' social memory: the environmental impact of settler and immigrant communities

The notion of 'exported' social memory refers to communities or individuals who have, for whatever reasons, left their familiar home communities. Such communities are usually referred to as 'settler communities'. Here, we need to distinguish between *voluntary settler communities* (e.g. including most European settlers who moved to the New World to improve their economic and social situation) and *forced settler communities* forced to leave their home territories by war, famine, social pressures or natural disasters. The latter include, in particular, war refugees who may settle permanently in a place not initially of their choice (e.g. current refugees from Darfur in western Sudan forced by war to settle in neighbouring Chad), original settlers of Easter Island (see Box 4.3) who, like many Polynesian settlers, were probably forced from their home islands due to war or diminishing resources linked to overpopulation (Flenley and Bahn,

2003) or, most recently, 'climate refugees' from low-lying islands threatened by sea-level rise linked to climate change (Adger *et al.*, 2003; Madaleno, 2010). The key issue affecting all these communities – whether through voluntary or forced migration – is the potential loss of social memory associated with their home communities and the repercussion this may have for community resilience in their new home territories, especially with regard to the creation of strong environmental capital.

One of the most interesting debates related to the impact and importance of social memory on community resilience relates to the impact of 'pioneer societies' on environmental capital in their countries of destination. A rich literature is available on the environmental impact of 'white settler societies' in North America, Australia and New Zealand (e.g. Wynn, 1979; Williams, 1989). Dating back to the nineteenth century, critical accounts by authors such as Thoreau (1851) or Marsh (1864) described the indiscriminate felling of forests by agricultural settlers in the New World, often described as 'wanton destruction'. In both the USA and New Zealand, for example, large tracts of forest were cleared in only a few decades of pioneer settlements as illustrated, for example, by McGregor (1988) for the Upper Delaware Valley (USA) where most of the accessible forests were clearfelled in only a few decades at the beginning of the nineteenth century. Possibly the most dramatic example of rapid deforestation by pioneer settlers can be found in New Zealand, where between 1860 and 1910 about 80,000 km^2, or about 60 per cent of all forests present at the time of European colonization, were removed (Wilson, 1990). In earlier work I highlighted that often standing forest rich in timber was simply burnt by settlers to create pasture for livestock, especially in areas where lack of infrastructure impeded the economic removal of logs (Wilson, 1993a). Not only did these clearfelling and burning practices decimate local wildlife and biodiversity, but also often led to erosion problems and loss of topsoil in the often rugged New Zealand terrain (McCaskill, 1973).

It is often argued that the social memory brought by these settlers to the unknown New Zealand forest environments partly explains the urge to rapidly clear forests and to often irreversibly degrade environmental capital in and near settler communities. Settlers brought with them social memory accumulated over generations in their home countries. Most settlers in New Zealand came from the deforested United Kingdom and were used to livestock and arable farming in 'open' cultural landscapes in which small woodlands were a relatively small and 'tamed' element of the landscape. In New Zealand, these settlers encountered a landscape that was still densely forested in most parts[1] and that was, therefore, very different from the landscapes they were familiar with (see also Diamond, 2006, for similar processes in once forested parts of Australia). Using original sources such as letters and diaries written by early settlers, authors such as Shepard (1969) or Wilson (1992) described how the settlers from the UK viewed the New Zealand forests as 'bush' and 'waste land' – a dark, brooding and wet vegetation cover that held no aesthetic value to early settlers, but that was merely seen as an encumbrance to productive agriculture that had to be removed (i.e. clearfelled or burnt) as quickly as possible. Some have argued that social memory linked to 'ideal' productivist agricultural landscapes of home led not only to removal of forest for the creation of livestock pastures, but also to additional forest removal to 'open up the view', to 'dry out the area' and to 're-create open landscapes of home' for homesick settlers (Wilson, 1993b). Box 4.5 describes in more detail the importance of social memory of Scottish settlers for pathways of deforestation among communities in the south-east of New Zealand's South Island.

Box 4.5 Exported social memory and forest clearance in the Catlins District, south-east South Island, New Zealand

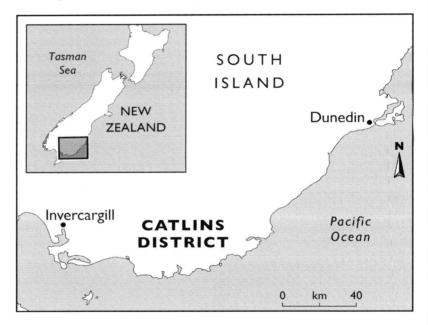

The Catlins District in south-east South Island, New Zealand, was entirely forested when it was first settled in 1861 by Scottish immigrants, most of whom had been given free passage to New Zealand and a free forest section (50 ha) for settlement. While forest clearance was slow between 1861 and 1880 due to inaccessibility of the terrain, most accessible forests were removed between 1880 and 1910 (Wilson, 1993b). Although most of the forest clearance can be attributed to the timber industry (at least on sections that were linked to the road network) and government grants encouraging settlers to convert the forested 'waste lands' into productive agricultural land, a study by Wilson (1992, 1993a), that included in-depth interviews with second- or third-generation residents who remembered the early days of forest clearance (i.e. some respondents were born around 1900), together with analysis of diaries and letters written by first generation settlers, revealed that settlers cleared more forest than was needed purely for agricultural purposes (including, for example, clearance of steep shady slopes that were never used for agriculture). Respondents suggested that first-generation settlers who had come directly from Scotland felt 'hemmed in' and 'overwhelmed' by the lush and wet native forest of the Catlins that contained only unfamiliar endemic trees. As a result, they set about 'opening up' the forests as quickly as they could, partly to make the area look more like their home country (Wilson, 1993b). In addition, the settlers introduced both European songbirds and garden plants from the British Isles to 'remind them of home'. Social memory related to specific landscape ideals brought by the settlers from their Scottish homelands provides a partial explanation for the landscape of the Catlins today, comprised of large cleared areas and small remnant 'woodlands' very similar to landscapes that can be found today north of Edinburgh or north-west of Aberdeen where many early Catlins settler families came from. The importance of 'exported' social memory became particularly evident through interviews with second- to fifth-generation descendants of the original settlers. Those who had been born in the Catlins had different attitudes towards their forests than first-generation settlers, and over the decades the appreciation of the scenic and practical value of remnant native forests on farms began to grow (Wilson, 1992). However, by the time attitudes began to change towards active conservation of native forests from the 1920s onwards, most Catlins forests had been cleared and only inaccessible upland areas remained forested (today designated as protected areas). Although local Catlins communities have benefited from deforestation through increased economic capital, the silting up of Catlins Harbour after 1900, linked to severe erosion problems, highlights that this had occurred at the expense of environmental capital. Because of increasing soil degradation problems on steep slopes, many of today's Catlins residents argue that 'too much forest was removed' and that not all their forebears had struck the 'right balance' between forest conservation and productivist agriculture. The result was that today's Catlins farmers comprise only about 15 per cent of the original number of settlers, with complete abandonment of some earlier farm communities and ultimate weakening of social capital in once tight-knit communities.

Examples of the impact of exported social memory are, however, not restricted to white settler societies. Another interesting example from New Zealand relates to the loss of social memory through forced settlement of South Island Maoris (people of Polynesian descent who had settled in New Zealand around AD 1000) to areas allocated to them by the state, and resultant 'lack of attachment' of Maori communities to these lands, with the result of unsustainable forest management on some of the Maori-owned sections. In 1906, landless Maori communities were given forested land by the colonial government as 'compensation lands' both for land requisitions by white New Zealanders and the near-decimation of the southern Maori population. These compensation lands were located in remote areas of New Zealand's South Island that had never been settled by white farmers due to remoteness of terrain and relative inaccessibility. In particular, these lands did not coincide with the 'ancestral domains' (lands originally inhabited and used by the Maori) of southern Maori tribes. A recent study has highlighted that, as a result, the southern Maori hardly used these lands for timber or agriculture and that they felt very limited 'connection' or 'association' with these lands (Wilson and Memon, 2010). Authors such as Park (1995), Kawharu (2000) or Stokes (2002) emphasized the importance of Maori connections to their tribal communities and the environment upon which they depended, expressed through notions of *kaitiaki-tanga* (Maori communities as environmental caretakers) and *taonga* (community resources as treasured environments), and to the preservation of forests used by Maori communities with important spiritual meaning. Often these close connections between Maori communities and their ancestral domains led to long-term sustainable management of forests. However, as with the example of excessive clearfelling of forests by white pioneer settlers disconnected from the land in the Catlins District of New Zealand (see Box 4.5), Wilson and Memon (2010) suggested that the allocation of land to the southern Maori that did not coincide with their ancestral domains (some Maori families had originally lived hundreds of kilometres away) may have led to excessively utilitarian attitudes towards forest resources by some of the Maori families. As a result, in the late twentieth century many Maori families allowed the chipmilling industry (owned by Japanese timber conglomerates which offered to build free road access to the remote sections) to clearfell their sections. Although a whole spectrum of forest management can be seen on the sections from complete conservation to complete forest destruction (with severe environmental degradation through erosion and loss of topsoil), many Maori respondents in Wilson and Memon's study agreed that their lack of connection and association with the allocated sections made it easier for them to decide to clearfell entire forest tracts – environmental management decisions which would have been almost unthinkable in their original ancestral domains. This example highlights that lack of social memory associated with non-ancestral domain lands, therefore, can be associated with excessive loss of environmental capital.

How can the often negative environmental impacts linked to exported social memory be explained? First, the moving of a community (or parts thereof) to another place or country (as in the case of New World settlers or dislocated Maori communities) disrupts pathways linked to local tradition and knowledge. As Box 4.5 highlights, immigrant settlers to New Zealand's forests initially lacked the knowledge how to sustainably manage the native forests they encountered – in other words, their experiences of farming and forest management acquired in Britain was of little use in their new environments. Indeed, for many decades white settlers to New Zealand (and to many other New World regions) thought that, due to slow growth rates, the forests they encountered lacked the 'vigour' of European tree species (Wilson, 1992). There was widespread belief that these forests were in the process of 'dying out' (early migrants misread evidence of abundant regeneration), and that they should be replaced with fast-growing 'exotic' species[2] (Wilson, 1993b). Only after two or three generations of settlers did local communities begin to realize the potential of New Zealand native forests for sustainable forest management.

Second, disruption of social memory linked to traditional resource use and knowledge also affects settler communities' perceptions of resilience thresholds. Evidence of these thresholds being exceeded is manifold in former settler societies such as the USA (e.g. the 'dust bowl' in the 1930s highlighted that the productivist agricultural frontier had been pushed too far west), Australia (adoption of agricultural practices ill-suited to drought-prone conditions) or New Zealand (severe soil erosion linked to deforestation of steep slopes), with complete disintegration of communities as a possible outcome (e.g. some drought-stricken rural communities in the Australian outback) (Diamond, 2006; Holmes, 2006). Third, and as highlighted above, the survival of settler communities was largely dependent on the pace of social learning processes – i.e. how quickly communities were able to adjust to their new environments using adaptive resource management techniques or, possibly more important, how willing these communities were to learn from already established pre-colonization communities about constraints and opportunities for environmental management in their new countries. In the context of New Zealand, for example, those settler families who were most able to quickly learn from early environmental management mistakes (e.g. excessive forest clearance) were also those most likely to maintain strong economic and environmental capital in the early phases of settlement – in other words, those families that were able to quickly develop a 'sense of place' for the territories they managed, which included the recognition that some forest had to be preserved for water management and soil protection reasons, were those most likely to survive (Wilson, 1993b).

Yet, in most cases, the issue of the importance of 'exported' social memory is less clear than in settler or colonial societies where settlement by a specific group (e.g. European settlers) occurred in a relatively homogenous manner with often little interaction between incoming groups and existing populations. Except for geographically closed communities such as Easter Island which are very rare (see Box 4.3), Section 2.4 highlighted that the socio-cultural boundaries of communities are usually 'open'. In other words, while new migrants continuously bring with them new social and cultural norms that will shape environmental pathways and transitions at community level, these norms will also continuously be shaped and re-shaped through challenges by already established populations and communities. Using multiresolution diffusion entropy analysis, Scarfetta and West (2004), for example, analysed the amount of memory left in time series in immigrant Hispanic and African communities in the USA. They highlighted that it usually takes one to two generations for residual social memory to be adjusted as a result of cultural change linked to immigration and exposure to 'new ideas' (similar to the example of the Catlins settlers discussed above), although fourth- and fifth-generation rural Hispanic communities also continued to cling to (some) traditional environmental pathways linked to the way they managed their farms. Similarly, Ward and Styles (2006) analysed a group of 154 British immigrants living in Australia to identify impacts of migration on residual social memory, and highlighted that migrants generally maintained a strong emotionally charged bond or 'residual link' to human and non-human elements of their homeland over several generations (see also Diamond, 2006).

The issue of 'exported' social memory suggests, therefore, complex patterns of human-environment interaction at community level over time. On the one hand, we see evidence where exported memory can be environmentally harmful (at least in the initial stages of settlement) due to ignorance about the new environments encountered and the legacy of (often misguided) cultural and environmental norms that may persist over several generations leading to a reduction in environmental capital. On the other hand, for settler or immigrant communities to survive and become more strongly resilient, a rapid adjustment phase is necessary predicated on learning and accepting that new skills for environmental management are needed in a new environment.

4.3.4 Rediscovering lost social memory

The discussion above has highlighted that social memory can be both a good and bad thing with regard to enhancing community resilience. Social memory can be particularly good in harnessing positive environmental pathways when it is rooted in skills, knowledge and tradition associated with strong environmental capital at community level. Yet, studies on the 'modern' and 'post-modern' era, on impacts of globalization, and on the erosion of social capital, argue that social memory has been increasingly lost in ever more globalized and international communities where individualism prevails over community-based actions (Bellaigue, 1999; Savage *et al.*, 2005). As Figure 3.6 emphasized, the loss of positive social memory may be a particular issue in 'communities gradually embedded into the global capitalist system', 'glocalized communities' and 'super-globalized communities' that have lost resilience. Harnessing past or lost social memory is, therefore, an increasingly important aspect for communities attempting to increase (or rediscover) resilience.

The rediscovery of lost social memory linked to more traditional local environmental management practices, and the rekindling of memories of 'how things were done in the past' through re-skilling of community residents, has become a particular feature of 'relocalized communities' (see Figure 3.6). As Chapter 3 highlighted, these communities are attempting to relocalize supplies of energy, food and housing materials by placing local communities at the heart of localized environmental management pathways (see also Chapter 5). As part of these communities attempting to relocalize environmental pathways, the global Transition Town Movement (TTM) has been particularly prominent (Bailey *et al.*, 2010; North, 2010). Hopkins (2008), one of the key leaders in this burgeoning movement, has lamented the loss of basic skills in many modern communities such as food preparation, vegetable gardening or tackling local crises linked to energy or food shortages. An important approach in the TTM, therefore, has been to uncover how positive social memory that may still be present in today's communities can help rekindle these skills (Box 4.6).

Box 4.6 Relocalized communities and the rediscovery of lost social memory: the Totnes Transition Town initiative

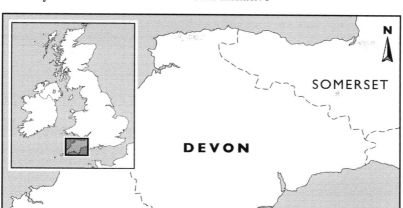

The Totnes Transition Town initiative, centred on the small market town of Totnes (about 20,000 inhabitants) in the south-west of England, is one of the most prominent examples of a community attempting to 'relocalize' (Bailey *et al.*, 2010; North, 2010). In his seminal book *The Transition Handbook: From Oil Dependency to Local Resilience* (translated into several languages), Hopkins (2008) has set out a vision for the ingredients needed for successfully relocalized communities based on the example of Totnes. His emphasis is on attempting to achieve (as much as possible) self-sufficiency in food, energy, building materials and, to a lesser extent, transport, in order to lessen community dependency on oil and to reduce individual carbon footprints. Although criticized by some as idealistic and reminiscent of 1970s alternative lifestyle philosophies (see Bailey *et al.*, 2010, for a detailed review of the literature), the harnessing of past social memory is a particularly interesting aspect of the TTM initiative. As part of a PhD research into the TTM initiative, Hopkins (2010) interviewed many Totnes residents who could remember times of 'enforced relocalization' during WW2, when food, energy and building materials were in short supply and when locals had to 'rediscover' ways to feed themselves and survive through harsh winters with little help from the 'outside' world due to severe rationing during the war (see also Section 6.4). Hopkins focused his questions particularly on how Totnes residents re-established community allotments and how heating materials were obtained locally, and he investigated the constraints and opportunities of enforced relocalization processes between 1941 and 1947 in particular. The aim was to tap the social memory of old people and to assess whether today's Totnes could rediscover pathways of resilience based on past social memory. The result has been that some relocalization initiatives that proved successful during WW2 could be more easily implemented than others. For example, the TTM initiative has relatively successfully persuaded some Totnes residents to re-use (or make better use of) existing garden spaces, either by enabling community access to private gardens for the planting of vegetables or by enlarging community-based allotment spaces akin to community initiatives in the 1940s. Hopkins (2010), therefore, argued that the relocalization of food production may be possible based on models from the past. What has proven much more difficult is to implement relocalized pathways for energy, largely due to highly centralized, and indeed globalized (especially with regard to gas and oil) energy networks. However, what emerges as most difficult – highlighting that past social memory cannot simply be superimposed onto existing development pathways (see also Chapter 5) – is that most Totnes residents' attitudes and worldviews are now so firmly embedded in a highly globalized and networked world that envisaging relocalization pathways has become very difficult for most individuals (psychological barriers). While residents may be interested in growing their own vegetables based on social memory from the past (many still have memories of vegetable gardens planted by their grandparents), most are reluctant to drastically alter their 'comfortable' capitalist and consumer-oriented lifestyles (Bailey and Wilson, 2009). This is particularly evident with regard to the problem of relocalization of transport (see also Chapter 6). While old residents in Totnes remembered times during WW2 when it was almost impossible to leave the immediate vicinity of the town, today's average Totnes family would find it difficult to live a life without car or holidays abroad. Barr (2008) referred to this selective appropriation of relocalization as 'compartmentalized relocalization' – i.e. where some aspects of relocalization (e.g. food production) are easier to implement than others (e.g. holiday or travel). Although Totnes can be seen as one of the most 'alternative' towns in the UK (Bailey *et al.*, 2010), relocalization based on past positive social memory is difficult to implement. The question, therefore, remains whether relocalization pathways can be implemented successfully at all if they are even difficult to implement in a 'progressive' town like Totnes?

The need for rediscovery of social memory is, however, not restricted to 'modern' communities that may have lost touch with basic community-level skills through modernization, technological change and globalization. There are also ample examples from around the world where vital skills linked to local traditions and belief systems as part of 'good social memory' have been lost over generations for a variety of reasons. Interesting evidence is, for example, beginning to emerge from the newly developing discipline of social volcanology which highlights that past "local traditions and belief systems can be extremely influential in volcanic regions, motivating local reactions during and prior to a crisis" (Donovan, 2010, p. 117). Donovan particularly discussed how various fatal volcanic eruptions over the past decades have highlighted the need to improve understanding of the complex interactions between lost social memory and the reasons why communities are willing to relocate and remain in volcanic hazard areas. By exploring the 'geomythology' – the extent of knowledge available within communities about past volcanic eruptions – of vulnerable communities, social volcanology attempts to understand why positive social memory linked to knowledge about the catastrophic effects of past volcanic eruptions in a given area may be lost, and the repercussions this has for community-level decision-making pathways (Vitaliano, 2007). Thus, "geomythology explores local knowledge to aid the compilation of volcanic eruptive histories, focusing on oral histories and traditional beliefs that retain information about hazard events" (Donovan, 2010, p. 118).

The example of rediscovery of lost social memory in Indonesia's volcanic areas is particularly instructive in this context. Indonesia is one of the most volcanically active countries in the world, with over 130 active volcanoes which have claimed over 130,000 casualties since 1800. It is, therefore, crucial to understand the role of social memory of communities living on the slopes of these volcanoes related to past eruption histories and experiences. Donovan (2010) conducted a study of communities living near Mt Merapi in Central Java, a volcano with over 20 eruptive episodes since 1900 (with large eruptions every 30–60 years), threatening over one million people. The volcano erupted again in 2006 and 2010, threatening hundreds of communities and killing over 150 people in 2010. The high recent death toll is linked to the fact that many communities refused to evacuate, choosing instead to rely on social memory based on traditional knowledge for seemingly strengthening community resilience during eruptions. Donovan highlights how this traditional knowledge is closely embedded in Javanese culture that attributes a sacred status to the mountain, expressed through myths, legends and ceremonies that have been in place for thousands of years. The harnessing of this ancient social memory reinforces attachment of people to their communities and leads to a reluctance to move. This has undoubtedly increased community vulnerability by exposing communities to potentially catastrophic impacts of volcanic eruptions (see above), but evidence from Donovan's study also suggested that community resilience is simultaneously strengthened through an intricate interweaving of volcanic mythology influencing the perception of hazard spaces that may challenge Western scientific assessments of volcanic hazards.

The rediscovery of oral histories linked to previous eruption events, in particular, has enabled the enforcement of taboos for those wishing to climb the volcano, or helped better understand the flow of lava streams and lahars threatening village communities, thereby reducing death tolls. This is often combined with intricate knowledge passed on through the generations about unusual animal movements or intense lightning storms as local indicators for imminent eruptive events. Donovan (2010, p. 122) concluded that "the geographical dispersal of hazard threats around the volcano shapes the development of oral traditions and myths, and offers clues into the ways indigenous populations react to different hazards". Yet, her study also highlighted ruptures in social memory of local communities, where past destructive eruptions appeared to no longer feature as part of the pantheon of community knowledge, possibly resulting in a false sense of security. This was best highlighted during the large Mt Merapi eruption of October/November 2010 where in one of the most affected villages the 'gatekeeper' – a key community member in charge of 'appeasing' the volcano – was killed (BBC News, October 2010). This suggests that the 'correct' calibration, and indeed rediscovery, of social memory with the factual history of volcanic eruptions (or other hazards and disturbances) is crucial for improved community resilience, and that communities where loss of 'good' social memory is not irreversible will usually have stronger resilience than those where these memories are completely lost.

4.4 Conclusions

Linked to the framework of community resilience and environmental transitions developed in Chapters 2 and 3, the aim of this chapter was to focus on the notion of 'social memory' to enable a better understanding of the importance of community learning, tradition and stakeholder networks for community resilience. The chapter argued that all communities have inherent qualities shaped by the 'memory' contained within the system which may be linked to individuals and/ or stakeholder groups within a community. The chapter analysed the importance of 'acquired memory' (how memory and learning are passed on from generation to generation to improve resilience) and 'communal memory' as the sum total of learning processes embedded in communities in the form of traditions, rites and local 'policies' often passed on informally and orally. Using examples from around the world, the chapter highlighted how social memory can act both as a malign and benign force in shaping environmental transitions at local community level. The notion of 'exported' social memory was explored as a possible explanation for the frequent mismanagement of environments in settler societies, as was the question of how 'lost' social memory can be 'rediscovered' to increase the resilience of communities.

Understanding the importance of social memory is a crucial building block for identifying ingredients needed for resilient communities. As this chapter highlighted, there is often a direct link between 'positive' (benign) social memory and strong economic, social and environmental capital at community level. Yet, as Figure 3.6 emphasized, many communities continue to lose resilience and may be 'locked' into pathways of vulnerability. Understanding social memory, therefore, forms the basis for better understanding interlinkages between 'path dependency' and local community resilience discussed in Chapter 5, and for understanding the importance of 'transitional corridors' analysed in Chapters 6 and 7.

5 Path dependency

'Lock-in' mechanisms, power
structures and pathways of the
(im)possible at community level

5.1 Introduction

Building on the discussion of social memory for understanding community resilience in the previous chapter, Chapter 5 focuses on the interlinkages between
'path dependency' and community resilience and vulnerability. The chapter will
focus mainly on path dependencies *endogenous* to communities (i.e. dependencies emanating from within communities themselves), while Chapters 6 and 7 –
which investigate the importance of 'transitional corridors' for community
resilience – will focus on *exogenous* processes and pathways (e.g. the importance of societal ideologies, policies and politics) that shape community resilience and vulnerability. Using Giddens' (1984) notion of structure-agency
interactions, the focus in Chapter 5 will be more on agency, while Chapter 6 will
emphasize structural factors shaping community pathways.

   Section 5.2 will, first, explain the notion of path dependency by providing
insight into wider debates in the critical transition literature. Section 5.3 will
then focus on endogenous 'lock-in' effects at community level that make
certain community pathways unthinkable and impossible to implement. Specific
emphasis will be placed on structural, endogenous economic and socio-
psychological lock-in effects. These highlight that, although many communities
would like to change their environmental trajectories, they are often impeded of
doing so because of path dependency inherent in the community itself through
factors such as entrenched customs, habits, conservatism, negative attitudes or
lethargic behaviour. In Section 5.4, two hypothetical examples of village communities from the developed and developing world will illustrate how path
dependencies and lock-in effects can affect economic, social and environmental
capital at community level. Building on transition theory (see Chapter 3),
Section 5.5 will then investigate the link between path dependency and 'transitional ruptures' at community level. Several case study examples from around
the world will be discussed to highlight how some communities have managed
to radically change their environmental trajectories, while other examples will
illustrate how many communities remain 'stuck' on pathways that may inexorably lead to increased vulnerability. Concluding remarks will be provided in
Section 5.6.

5.2 Understanding path dependency at community level

The notion of path dependency is intricately connected with both transition theory and social memory. A pathway can be seen as a process where 'memory' (i.e. knowledge, experience, accumulated wisdom) can be passed on from generation to generation or from actor to actor (Stark, 1992; Forbes *et al.*, 2009). As Folke (2006, p. 257) argued, "non-linearity generates path dependency, which refers to local rules of interaction that change as the system evolves and develops". Building on the discussion in Chapter 3, Figure 5.1 highlights that path dependency is based on the assumption that specific 'pathways' of change can be identified over space and time at community level. A pathway should hereby be understood as a simplified version of complex processes occurring within a community, and the pathway shown in Figure 5.1 represents the sum total of cumulative actions at individual and stakeholder group levels. As the figure suggests, these pathways are rarely static and usually fluctuate based on various factors of change (see Chapter 3). The figure shows that changes in the direction of a pathway can be associated with 'nodes' of decision-making (nodes 1–11 in the figure), i.e. points on a pathway indicating a qualitative change in direction. Cumming *et al.* (2005, p. 984) refer to these as 'levers' "at which changes in the system trajectory could be brought about". Path dependency is hereby defined as the general direction of the pathway trajectory, taking into account upward and downward qualitative shifts in decision-making over time. With regard to community resilience, this may mean a change in the direction of a pathway towards either weaker or stronger resilience. Figure 5.1 shows a general tendency towards weaker community resilience (Section 5.4 will discuss in more detail one example of a village community directly associated with pathways shown in the figure). As Martens and Rotmans (2002) highlighted, the longer the period of observation and the more detailed knowledge is available about nodal points of decision-making over time, the more accurately can the loss/gain of community resilience be assessed (see also Section 2.5).

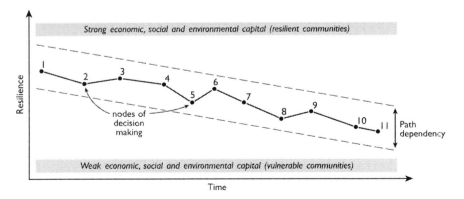

Figure 5.1 Path dependency, resilience and nodes of decision-making (source: author).

Chapter 2 highlighted that any community will be at its specific starting point in a transition precisely because of the history of decision-making pathways *preceding* that starting point (Stump, 2010). As Stark (1992) emphasized, path dependency is, therefore, a process in which the next steps or nodes of change are determined by the previous ones. In Figure 5.1 the general 'downward' tendency (i.e. decisions made at community level that lead to gradual loss of resilience) can be explained by the fact that the starting point for each nodal section already carries with it the *memory* of a gradual decline in resilience (e.g. linked to specific traditions in a community or associated with lack of skills among community members; see Chapter 4 and Section 5.4). In other words, social memory is key for the direction of path dependency, and any system carries with it the memory ('baggage') of previous decision-making pathways. In human systems in particular, therefore, *history and memory matters*, and path dependency means that system trajectory is a function of past states and dependent on previous (and subsequent) probabilities of change (O'Sullivan, 2004; Stump, 2010). However, as Section 5.5 will discuss, path dependency is not predetermined, and a general loss of resilience as shown in Figure 5.1 can be reversed if appropriate positive action is taken (adaptive capacity) and carried by a sufficiently large number of community stakeholders. Indeed, Figure 5.1 already suggests that, at times, a 'rupture' towards stronger resilience is possible (e.g. between nodes 5 and 6; see Section 5.4), even within a general tendency of loss of resilience (e.g. through implementation of innovative policies or enlightened environmental management practices).

Four key issues are important when investigating notions of path dependency. First, Section 4.2.2 highlighted that pathway changes are often associated with changing 'learning pathways' which often streamline transitional processes but which, at the same time, can be difficult to change (Dahle, 2007). Transition theorists with roots in evolutionary political economy particularly point to the importance of community-level forms of learning and to the fact that personal choices can be self-reinforcing and may, therefore, lead to self-fulfilling pathways (Stark, 1992; Grabher and Stark, 1997). As Section 5.3 will discuss, means may become ends and alternative pathways may not even be considered – which explains the term 'path dependency' as an often irrevocable self-determining process in community development. There are parallels here with the notion of *self-organized criticality* that originated in physics to explain organizational patterns in natural systems based on the notion of a self-organized critical state (or threshold) beyond which a 'new' discrete level or pathway of development is reached (Frigg, 2003; see also Gunderson and Holling, 2002). This means that outliers beyond specified community pathways are often seen as 'aberrations' and difficult to implement (the notion of 'unthinkable pathways'). However, where pathway change at community level does occur (e.g. nodal change between Points 5 and 6 in Figure 5.1), it may also act as a catalyst for macro-level transitional changes beyond the community ('snowball' effect) (see Chapter 6).

Second, the notion of community path dependency often simplifies what are usually complex stakeholder interactions based on intricate power structures within communities (see also Section 4.2.4) (Allen, 2003). This means that there usually are *multiple* stakeholder pathways within communities, with multiple and often overlapping path dependencies. Only parts of a community may move towards stronger resilience pathways, suggesting that *compartmentalized resilience* – pathways characterized by different stakeholder groups moving at different pace through environmental transitions – may be a key feature of most communities. Bailey and Wilson (2009) have, therefore, warned of the overlapping nature of stakeholder pathways that often lie submerged beneath stylized portrayals of polarized transitional pathways. Rotmans *et al.* (2002, p. 4) thus argued that pathways are "a mélange of fast and slow dynamics, the tempo and direction of which are ultimately constrained by the slowest processes" – in other words, multiple resiliences may emerge in what are often non-linear community transitional processes (Wilson, 2007).

Third, due to its close association with conservatism, lethargy and a lack of willingness for change, path dependency is often associated with *negative* community development processes (Scheffer *et al.*, 2003). As Davidson (2010, p. 1139) emphasized from a historical perspective,

> accounts of several societies in premodern times point to the decreasing likelihood of abandoning a course of collective action when there are higher historical investments in that course of action in terms of economic and social capital, [thereby] decreasing adaptive capacity

(see also Diamond, 2006). Indeed, Section 5.3 will highlight that such 'lock-in' effects, closely associated with path dependency, often result in negative processes that, as the term implies, lock stakeholder groups or entire communities into pathways from which it may not be easy to 'escape' (see also examples of two village communities discussed in Section 5.4). However, Section 5.5 will suggest that 'transitional ruptures' are possible, i.e. where stakeholder groups or entire communities radically change pathways to increase (or at times suddenly decrease) community resilience. Such community-level transitional ruptures are possible because endogenous transitions (i.e. from within the community) may be more rapid to implement than macro-structural changes linked to often slow institutional, policy-related and political change (see Chapters 6 and 7).

Fourth, chaos theory suggests that small effects can lead to substantial changes in pathways. For example, American meteorologist Edward Lorenz suggested in the 1960s that in non-linear systems (e.g. community transitions) small changes in the early stages of a transition can be amplified over time, leading potentially to 'chaotic' behaviour of a system (e.g. the flapping of the wings of a butterfly in one locality could lead to a hurricane in another part of the world – a process coined the 'butterfly effect'). This may also affect community-level transitional pathways, as what may seem a small decision at the time (e.g. the election of a specific community leader) may, ultimately, define community pathways for decades to come, for example through the leader's family establishing itself as part of the power elite for several generations (see Bodin and Crona, 2008, for resilience issues linked to leadership in a Kenyan fishing community, or Goldsworthy, 2010, for a detailed analysis of interlinkages between leadership and resilience in ancient Roman communities). At community level, therefore, the butterfly effect may be particularly associated with the notion of 'power breeds power' – in other words, once specific stakeholders or stakeholder groups gain power from relatively powerless starting points, they themselves perpetuate their power (and that of their cronies) to the expense of other community voices (Allen, 2003). Critics, however, may argue that even the seemingly 'random' butterfly effect is connected in time and space to antecedent pathways, and that, therefore, 'chaotic' behaviour of non-linear systems is, in fact, nonchaotic and can be explained through 'self-organized criticality' associated with detailed knowledge of path dependencies preceding a seemingly 'random' effect (e.g. Frigg, 2003).

Path dependency is evidently a complex process which emphasizes that interlinkages between stakeholder interactions within a community need to be understood to fully grasp the potential for resilience at community level. As the next section will discuss, path dependencies are often shaped by so-called 'lock-in' effects which shoehorn stakeholder groups, or entire communities, into positive or negative pathways of change.

5.3 Lock-in effects at community level

Let us investigate in more detail what specific form path dependency may take at community level. Using examples, the following discussion will focus on four intertwined 'lock-in' effects: structural, economic, political and sociopsychological lock-ins. These highlight both the complexities of path dependencies and the resultant difficulties for communities to choose 'alternative' pathways.

5.3.1 Structural lock-in effects

'Structural lock-in effects' can be understood as pathway-related lock-ins associated with processes usually beyond the control of individual communities, including, in particular, moral codes, traditions, religion and rites. These include the embeddedness of communities into the capitalist world and/or into neoliberal mindsets and thinking (as an important part of contemporary moral codes in many parts of the world), the general political orientation of a community, and other moral and behavioural codes associated with, for example, gender relations or property rights within a community. Structural lock-in effects are also associated with 'structural' factors often beyond the direct control of communities, such as the embeddedness of communities within transport, food and energy networks, or the geographical location of a community with associated constraints and opportunities for economic development (see Chapter 6). Many structural lock-in effects, therefore, permeate the boundaries between the local community and society – possibly with the exception of communities that are more or less 'closed systems' with little interaction with their region or the nation state within which they are embedded (as Section 2.4 discussed, such communities are almost non-existent in today's world).

Chapter 4 already discussed the importance of moral codes, traditions, religion and rites as part of the social memory of communities. How do these affect path dependencies at community level? Moral codes in general define the philosophical basis upon which community action takes place, and usually find expression through traditions and specific rites. Moral codes are often shaped by religious beliefs, but are also influenced by political beliefs. For example, in many areas of the developed world, rural communities (as opposed to urban communities) are often characterized by an inherent conservatism that may stifle innovation. As one of the village examples described in Section 5.4 will demonstrate in more detail, many studies have highlighted that in the UK, for example, an important aspect of the notion of the 'rural idyll' is to preserve the 'charm' of the countryside and to 'keep things as they are' (Robinson, 2004; Woods, 2005). Although this may, at times, result in relatively strong community resilience (see Chapter 3), it may also explain a pronounced path dependency regarding resistance to change and innovation. Similarly, as Chapter 4 already alluded to, decision-making pathways in staunchly religious communities (e.g. Amish communities in the USA) may inadvertently reinforce path dependencies predicated on traditional norms that may prevent the introduction of innovative environmental management practices at community level (Beit-Hallahmi and Argyle, 1997; Wade, 2009), thereby potentially weakening environmental capital.

Chapter 3 highlighted the impacts of globalization and capitalism on community resilience, and the embeddedness of a community into the global capitalist system usually creates multiple path dependencies. First, it changes community-based norms and conventions related to the generation of economic capital and may also lead to the erosion of social and environmental capital – the 'globalization bottleneck' affecting community resilience highlighted in Chapter 3. However, global capitalism may also enable 'positive' path dependency in that it may enable communities to raise sufficient income to improve social and environmental capital (e.g. by funding local-level soil or water management projects) (see Figure 3.6). Community-level path dependencies associated with neo-liberalism,[1] meanwhile, are more difficult to gauge (Larner, 2003; Castree, 2008a, 2008b). Here, studies have shown that neo-liberalism has several characteristics that usually lessen community resilience, in particular by encouraging vertical as opposed to horizontal stakeholder interactions (loss of social capital) (Mansfield, 2004), by restructuring local trade flows and exchange of goods based on neo-liberal free market ideals (often exacerbating existing power imbalances within communities) (Harvey, 2005), and by encouraging a mindset that foregrounds the market as the solution to problems as opposed to investments into less economically tangible social capital (leading to the erosion of traditional networks of trust and neighbourhood characteristic of strong resilience) (Heynen *et al.*, 2007;

Castree, 2008a). Bardhan (2006, p. 1400), for example, argued that "liberalization damages the poor by encouraging overexploitation of the fragile environmental resources … on which the daily livelihoods … of the rural poor depend". However, critical commentators also argue that neo-liberalism can be associated with the creation of 'self-sufficient' communities with the cultivation of an ethic that emphasizes less reliance and dependency on state-provided services, with a strong focus on individual communities' rights to maximum freedom and responsibility for their own affairs – processes that can both strengthen or weaken community resilience, depending on local socio-economic circumstances (Barnett, 2005; Harvey, 2005). A case in point is Mansfield's (2007) analysis of the 'neo-liberalization' of fishing quotas to Native Americans in Alaska, which gives a portion of fisheries income back to poor communities and, therefore, helps raise both economic and social capital in previously vulnerable communities. McCarthy's (2006) study of neo-liberalism and community forestry in the USA and Canada also suggested that timber resources have been returned to communities under neo-liberal policy agendas, thereby providing a vital basis for strengthening economic and social capital in vulnerable timber-based communities (Box 5.1). By arguing that "recognition of such complexity … makes … identifying the neo-liberal component of particular ensembles quite difficult", McCarthy (2006, p. 87) emphasized the hybrid and multidimensional impacts of neo-liberal and capitalist thinking within local communities (see also Bardhan, 2006).

Path dependency at local community level can also be closely associated with 'political lock-in' mechanisms. Closely related to other macro-structural path dependencies (e.g. capitalism, religion; see Chapter 6), the political orientation of a community[2] may either stifle or improve community resilience. There is a particularly close link between path dependency and political views, especially because political views at community level tend to change slowly and are, therefore, 'path dependent' themselves (Dobson, 2007). While boundary changes to constituencies (e.g. in the UK) or in- and outmigration of people with specific views can change political allegiances within communities, it usually takes several electoral cycles (or even generations) to change the general political orientation of a community (see also Section 5.4). Although it is impossible to associate specific political views with strengthening or weakening community resilience (i.e. examples could be found across the world of strongly resilient communities that adhere to both extreme right- or left-wing politics; e.g. Dobson, 2007), there is nonetheless a tendency that relocalized communities (see Figure 3.6) are often associated with more liberal and left-wing political lock-in pathways. Transition Town Totnes in the UK, for example, which is attempting to disengage from external energy and food dependency by 'relocalizing' environmental management processes, can be classified as a relatively 'liberal' town decried by its neighbours as a 'hippy town full of lefties' (Bailey *et al.*, 2010; Hopkins, 2010). Positive path dependency may be evident in Totnes, precisely because the social memory of the community is already closely associated with attempts – past and present – to find alternative solutions towards relocalization (see Box 4.6).

Box 5.1 British Columbia's Community Forestry Project: how neo-liberal agendas can engender positive path dependencies

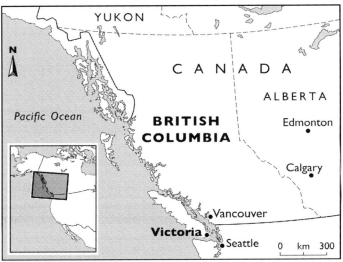

Calls for community-based forestry in British Columbia (Canada) have grown in urgency since the 1990s, especially since the state-led forestry approach had often led to a loss of control of communities over forest resources surrounding their communities. McCarthy (2006) highlighted that nearly a hundred Canadian forest communities expressed interest in taking more control of their forest resources, including native Indian First Nation communities. Tenure over forest resources was particularly awarded to those communities committed to eco-forestry, to communities with sound management plans and to groups who could demonstrate that logging of forests would benefit the community by strengthening economic capital. McCarthy suggested that First Nation communities particularly benefited from receiving tenure over their forest resources, some obtaining the rights to use up to 50,000 ha of forested lands. As a result, some communities prioritized environmental goals (e.g. the Bamfield-Huu-ay-aht First Nation community on Vancouver Island), emphasizing watershed protection and recreational uses of forests. According to McCarthy, these 'neo-liberal' agendas thereby strengthened environmental capital of some communities, compared to the situation before in which state-owned logging companies often depleted timber resources. This can be seen as a key example of 'positive' path dependencies, especially as

> community forests and other efforts to wrest some control away from state bureaucracies may, then, be seen as struggling steps toward a more democratic and sustainable future, evidence that communities have learned better than to leave their social and ecological destinies in the hands of overweening and self-interested states.

> (McCarthy, 2006, p. 100)

Path dependency is also closely associated with other moral codes at community level associated, for example, with gender relations or property rights within a community. Such path dependencies are often enshrined within religious moral codes (e.g. gender relations) or traditions (patriarchal property rights), which can have negative impacts on community resilience. As Chapter 2 highlighted, different cultural perceptions make it difficult to provide value judgements about 'positive' and 'negative' gender relations, although there may be a tendency for communities with gender roles unequally skewed towards patriarchal power structures (e.g. many Middle Eastern communities) to have weaker social capital. Path dependencies in these instances are closely associated with traditions, land ownership patterns and community organization patterns that marginalize and disenfranchise women – community processes which may be difficult to break down in the short and medium term (Liepins, 1998; Reynolds, 2002). Gendered spaces of difference may, therefore, be a particularly apt example to illustrate problematic path dependencies that can be seen to gradually erode community resilience (Janssens, 2010).

Structural lock-in effects are also linked to 'structural' path dependencies faced by communities, in particular related to transport, food and energy networks that are most commonly relatively centralized (i.e. central energy grid, national transport networks and infrastructure). The example of relocalized communities is, again, a case in point. As Hopkins (2008, 2010) highlighted, even if communities may wish to disengage from contemporary dependency on 'external' energy, food and transport, it is often impossible for these communities to simply de-link themselves from existing networks. Figure 5.2 shows for the south-west of the UK how complex and overlapping 'foodsheds' of individual communities are (the largest circle shows the foodshed of the city of Bristol) and how difficult it would be for communities to source food entirely from within their own foodsheds (see also Section 6.3.2). Although Chapter 4 highlighted that food self-sufficiency may (arguably) be the easiest to achieve,[3] community path dependencies are particularly pronounced with regard to energy networks (i.e. most communities in the developed world obtain their energy from national/ supra-national power grids) and transport networks (most communities are closely interlinked by road, train and airplane with other localities). While partial disengagement from transport may be possible (e.g. abandoning the private car), research has shown that people simply switch to other intra- and extra-community forms of transport (Barr, 2008).

Community location is an important aspect of transport-related path dependencies, and a lively debate has emerged around the question whether urban communities may be more resilient with regard to transport dependencies than rural communities (Forrest, 2001; Bulkeley, 2006). A key argument here is that while it may be more difficult for residents in large urban conurbations to quickly leave urban environments (e.g. for those living in or near central London it takes a good hour to reach the outskirts of the suburbs), travel within the urban conurbation is often relatively efficient due to high density and frequency of public transport (Hall, 2002). People in rural communities, meanwhile, usually face

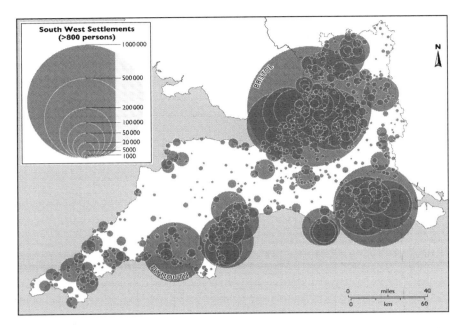

Figure 5.2 Foodsheds in the south-west of the UK for villages and towns with a population >800 (source: after Hopkins, 2010, p. 180).

higher dependencies on cars due to poorly developed public transport (see also case studies discussed in Section 5.4). Even more difficult is for communities to break out of path dependencies related to energy supplies. Although various schemes are now available in most developed countries (and increasingly in the developing world) that encourage individual households to generate their own energy (e.g. through wind turbines, ground heat pumps or photovoltaic cells), evidence suggests that the total energy produced through localized devices is still well below 10 per cent for most communities around the world – emphasizing path-dependent energy lock-ins that will take several generations to shift (WADE, 2003; Walker, 2008). In addition, the geographical location of a community is associated with structural lock-in effects linked to constraints and opportunities for economic development of a community ('geographical capital'). This is well illustrated through opportunities offered for the development of the tourist industry for communities wishing to raise economic capital from tourism revenues – pathways only possible for communities that contain some positive tourist assets either within the community itself (e.g. historical sites) or linked to the geographical location of a community (e.g. within scenic mountain scenery or in a coastal location that can attract tourists) (Wilson, 2007).

The latter examples highlight that structural lock-in effects are particularly problematic for communities wishing to break the deadlock of negative path dependency. Many communities are 'stuck' in specific pathways because of structural problems linked to contemporary globalized and capitalist lifestyles, political and infrastructural lock-ins, geographical constraints, and adherence to often conservative norms and conventions that may stifle the willingness for change (Scheffer *et al.*, 2003; Turner, 2009). While change may not be necessary in communities that are already taking active steps to strengthen resilience, it is usually those communities that are on a downward spiral – Marsden's (2003) notion of 'race to the bottom' – that will be hampered most by structural lock-ins in their attempts to reduce vulnerability.

5.3.2 *Endogenous economic and political lock-in effects*

'Endogenous economic lock-in effects' are pathway-related lock-ins endogenous to communities directly associated with economic capital at community level. With exception of subsistence farming communities (see Figure 3.6), endogenous economic lock-ins are closely linked to globalization processes and the spread of global capitalism and how these constrain or enable economic development at community level (Robertson, 1992; Turner, 2009). Endogenous economic lock-ins are particularly associated with path dependencies related to a spectrum ranging from extreme poverty to extreme wealth at community level, the latter often linked to profit-driven pathways engendered by increasing embeddedness of communities into the global capitalist system (Aggarwal, 2006).

Figure 3.6 in Chapter 3, showing the horizontal-hourglass-shaped transition from subsistence farming communities to relocalized, glocal and super-globalized communities, can be used to illustrate different micro-economic lock-in effects related to poverty, wealth and profit maximization. For example, subsistence farming communities that are not or only weakly embedded into the global capitalist system are often characterized by poverty (Bardhan, 2006; Rigg, 2006). As Jazeel and McFarlane (2010) emphasized, 'poverty' in this context is a relative term (i.e. no absolute levels of poverty can be established) and globally poverty usually refers to an economic measure based on income and expenditure below which a minimum nutritionally adequate diet plus essential non-food requirements are no longer affordable (often measured as daily household income of < US$2; cf. Millennium Ecosystem Assessment, 2005). The UNDP (annual) estimates that over one billion people live on less than US$2/day and that in countries such as Yemen, Somalia or Mozambique about 50 per cent of all households are below the poverty line, although the UNDP also highlights large income disparities within most communities (see below). Although – as Chapter 3 highlighted – social and environmental capital may be relatively well developed in these communities, economic capital is often underdeveloped. Indeed, in many subsistence farming communities around the world, non-monetary forms of exchange (e.g. bartering, trade through exchange of goods) are still predominant.

Both Rigg (2006) and Chaskin (2008) highlighted that poverty is probably the most important constraint for community development and, therefore, a key component of vulnerable communities. Indeed, it is difficult for many subsistence farming communities caught in the poverty trap to find ways to raise resilience, as most of their day-to-day activities will be focused on raising sufficient income for survival (Parnwell, 2007). Negative path dependency is, therefore, closely associated with poverty, as the lack of financial resources often means that these communities have little opportunity to actively shape environmental transitions, either in the form of improved environmental management strategies regarding soils, water or community forest resources (which can be financially costly), or with regard to the ability to devote sufficient time and energy beyond basic and immediate survival needs for building strong(er) environmental capital. Micro-economic lock-ins linked to poverty are, thus, closely linked to Maslow's (1943) 'hierarchy of needs', where conservation of environmental resources may be a 'luxury' of those whose livelihoods are secure. Nonetheless, as Figure 3.6 highlighted, environmental capital can be high in subsistence farming communities, precisely because these communities are not linked to globalized capitalist markets, and because these communities often lack the financial wherewithal to exploit the environment to the maximum (see also first community example discussed in Section 5.4). Nonetheless, the economic fragility of these communities also means that pressure for maximum exploitation of environmental resources is always a threat (Carrier, 2004; Bryant, 2005).

As Figure 3.6 highlighted, communities gradually embedded into the global capitalist system are often characterized by reduced environmental and social capital but also by increasing economic capital (see, for example, Macleod's (2002) case study of a Canary Island fishing community). At community level the availability of regional, national and global markets for community-based products can substantially increase the wealth of communities. However, it is also in these communities that income disparities between wealthy and poor residents may be particularly pronounced. Poverty among urban communities is commonplace, but with 'poverty' as a relative term that highlights pockets of deprivation (with many below the poverty line) within often wealthier urban conglomerations (Thrift, 2005). In these communities, endogenous economic lock-in effects are, therefore, complex, and profit-driven lock-ins become particularly evident as certain stakeholder groups increase their dependence on the global market and may find it increasingly difficult to 'break out' from profit maximization pathways (e.g. from globalized pathways in megacities in the developing world) (Harvey, 2005). Increased depletion of community forest resources may be a case in point, as deforestation often increases once local stakeholders (often with the help of multinational corporations) attempt to maximize profits from sale of timber on national/global markets (Wilson and Bryant, 1997; Bardhan, 2006; see also Section 5.4). Unsustainable resource use and weakening environmental capital are, therefore, often the result. Yet, poverty-driven lock-ins can also remain prominent in communities gradually embedded into the global capitalist system, especially with regard to *lack of access* to environmental resources because of lack of monetary funds by community members (e.g. the enclosing and pricing of previously unpriced open-access resources by powerful and wealthy community elites), leading to increasing exclusion of parts of the community (Davidson, 2010).

Super-globalized communities, meanwhile, are the most prominent example of profit-driven lock-ins, as these communities are closely associated with globalization and capitalist accumulation often predicated on neo-liberal agendas (Robertson, 1992). Endogenous economic path dependencies are particularly associated with the influence exerted by powerful national or multi-national corporations upon community stakeholders. As a wide variety of critical literature emphasizes, such corporations may lead to the substitution of local businesses (e.g. through establishment of 'chain stores' prominent in most European towns and communities), the loss of local economic self-identity and regulation (dependency upon national/international decision-making and markets), shifts in patterns of community-level production from local/regional to national/global, and lock-in effects associated with the loss of alternative economic pathways for local stakeholder groups (Korten, 1995; Gray, 2002). As a result, and as Chapter 3 highlighted, super-globalized communities are often characterized by weakly developed social and environmental capital, although economic capital is usually well developed, albeit with often large income disparities between stakeholder groups. As the global economic crisis of 2008–2011 highlighted, these communities, which have focused almost entirely on developing economic capital at the expense of social or environmental capital, will often be vulnerable despite the fact that some individuals within this community may benefit disproportionately in financial terms.

Relocalized communities, on the other hand, are attempting to break out of economic path dependency linked to globalization and capitalism (Hinrichs, 2003; Porritt, 2007). In many ways, the attempt to break out from economic lock-ins is the *raison d'être* for these communities (Hopkins, 2008). As a result, and as both Bailey *et al.* (2010) and North (2010) emphasized, these communities are often characterized by both attempts to disengage from profit-driven lock-ins and by anti-capitalist discourses and community actions. They often, for example, are associated with 'alternative currency' schemes as part of local exchange trading systems (LETS) with individual currencies that can only be used within the locality (e.g. the 'Bobbins' in Manchester or the 'Totnes Pound' in Totnes, UK) (Cahn, 1999). Yet, endogenous economic lock-ins are also evident in these communities, as evidence so far has shown that it is almost impossible to disengage completely from capitalist globalized lifestyles (see also Box 4.6 and Section 6.3.4). Indeed, alternative currencies themselves can be seen as part and parcel of self-enforced endogenous lock-in mechanisms that tie community residents to a specific economic ideology, mindset and 'enforced localism' that may not chime with the wide spectrum of economic interests and networks usually found within communities (North, 1999; Winter, 2003). In particular, LETS schemes may struggle to compete with the efficiency, choice and global reach of the 'formal' economy, and may be abandoned or never taken up by more mobile and globalized community residents (Bowring, 1998).

'Endogenous political lock-in effects', meanwhile, are associated with specific political pathways adopted by powerful individuals or groups within communities (see also Section 6.3.1 for a more detailed discussion). Although these pathways may be benign (a community leader adopting endogenous political decisions 'for the common good'), often they are malign and may stifle innovation and the implementation of alternative community pathways (Box 5.2) (Tews, 2005). The impact of endogenous political lock-in effects depends largely on the political organization of a community, power structures of decision-making and the level of transparency that define whether all community voices can be heard (Bryant, 2005; Davidson, 2010). Path dependencies become particularly apparent when individual community-based family 'clans' manage to cling on to power for generations, without allowing dissenting voices to be heard. Although political decisions at community level are usually closely intertwined with political decision-making at regional/national level (see Chapter 6), in remote communities such external political influences can be relatively weak, thereby delegating much political decision-making power to local elites. As Box 5.2 suggests, endogenous political lock-ins may lead to political fossilization of community structures and networks, with often negative impacts on community resilience.

Box 5.2 Endogenous political lock-in mechanisms and community resilience in the village of Fanlo, southern Pyrenees, Spain

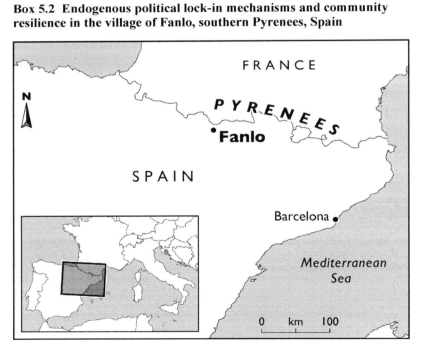

The village of Fanlo, located in a remote valley in the southern Pyrenees (Spain), comprises about 40 households and is located at an altitude of 1300 m. Research undertaken as part of the LEDDRA (2011) Project has highlighted that the mayor of Fanlo is in a powerful political position, as a member of a family that has been in power in the area for several generations. Endogenous political lock-in mechanisms are evident through the mayor's position as the key person who decides who may, or may not, move into the village. Many houses in the village are abandoned (due to outmigration) and could, in theory, be sold to 'outsiders'. However, the mayor will only allow newcomers to settle in the village who are likely to support him politically (especially at local elections), and who are associated with the powerful hunting lobby of the area (a network within which the mayor is closely embedded both politically and economically). The result is *political fossilization* of community structures and networks in Fanlo as few innovations reach the isolated community, and conservative values about village-level environmental management practices continue to predominate. The outcome has been a partial breakdown of traditional sustainable mountain grazing systems with associated disappearance of biodiversity-rich ecosystems, and the favouring of landscapes that favour hunters (e.g. biodiversity-poor open landscapes) at the expense of more biodiverse environments (e.g. mixed forests). Inevitably, this weakening of environmental capital has led to a relative loss of community resilience, and the future of the village looks increasingly uncertain.

5.3.3 Socio-psychological lock-in effects

'Socio-psychological lock-ins' refer to pathway-related lock-ins associated with community-level endogenous social and psychological factors. In contrast to structural and endogenous economic and political lock-in effects, socio-psychological lock-ins at community level are probably the most difficult to assess, but also the most interesting to evaluate, in particular as any analysis of socio-psychological factors relies on research from a multitude of different disciplines including sociology, psychology (especially social psychology), anthropology, political sciences or human geography (e.g. Bonnano, 2004; Rival, 2009; Davidson, 2010). The literature points towards four key issues in this respect: the metaphor of addiction with regard to specific path dependencies (e.g. oil and energy dependency), interlinkages between power and 'follow-the-leader mentalities', psychological conservatism (sticking to pathways that appear to have been 'best' for generations), and evidence for selective or compartmentalized transitions in which the socio-psychology of only a part of the community is ready to embark on pathways that may lead to stronger resilience.

First, the *metaphor of addiction* has become a powerful lens through which to understand the reluctance of many communities (and stakeholder groups within communities) to break lock-ins and change towards more resilient pathways. In particular, psychological models from addiction studies have been used to explore how communities attempt to acquire more resilient behaviours (DiClemente, 2003). One such model is the trans-theoretical change model, a framework for identifying the stages individuals must go through to implement behavioural changes, including pre-contemplation (developing awareness of the need to change), contemplation (increasing arguments for, and countering arguments against, change) and preparation (commitment and planning of the changes to be attempted). Although such models often focus on individual change, some organizations have argued that the trans-theoretical change model may also be effective in catalysing community-scale pathways towards stronger resilience (e.g. CPRC, 2006). Path dependency in the context of the metaphor of addiction is particularly pronounced with regard to dependencies of communities on oil and other carbon-based fuels and energy (Dahle, 2007; Bumpus and Liverman, 2008). In this context, 'despair and empowerment approaches' provide a framework for helping communities explore their 'grief' at losing the services cheap energy provides and to highlight the possibly positive aspects of relocalization (Macy and Brown, 1998). Bailey *et al.* (2010) used the addiction metaphor to emphasize how the social memory of many communities is locked into complex global/national energy, transport and food dependencies, and that most community members have become 'addicted' to capitalist and globalized lifestyles associated with these dependencies. The reluctance of individuals to leave such pathways is perceptible in communities gradually embedded into the global capitalist system (in many ways globalization enables access to such pathways in the first place), is particularly evident in super-globalized communities (often with little questioning of high energy and transport-dependent pathways), but can also be found in glocal communities where the majority of stakeholders are on pathways of dependency regarding energy, transport and food networks (Robertson, 1995; Seyfang, 2006). Yet, even in relocalized communities, addiction studies suggest that people who are contemplating leaving established lock-ins based on extra-community transport, energy and food dependencies feel real sadness, pain and 'withdrawal symptoms' when embarking on relocalized pathways (Hopkins, 2008; Bailey *et al.*, 2010). Addiction to globalized lifestyles is, therefore, one of the most powerful explanations for the difficulties many communities face in embarking on more resilient pathways.

Second, issues of *power* and *follow-the-leader mentalities* also often explain why communities may be reluctant to embark on more resilient pathways. Especially in tight-knit communities, political structures of stakeholder interactions linked to the relative power positions of individuals can be crucial for understanding chosen community development pathways (Lebel *et al.*, 2006; Bodin and Crona, 2008). 'Follow-the-leader mentality' is a particularly powerful process in this respect, as in most communities specific leaders emerge whose individual visions, plans for the future and drive can strongly influence how a community evolves (as the example in Box 5.2 illustrated). As with social memory, such 'leadership' can work both ways by either enhancing or reducing community resilience. Powerful leaders with charisma, positive plans for community resilience and able to control powerful networks at community level can often engender positive change (Folke, 2006; Magis, 2010). As examples in Section 5.4 will illustrate, such 'positive plans' may include the willingness to embark on green technology and energy pathways, or the ability to harness community power to prevent unsustainable resource use (e.g. felling of community forests) by external actors. On the other hand, powerful community leaders who lack a vision for resilience may 'drag down' a community through their involvement with powerful actor groups that may increase community vulnerability, for example by being closely aligned with multinational corporations intent on maximum exploitation of community natural resources (see Bodin and Crona, 2008, for an example from a Kenyan fishing community). A follow-the-leader mentality at community level is, in turn, based on complex socio-political and psychological factors that can be highly dynamic (i.e. power is relational and stakeholder allegiances can change quickly) (Allen, 2003). Factors highlighted in Table 2.1 such as wealth/poverty, gender roles or the internal structural complexity of communities can all influence whether and how follow-the-leader mentalities are developed and expressed. For example, a community will often be comprised of multiple leaders, often with different factionalized views and visions about community development. Path dependencies can become particularly entrenched in communities with pronounced follow-the-leader mentalities, and it may be difficult for these communities to leave pathways decided by only one or a handful of powerful leaders – in some cases, resulting in path dependencies defined by ruling families/elites over many generations (Davidson, 2010; Goldsworthy, 2010).

Third, *psychological conservatism* (with a small 'c') can be another important socio-psychological lock-in mechanism, often also referred to as 'cultural resistance' (e.g. Bonnano, 2004; Burton *et al.*, 2008). Although adopting new technologies to 'fix' community problems may be relatively easy, developing a new attitude and moving the culture from one mental mode to another is difficult. While communities may be given solutions to raise resilience, the great irony is that even though people may be unhappy, they have high levels of inertia – people do not like change unless it is enforced upon them (Hopkins, 2008). This highlights that, in many ways, psychological conservatism is closely associated with social memory of a community, as it is often closely related to 'doing what has been seen as best for generations'. As Chapter 4 highlighted, the perception of 'doing what is best' is not necessarily associated with resilient pathways but can be related to environmentally malign traditions, rites and conventions at community level. Some of the most poignant examples of psychological conservatism come from the critical literature on 'traditional' farming communities, highlighting that farmers, in particular, due to their strong embeddedness with farming lifestyles, local landscapes and communities, often resist change (Wilson, 2007, 2008). Although, as Box 5.3 highlights, such conservatism can also be positive for environmental management at community level (e.g. by adhering to environmentally friendly 'traditional' farming practices'), it can also stifle innovation regarding the strengthening of social and environmental capital in productivist/super-globalized farming communities. The resilience literature suggests, in particular, that during crises such communities are often less open for new ideas, and only when things improve can change be productively turned into 'positive' development (Diamond, 2006). In other words, vicious circles of psychological conservatism may be in operation precisely when communities may be in most need to innovate and be open-minded (e.g. at times of crisis). The frequent dominance of psychological conservatism at community level means, therefore, that *timing* is key for success of new ideas and innovations: too early attempts for change may mean that ideas dissipate, while too late attempts may mean that pathways of vulnerability can not be reversed. Visionary community leaders (and visionary external agents like policy-makers; see Chapter 7) may, therefore, be those who recognize the best time and pace for introducing change in conservative communities (see, in particular, Hopkins, 2008).

Finally, socio-psychological lock-ins may be related to *selective* or *compartmentalized transitions* within individual communities, where only a sub-section

---

Box 5.3 Psychological conservatism and path dependencies in farming communities

Critical rural literature has highlighted that many farming communities are relatively 'conservative' in the way they address the need for change and innovation (e.g. Marsden, 2003; Robinson, 2008). Farmers tend to stick to 'what they know best', to 'how their parents and grandparents farmed' and 'to how things have always been done' (Wilson, 2007). These attitudinal path dependencies can be largely explained by the fact that farming communities are often relatively stable with regard to stakeholder structures (i.e. families and neighbours have often known each other for generations) leading to internal inertia, have a strong sense of embeddedness in both the community and farmed landscape, and are often sceptical of change imposed from 'outside' (Burton *et al.*, 2008). Psychological conservatism of farming communities is particularly evident with regard to attempts by policy-makers to implement 'innovations' aimed at improving community resilience. In particular, many farming communities in the developed world have strongly resisted implementation of non-productivist agri-environmental policies aimed at reducing farming intensity and raising environmental capital. Resistance by farmers to these policies is especially linked to their perceptions that such policies force them to change their identities as farmers away from food and fibre production towards becoming 'landscape gardeners' (Wilson and Hart, 2000; Burton and Wilson, 2006). Burton *et al.* (2008) referred to this as the 'cultural resistance' of farmers to adopt policies seen to go 'against the grain' of established farming pathways. In productivist farming communities, this resistance/conservatism may enhance existing path dependencies that may, ultimately, lead to irreversible erosion of environmental capital, as already evidenced in some of the least environmentally sustainable farming landscapes of the American Midwest, the Paris Basin, the intensive arable belt in Australia or the Ukrainian wheat belt (Diamond, 2006; Wilson, 2007).

of the community is willing to risk embarking on more resilient pathways. Closely interlinked with the above notions of follow-the-leader mentality and psychological conservatism, in most communities a groundswell or momentum of 'readiness for change' is necessary for a community to agree to adopt more resilient pathways. Subtle psychological forces are at play here, especially as wrong timing, excessive pressure for change exerted upon conservative elements in the community or misguided lobbying may tip the balance away from decisions for change (Scheffer *et al.*, 2003). Notions of power and community leadership are, again, crucial in this respect, as politically and psychologically astute leaders well embedded within their communities will be able to both understand the signals emanating from community stakeholder groups and to perfectly time their suggestions for change towards more (or less) resilient pathways (Bonnano, 2004). Stryker's (1980) work in social psychology particularly pointed towards the fact that certain stakeholder identities come to the surface under certain conditions, and that people are only ready for change when these changes coincide more or less with the dominant identities of specific stakeholder groups (e.g. identities that embrace rather than resist relocalization processes). As a result, even in some of the most 'relocalized' communities in the developed world (e.g. Transition Town Totnes; see Box 4.6), transitions towards stronger resilience are only partial, as only certain stakeholder groups are willing to engage with relocalization agendas (e.g. Hinrichs, 2003; Hopkins, 2010). So far, evidence suggests that in none of the 1000+ transition town initiatives has there been enough momentum that entire communities have been willing to shift towards relocalized pathways of resilience (Bailey *et al.*, 2010). Community transitions to resilience are, therefore, inevitably characterized by hybridity, complexity, selectivity and non-linearity.

5.4 Endogenous path dependency at community level: examples from the developed and developing world

In this section, I wish to show how the more abstract discussion of path dependency can be illustrated through two hypothetical examples of endogenous pathways at community level. To this end, I have chosen one example of a community in the developing world gradually embedded into the global capitalist system (Indonesia), and one from a glocal community in the developed world (United Kingdom). As the following discussion will highlight, both communities face different types of path dependencies and lock-ins, but both share the fact that community resilience is threatened by various structural, endogenous economic and socio-psychological lock-ins. The discussion below will not only illustrate the utility of visual conceptualizations of path dependencies and nodal transitional points (e.g. Figure 5.1), but will also highlight the applicability of such transitional concepts across different cultural settings (e.g. developed and developing world) in which there may be similar loss of community resilience, but where drivers of change and lock-in effects may be rather different.

5.4.1 An Indonesian community: tropical deforestation, path dependencies and weakening environmental capital

Imagine a small agricultural village (Village 'X'; *c.*1000 inhabitants) in a tropical forest setting somewhere on the west coast of Sumatra (Indonesia). Based on Figure 5.1, at nodal point 1 in the early 1980s this village had relatively well-developed social capital based on several of the indicators of strong social capital highlighted in Table 3.1. For example, it was a tight-knit community with relatively strong kinship and neighbourhood networks and reasonably well-developed levels of trust among village community members. However, power relations were complex, and there was inequality with regard to both ownership of land, gender relations and the existence of a relatively powerful village elite in which the majority of members inherited rather than 'earned' their powerful positions in the community. At times, political lock-in effects, therefore, stifled 'democratic' endogenous decision-making processes. Simultaneously, economic capital was relatively weak, as Village X was not well connected to the wider world (poor road network, impassable during the wettest part of the season), and travel to the nearest large city (Padang) took several days. Monetary means of financial exchange were, therefore, rare, and for most of the year community members exchanged and bartered goods (especially locally grown agricultural products) and services. Environmental capital, meanwhile, was well developed, especially as the surrounding tropical forest, although modified and selectively logged in the immediate vicinity of the village, had survived relatively intact and provided an important source of additional food through hunting and gathering. At nodal point 1 (Figure 5.1), the combined effect of strong environmental capital, relatively strong social capital but weak economic capital situated Village X towards the stronger end of the resilience spectrum (with a relatively large 'resilience triangle'; see Section 2.5), placing the village in a relatively good position of resilience with regard to key disturbances (e.g. weather-related disasters or disturbances linked to globalization or economic and socio-political disturbances).

A gradual reduction in community resilience was evident between nodal points 1 and 2. In Village X, this could be attributed to the building of an all-weather road in the mid 1980s which opened up new opportunities for the village community, some of which resulted in increased resilience, but many of which led to a gradual reduction in community resilience (see Cumming *et al.*, 2005, 2006, for discussion of positive and negative impacts of infrastructure projects on community resilience). While economic capital in the form of availability of 'hard' currency improved for most community members who could now sell surplus agricultural products in nearby markets, environmental capital was negatively affected as the logging of large timber trees near the village was intensifying. Individual stakeholder groups in the village began to sell cutting rights to local timber companies who used damaging logging practices resulting in erosion and localized destruction of soils (nodal point 2). Logging was briefly interrupted in the early 1990s due to protest by some village women who argued that their agricultural plots were affected by increased erosion and desiccation of soils. The women's actions were, thereby, temporarily raising environmental capital or at least halting further loss of environmental capital (nodal point 3) (see also Agrawal and Gibson, 1999). Yet, lock-in effects linked to unequal power relations within the village, and the relatively marginal economic position of many of the affected women, resulted in an intensification of logging activities aided and abetted by the powerful village elite who benefited financially from logging revenue (nodal points 4 and 5). The latter point highlights the importance of understanding processes underlying selective or compartmentalized transitions where only a small proportion of a community (i.e. the village elite) may define pathways, overall resulting in weakening community resilience.

Nodal point 6, showing temporary strengthening of community resilience, formed an important turning point for Village X. The continuing logging operations damaged a sacred village burial ground which held a special role in community traditions and rites. As a relatively remote community, animist religion survived in the community, and the veneration of ancestors formed a key religious and ritualized (possibly positive) lock-in effect that still defines most of the worldviews of Village X community members today. As a result, the village briefly stood united against further logging activities that would have destroyed 'holy sites' near the village, resulting in the complete withdrawal of local logging companies by the mid 1990s. Simultaneously, the crisis over destroyed burial sites brought the village community closer together, thereby temporarily strengthening social capital.

Nodal points 7 and 8, however, are indicative of the increasing embeddedness of the community into the global capitalist system. Based on the improved infrastructure of the formerly remote village to towns and cities on the coast with access to harbour facilities for export, Japanese chipmilling conglomerates began approaching village leaders from the mid 1990s with the aim of purchasing rights to cut timber within the 'ancestral domains' of the community.[4] Chipmilling contracts can be attractive to poor village communities, as the logging companies often offer to build road access to inaccessible parts of the territory and pay a flat rate for the complete clearfelling of forest (total forest utilization irrespective of timber species) (Schreuder and Anderson, 1988). The result was the sale of ancestral domain land by the village elite likely to gain most financially from the deal, suggesting that endogenous economic lock-ins linked to poverty and the absence of clear property rights (ancestral domains are often managed as a common property resource by village communities) can override positive lock-ins linked to rites and rituals associated with more sustainable forest management (see Lebel *et al.*, 2006, for a similar example from the Malinau District, East Kalimantan, Indonesia). After only a few years of logging until the early 2000s, the outcome was complete removal of forest cover in all accessible parts of the village's ancestral domain, associated loss of biodiversity, lowering of the water table with associated desiccation of the ground, and high levels of soil erosion. By nodal point 8, this almost complete loss of environmental capital led to a loss of traditional forestry practices and the almost complete destruction of the agricultural livelihood base of the village.

A brief respite was offered at nodal point 9 (in 2004) when the international woodchipping market collapsed due to tightening regulation in most countries exploited by Japanese woodchipping multinationals (see also Wilson and Memon, 2005, for New Zealand), resulting in the abandonment of logging sites on Village X's territory. However, the destruction of environmental capital had by then engendered an almost irreversible downward spiral of loss of resilience, associated in particular with the outmigration of a large part of Village X's population, especially young people. Nodal points 10 and 11, situated close to extreme vulnerability thresholds of community survival (see Figure 5.1), highlight that the remaining village population is no longer capable of supporting itself from its degraded soils, and is increasingly dependent on remittances sent by relatives working in nearby urban centres (e.g. Padang). The rapid weakening of environmental capital has led to a concurrent weakening of social and economic capital. Within only three decades, at nodal point 11 Village X has lost most of its resilience, and it is difficult to imagine a 'rediscovery' of stronger resilience pathways in the near future.

Although the example of Village X is hypothetical, the critical literature on community resilience describes many examples that echo the rapid loss of resilience at community level described here (see Peluso 1992, 1995; Bryant, 2005; and Pretty, 2007, for discussion of similar examples in South-East Asia). As Parnwell (2007) and Rigg *et al.* (2008), in particular, emphasized, the example of Village X shows how poverty and unequal power relations often predetermine pathways of declining resilience. Although positive social memory may exist at the outset of a transitional pathway in the form of long-established traditions and rites (e.g. linked to sustainable logging of forests within ancestral domains), the greed of a powerful village elite, combined with the gradual embeddedness of communities into the global capitalist system (see Chapter 3) have combined in negative ways to result in rapidly diminishing resilience. 'Scale mismatches' between the local and global are, therefore, particularly evident in this case study, severely affecting community resilience (Anderies *et al.*, 2006; Cumming *et al.*, 2006). The example of Village X also particularly exemplifies that poverty, as a key determinant of transitional pathways in the developing world (and beyond), is relational. Indeed, before embeddedness of Village X into the global capitalist system (especially through the building of a road enabling access for multinational logging companies), poverty was not necessarily perceived as 'negative' by the village community as almost everybody was equally poor. However, once embedded in capitalist processes and worldviews, the need to accumulate economic capital often overrides positive social memory associated with conscious and subconscious efforts at preserving environmental capital (Stiglitz, 2002; Young *et al.*, 2006).

5.4.2 A UK community: counter-urbanization, conservatism and (im)possible green energy pathways

Imagine a small village community (Village Y) somewhere on the south coast of the county of Devon in the south-west of the UK. Figure 5.3 suggests that at nodal point 1 in the 1870s the small community (a few hundred inhabitants) was relatively resilient, with well-developed social and environmental capital based on a semi-subsistent fishing economy and some extensive livestock agriculture (see also Macleod, 2002, for a similar example from the Canary Islands). In relative terms, however, Village Y was a poor village (relatively low economic capital) bypassed by rapid industrialization characteristic for the UK in the late nineteenth century. Social networks were strong, especially as fishing and farming families were often reliant on each other to get through 'the hard times', particularly during periods of poor fish catches and poor agricultural returns – indicative of positive path dependencies related to centuries-old rituals and unwritten moral codes of self-help and neighbourhood support in remote rural areas of Europe (Rival, 2009). The economy was largely based on self-sufficiency, with excess produce sold in the local market of a nearby town.

At nodal point 2 community resilience was slightly increased based on the arrival of wealthy 'tourists' in the 1880s from the London area who discovered the 'charms' of traditional rural English life. These tourists provided the first substantial opportunity for wider capitalist embeddedness of Village Y, in particular as they brought with them innovative ideas (e.g. creation of a coastal pathway that enables visitors to see the idyllic coastal cliff scenery), money (some of which was spent within the village through the building of new houses/second homes and employment of locals), and new knowledge and communication networks (e.g. extension of village school). Social networks

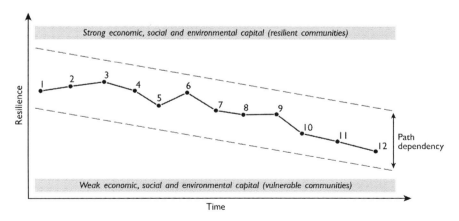

Figure 5.3 Hypothetical path dependency and nodal points of change in a small coastal village community (UK) (source: author).

were not greatly disrupted by these newcomers, while economic capital was partly strengthened. These pathways were strengthened further at nodal point 3 in the 1920s when Village Y was connected for the first time with an all-weather road to the nearest city (Plymouth) and to an emergent network of national roads. This sparked a house-building boom, as wealthy workers from Plymouth chose to move out of the crowded and polluted city into the country-side (first wave of counter-urbanization; see Woods, 2005). While, on the one hand, this provided new opportunities for Village Y through increased demand for local services (e.g. new shops; more children in the local school), it also sparked a first wave of outmigration of young people seeking better job oppor-tunities elsewhere (nodal point 4). The latter set in motion pathways of steady erosion of social capital (greying of the community) that has lasted to the present day.

At nodal point 5, overall resilience of the community had declined below that at the starting point in the 1870s. The recession of the late 1920s and early 1930s particularly affected Village Y, signalling that the village was now more firmly embedded within the global capitalist system with all its positive and negative effects. Some of the newcomers went bankrupt during the recession, the housing market partly collapsed and the village lost further population to nearby urban centres. In addition, coastal pollution from nearby industrial areas, combined with overfishing of coastal waters, began to erode environmental capital (fisher-ies) upon which part of the community had relied for centuries. The result was a relatively rapid decline of fishing as a local economic activity during the 1930s – an activity that had almost completely disappeared by the end of the twentieth century.

At nodal point 6, however, WW2 provided some interesting opportunities for raising community resilience, despite the devastations caused by the war in nearby urban centres. Due to energy (especially fuel) and food shortages, the war *forced* communities like Village Y to relocalize. Food had to be sourced and grown more locally, as national/global food networks were disrupted and local timber was used more frequently (and sustainably) for heating rather than coal imported from the north of England or beyond (see also Chapter 6). The fact that villagers had to 'stick together' to survive the war also led to a strengthening of social capital, helped by the fact that more villagers met each other on a daily basis as part of relocalized food production initiatives (e.g. the village green was transformed into a large allotment for local food production).

After the war, changes accelerated. During the 1950s to the 1970s (nodal points 7 and 8), Village Y lost its status of 'remote' community and was increasingly drawn into the sphere of influence of Plymouth as the neighbour-ing large city. Lax planning legislation led to a relatively uncontrolled house-building boom, with some houses built in a way that no longer fitted the traditional 'rustic' image of the village. As a result, the formerly tight-knit village community was eroding fast, with newcomers quickly outnumbering the 'locals' (second wave of counter-urbanization). Although economic capital was strengthened (for some stakeholder groups), social (and environ-mental) capital was further eroded. Nonetheless, at nodal point 9, tighter planning legislation (since the late 1970s) prevented further urban sprawl, and Village Y was prevented from further expansion thereby 'fossilizing' its housing landscape and geographical boundaries to those of the late 1970s. To some extent, this enabled a stabilization of further social capital erosion, although it did not prevent accelerating counter-urbanization. During the 1980s and 1990s (nodal point 10), the village changed from a relatively affordable place to live to an exclusive playground of the wealthy, with nearly 50 per cent of the village housing stock sold as second homes (third wave of counter-urbanization). Today, the maintenance of 'traditional' social net-works is increasingly difficult (most people no longer know their second-home neighbours), and community services such as the school also begin to suffer as families with young children can no longer afford to purchase prop-erty in the village.

This loss of resilience is further exacerbated by psychological lock-in mech-anisms related to entrenched pathways of conservatism, partly linked to the type of wealthy newcomers to the village (mainly second-home owners) who wish to preserve the status quo of the 'rural idyll' they see embodied by Village Y. In the 2000s and 2010s, other psychological lock-in effects linked to high depend-ency on car ownership – most households have two cars due to the remote geo-graphical location of Village Y and poor public transport infrastructure – combined with the resistance by the conservative village elite to contemplate greener energy pathways (e.g. through wind turbines), suggest that Village Y is further losing resilience (nodal points 11 and 12) (see also Scheffer *et al.*, 2003). Although there are still opportunities for the community to raise both social and environmental capital (e.g. through the adoption of green energy pathways or relocalized food networks), it appears that at nodal point 12, social capital has been eroded to such an extent that Village Y can be classified as a 'vulnerable' community with limited adaptive capacity to withstand many of the disturbances highlighted in Chapter 1.

Village Y thus epitomizes problems associated with the problematic combi-nation of an almost complete change in the socio-economic structure of a small community over a relatively short time span (i.e. less than four or five genera-tions), with remnant path dependencies (e.g. entrenched conservatism linked to inmigration of residents or second-home owners seeking the rural idyll) that often prevent the implementation of innovative pathways (e.g. alternative green energy pathways) (Tews, 2005).

5.5 Path dependency and transitional ruptures at community level: pathways of the (im)possible?

This chapter has so far explored patterns and processes associated with path dependencies that assume that transitions are relatively linear and 'smooth'. However, as Figure 3.4 (Chapter 3) highlighted, community transitions can also be characterized by 'transitional ruptures' (or 'regime shifts') where the quality of resilience is abruptly changed (positively or negatively). In this section, I wish to explore in more detail the complex interlinkages between transitional ruptures and path dependency. I will argue that, over longer periods of time, transitional ruptures are *always* a feature of transitional pathways (non-linearity). Indeed, rather than focusing on responses to 'everyday' transitions to resilience, it is how communities tackle transitional ruptures that is the true test of a community's adaptive capacity (Cutter *et al.*, 2008). Section 5.5.1 will first investigate the nature of transitional ruptures, while Section 5.5.2 will discuss how communities can best manage such ruptures.

5.5.1 Understanding transitional ruptures

Figure 5.4 shows a conceptual model of a community pathway characterized by two transitional ruptures (community resilience and vulnerability on y-axis, time on x-axis). First, the model shows that pathways of community development/evolution can be shown as probability pathways characterized by a bell-shaped curve of decision-making possibilities centred broadly against the middle of the decision-making corridor. These corridors suggest that most (possibly even all) community decisions with regard to economic, social and environmental capital are made within these 'pathways of the possible' (Shucksmith, 1993). The transitional pathway in this context has to be understood as comprising a myriad of transitions, the sum total of which is shown by the lines a1–a3 in the figure. This highlights that usually community development pathways would be located towards the centre of decision-making corridors, and that pathways that stray beyond or outside these corridors (b1–b3 and c1–c3) are often 'pathways of the impossible' – either unthinkable pathways as they are beyond the realm of a community's imagination, or pathways that would be impossible to implement as they may be perceived as being too 'radical' (see also Chapter 6). Although 'radical' individual voices or 'radical' individual stakeholder groups within communities may wish for the community to embark on pathways that break away from the norm and that may induce vital change towards improved community resilience, pathways a1–a3 are the more likely pathways often (but not always) representing the *majority* view of stakeholders within the community embedded within a specific paradigm.[5] The further a decisional pathway varies from the 'norm', the greater resistance it is likely to face (Dryzek, 2001). Indeed, the notion of 'radicalism' usually implies – whether at community or other levels – attempts by a minority to break away from 'traditional' pathways at the centre of transitional corridors. As the discussion above highlighted, the key explanation for the reluctance of communities to embark on 'pathways of the impossible' lies in various structural, economic and socio-psychological lock-in effects. Indeed, the fact that pathways towards the centre of the transitional corridor tend to be the ones most frequently chosen by a community is closely associated with the frequent

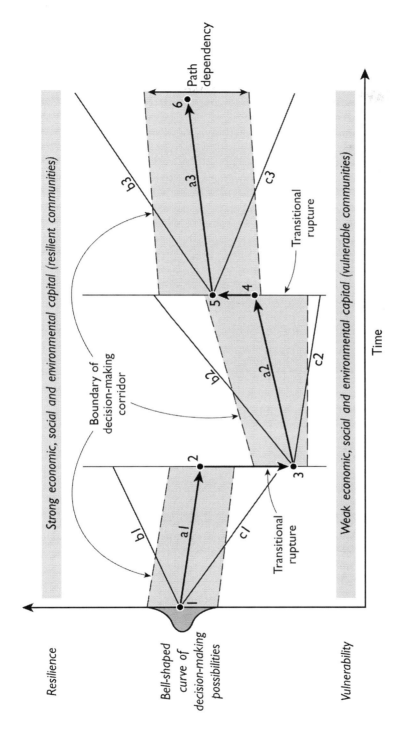

Figure 5.4 Conceptual model of a community pathway characterized by two transitional ruptures (source: author; after Wilson, 2007).

conservatism associated with community transitions (for better or for worse for community resilience) discussed in Sections 5.3 and 5.4.

Second, the model shows a community pathway characterized by two *transitional ruptures* (sometimes also referred to as 'regime shifts'; see Folke, 2006) where the 'quality' of resilience/vulnerability suddenly changes. While community transitions are usually characterized by slow and gradual change over time (linearity), transitional ruptures suggest that community resilience can change rapidly from one moment to another. Most often such ruptures are associated with a sudden loss of resilience (i.e. abrupt 'downward' shift of resilient quality; the first transitional rupture shown in Figure 5.4), but the figure also shows a second 'upward' transitional rupture in which resilience is suddenly increased. Downward ruptures are usually (but not exclusively) associated with 'disturbances' exogenous to the community itself (Figure 1.1 showed examples of such anthropogenic and natural disturbances affecting communities). These include catastrophes such as weather-related disasters (e.g. hurricanes, tornados) or geological disasters (e.g. tsunamis, volcanic eruptions) (Box 5.4). Davis (2004), for example, suggested that severe El Nino events in the late nineteenth and early twentieth century caused pronounced negative transitional ruptures, which led to a substantial reduction in community resilience in India, China and many parts of Africa and South America which, in turn, allowed imperial powers to exert more political pressure on colonial states than would have otherwise been possible. Similarly, the magnitude 9 earthquake and tsunami that affected north-east Japan in March 2011 created a distinctive transitional rupture for affected communities from which it will be difficult to recover in the near future.

On the other hand, possibly with the exception of wars and revolutions, anthropogenic disturbances (e.g. human mismanagement of the environment such as climate change, governance shifts, economic disturbances such as recessions) or disturbances linked to globalization, are usually akin to 'slow-onset hazards' associated with linear loss of community resilience, rather than nonlinear transitional ruptures. Yet, human factors can also contribute towards transitional ruptures where pathways are suddenly elevated/lowered towards stronger/weaker levels of resilience. Examples for upward transitional ruptures linked to anthropogenic drivers are closely related to Table 2.1 (Chapter 2) and may include sudden changes in community governance structures (e.g. the overthrowing of an unpopular elite that stifled developments for improved community resilience), abrupt changes to structural lock-ins (e.g. a community implementing green energy pathways through a community-based wind farm project or successful food relocalization initiatives) or the sudden opening up of new community development/economic opportunities (e.g. sudden strengthening of economic capital). Upward transitional ruptures induced by anthropogenic factors, therefore, can contribute towards breaking established path dependencies (see Section 5.2) and 'elevating' community pathways to a stronger level of resilience.

Box 5.4 Transitional ruptures and the Indian Ocean tsunami 2004

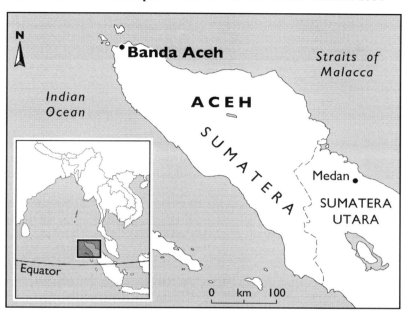

The Indian Ocean tsunami of December 2004 that affected countries around the Indian Ocean and that killed over 250,000 people is a typical example of a geological disaster that led to pronounced transitional ruptures in affected communities (Rigg *et al.*, 2005). The most affected community that received substantial media coverage was the town of Banda Aceh (35,000 inhabitants) at the extreme northwestern tip of the island of Sumatra, Indonesia. Within an instant, a 20–30m tidal wave destroyed 95 per cent of the housing stock and killed about half of the residents. The massive death toll, combined with the near complete destruction of infrastructure, inevitably led to a sudden lowering of community resilience. Indeed, for months after the disaster discussions focused on the question whether the community of Banda Aceh could survive at all or whether the surviving residents should be resettled elsewhere (Miller, 2008). Loss of resilience was associated with a sudden weakening of all three types of capital. Economic capital was substantially reduced as the community was no longer able to use and sell traditional goods such as fish (the entire fishing fleet of Banda Aceh was destroyed) or agricultural products (although some of the agricultural land had not been affected by the tidal wave, the massive death toll meant that there was insufficient agricultural labour to tend the fields). Social capital was affected because most families had lost members, social networks could not be maintained or were substantially changed, and community-level power structures had inevitably shifted (many families were dead or had moved out). Environmental capital was considerably weakened especially along the coast (the geomorphology of the coastal area had been changed; productive reefs have been damaged or severely affected). Yet, at the time of writing (2011) the community of Banda Aceh *has* survived and the infrastructure has been largely repaired (partly linked to generous international donations). Political capital for the region may have even been *enhanced* by the catastrophe as the Free Aceh Movement in the north-west of Sumatra was substantially weakened by the catastrophe (more political stability), and economic capital may have also increased for some community members benefiting from the influx of 'catastrophe tourism' (Miller, 2008). It appears that the adaptive capacity of Banda Aceh was sufficient to ensure survival of the community, despite the substantial transitional rupture created by the tsunami.

5.5.2 Transitional ruptures and adaptive capacity

How can transitional ruptures be understood in light of adaptive capacity of communities? Chapter 3 highlighted the importance of understanding adaptive capacity as the potential of a community to survive transitional ruptures. Figure 5.5 emphasizes that adaptive capacity after downward transitional ruptures, or the 'elevation' of transitional pathways after upward transitional ruptures, depend heavily on conditions *before* the rupture. Figure 3.4 (Chapter 3) already highlighted that a community is only able to recover from the trauma of a catastrophic rupture if that community can successfully implement a 'period of readjustment' (usually characterized by more chaotic pathways) and a (possibly more linear) 'period of recovery'. This may enable the community to 'rediscover' and build upon more resilient pathways it enjoyed before the catastrophe.

Figure 5.5 shows a stylized model of community recovery options after a transitional rupture. Different adaptive capacity is shown through lines 'a' (rapid readjustment and recovery), 'b' (slow or gradual readjustment and recovery) and 'c' (inadequate readjustment and recovery). These different adaptive capacities are strongly dependent on antecedent conditions before the rupture and the strength of social memory, path dependencies and lock-in mechanisms (Smit and Wandel, 2006). The rediscovery of resilience may be easier for communities where economic, social or environmental capital were relatively well developed *before* the onset of the transitional rupture. In particular, communities located towards the stronger end of the resilience spectrum often find it easier to implement rapid readjustment and recovery pathways than already vulnerable communities (see example of Banda Aceh in Box 5.4). Communities with well-developed economic, social and environmental capital can usually harness sufficient adaptive capacity to rediscover resilience pathways, even after a short period of time (Magis, 2010). Although debates are complex, there may also be a tendency for communities with fewer path dependencies linked to conservatism or established rites and rituals (be they religious or not) to 'bounce back' more quickly, as the relative open-mindedness of community members may enable them to 'think outside of the box' at times of crises. Similarly, positive social memory will usually be beneficial for the more rapid implementation of readjustment and recovery trajectories.

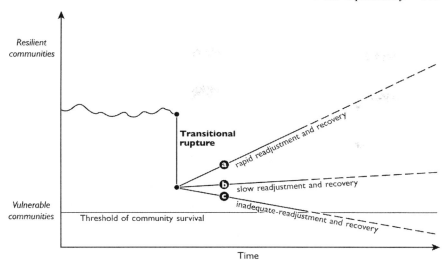

Figure 5.5 Stylized model of community recovery options after transitional rupture (source: author; after Adger, 2000).

Although slow readjustment and recovery pathways (path 'b' in Figure 5.5) can be problematic as they may reduce development and resilience options of communities for generations, it is communities along pathway 'c' – with inadequate readjustment and no recovery options – that are the most problematic. However, conceptualizations of pathway 'c' are highly dependent on definitions of thresholds of community survival and, as Chapter 3 highlighted, any assessment of community vulnerability is ultimately linked to *normative* assumptions and the positionality of commentators dependent on cultural factors. Aid agencies coming in from 'outside' may often misread endogenous potential of communities, due to misinterpretations of cultural signifiers of adaptive capacity, such as the strength of community networks and trust, power structures or specific livelihood needs (Abel *et al.*, 2006). Nonetheless, in the most extreme cases it is relatively easy to identify 'bad' community trajectories, especially those associated with *complete annihilation* of communities. Along trajectory 'c', therefore, thresholds will be linked to an inability of a community to recreate a qualitatively different but successful alternative pathway, and an associated inability to implement a period of readjustment and recovery, as the disturbance may have been so large that it has overwhelmed local capacity (as may be the case for some coastal communities affected by the Japanese mega-tsunami of March 2011).

As Chapter 3 suggested, the outcome for communities along pathway 'c' may be a complete disintegration of social support networks, outmigration and possible complete reconstitution of community boundaries and spaces of community ownership. These communities have, therefore, fallen below the 'resilience threshold', and will not be able to bounce back and survive. Examples for the rapid disappearance of such communities are manifold and – as high-lighted above – are usually associated with rapid-onset natural disasters (ruptures) such as droughts, volcanic eruptions, tsunamis, floods or earthquakes. Box 5.5 highlights the example of the Anaszasi communities in the Chaco Canyon of north-western New Mexico (USA), where settlements were suddenly abandoned in a matter of a few years due to severe drought, and were never re-settled again.

As Figure 5.4 highlighted, transitional ruptures are, however, not only associated with loss of resilience, but may also lead to a sudden strengthening of community resilience. Ruptures can, therefore, lead to both a loss or increase of community resilience (Dorfman *et al.*, 2009). As a result, some of the most interesting discussions currently revolve around the management of 'upward' transitional ruptures, i.e. where communities are attempting to suddenly break with established path dependencies of weak(er) resilience. Such 'positive

---

Box 5.5 Transitional ruptures and lack of adaptive capacity among the Anaszasi in Chaco Canyon, north-western New Mexico (USA)

Chaco Anaszasi communities flourished from about AD 600–1100 and then suddenly disappeared between AD 1150 and 1200. Diamond (2006, p. 143) described the Anaszasi as "a complexly organized, geographically extensive, regionally integrated society that erected the largest buildings in pre-Columbian North America". Early negative path dependencies were created in Anaszasi communities based on technologically advanced irrigation-based oasis agriculture (corn, squash, beans) that relied on steady supplies of water (high alluvial groundwater levels). Although this enabled intensive farming in a semi-arid environment, overintensive farming and rapid deforestation from AD 900 resulted in a lowering of water tables, which made irrigation even more important. All these factors led to a considerable weakening of environmental capital over time, with relatively large populations living close to thresholds of community survival. Diamond (2006) argued that a severe transitional rupture occurred around AD 1150 when problems caused by the anthropogenic degradation of the environment were exacerbated by a prolonged drought. This drought was the key factor that overwhelmed Anaszasi adaptive capacity and that pushed Anaszasi communities on a pathway of inadequate readjustment beyond community recovery potentials. The drought was "the proximate cause, the proverbial last straw that broke the camel's back ... that finally pushed [the Anaszasi] over the edge" (Diamond, 2006, p. 156). The result was complete abandonment of all sites in Chaco Canyon (and beyond) and the complete collapse of Anaszasi society.

ruptures' are almost always associated with anthropogenic factors (i.e. human change from within the community), although some natural factors may also, at times, result in a positive transitional rupture.[6] 'Adaptive capacity' in this context is, therefore, more closely associated with 'adaptive human potential', i.e. an expression of how well a community is socially and psychologically prepared to abruptly change direction towards stronger resilience by leaving established pathways. As a result, positive transitional ruptures are highly dependent on the 'right timing' of the 'right ideas'. As innovation diffusion theory amply demonstrates (e.g. Rogers, 1995; Tews, 2005), following a charismatic and forward-thinking community leader is not always possible, especially if dogmatic ideas based on conservative adherence to established pathways continue to dominate (Scheffer *et al.*, 2003). As highlighted above, 'radical' questioning of established pathways can, therefore, be dangerous and, in extreme cases, may destroy authority, resulting in further loss of community resilience. As a result, the skills of good community leaders of 'reading the signs' well, and choosing the appropriate rhetoric and timing for implementation of sudden change, are crucial for raising resilience (see Hopkins, 2008, 2010). Positive transitional ruptures are, therefore, only possible if there is enough *momentum* for change and – as Chapters 6 and 7 will discuss in more detail – if such change is also supported at the meso- and macro-levels (e.g. through supportive policies).

5.6 Conclusions

Building on the discussion of the importance of social memory, this chapter focused on understanding notions of path dependency in community transitions. The chapter highlighted that path dependency can be understood as both positive and negative for community resilience, although path dependencies often stifle the implementation of innovative pathways. In particular, endogenous 'lock-in' effects at community level (structural, endogenous economic and socio-psychological lock-ins), that make certain community pathways unthinkable and impossible to implement, can be severe hindrances for raising community resilience. Although many communities would like to change their development trajectories and levels of resilience, they are often impeded in doing so because of path dependencies inherent in the community itself through factors such as entrenched customs, habits, conservatism, negative attitudes or lethargic behaviour. Pathways with highest levels of resilience may therefore be difficult, if not impossible, to implement.

Two case examples from a hypothetical village community in both Indonesia and the UK were used to illustrate how path dependencies and lock-in effects affect economic, social and environmental capital at community level, highlighting in particular the importance of power and psychological conservatism for reducing community resilience over time. The chapter also highlighted that transitional pathways at community level can also be characterized by 'transitional ruptures'. While these are usually caused by sudden natural catastrophes, anthropogenic factors (e.g. wars, revolutions) can also cause sudden ruptures in transitional pathways. The chapter highlighted that such ruptures are usually associated with negative pathways (i.e. loss of resilience), although examples of 'positive ruptures' are also common.

This discussion of path dependencies was predicated on the assumption that most pathways are driven by endogenous factors emanating from the community itself. However, communities do not operate in isolation from wider regional, national or global forces shaping community resilience. How are community-level path dependencies, therefore, shaped and influenced by forces *exogenous* to communities? By investigating in detail notions of transitional corridors, Chapter 6 will discuss the importance of macro-scalar influences in community-level transitions, while Chapter 7 will analyse the role that national policies can play in raising community-level resilience.

6 Transitional corridors

Macro-structural influences and community resilience

6.1 Introduction

Chapter 5 discussed interlinkages between 'path dependency' and community resilience and vulnerability, with a focus on path dependencies *endogenous* to communities (i.e. dependencies emanating from within communities themselves). Chapter 6 investigates the importance of 'transitional corridors' for community resilience. As Martens and Rotmans (2002) emphasized, transitional corridors can be interpreted as macro-scalar *exogenous* processes and pathways that shape human decision-making at multiple scales (i.e. structural factors shaping community pathways) and that also greatly influence community-level environmental and societal transitions. Transitional corridors, thus, are characterized by *indirect expressions of resilience* (e.g. policy and planning, societal ideological pathways) that inform and influence *direct* resilience action by individuals/households at community level. As Section 2.4 highlighted, almost all communities on Earth are embedded in wider regional, national and global flows and processes of material and mental exchange, suggesting that endogenous transitional pathways described in Chapter 5 will almost always be influenced by exogenous forces. Transitional corridors are, therefore, an important concept to describe the importance of societal ideologies, macro-economic processes, and policies and politics that shape community resilience and vulnerability.

Section 6.2 will, first, analyse the notion of 'transitional corridors' and will highlight that these corridors of decision-making are, inevitably, wider and, arguably, fuzzier than endogenous transitional pathways discussed in Chapter 5. Section 6.3 will then revisit the notion of 'lock-in' effects, with a focus on lock-ins *external* to communities and how these can shape community pathways and resilience. The discussion here will particularly include the importance of political and policy-based lock-ins, macro-structural lock-ins (e.g. oil dependency of most communities), ideological lock-ins at societal level (e.g. religion, conservatism) and macroeconomic lock-ins (e.g. globalization, global capitalism). Section 6.4 will focus specifically on the interlinkages between 'transitional ruptures' and macro-scalar transitional corridors, and how such large-scale ruptures can influence community-level attempts to raise resilience (e.g. abrupt changes in political organization of a country). Conclusions are provided in Section 6.5.

6.2 Transitional corridors

The notion of transitional corridors is closely connected with transition theory, social memory and path dependency. Chapter 5 highlighted that a pathway can be seen as an *endogenous* process where 'memory' (i.e. knowledge, experience, accumulated wisdom) can be passed on from generation to generation or from actor to actor at community level. Transitional corridors, on the other hand, are linked to *exogenous* processes influencing decision-making at community level. Such transitional corridors can be seen to embody mainstream ideology and thinking *external* to the community. Transitional corridors, therefore, are linked to outside forces that shape community transitions – forces upon which communities often have little influence, but that can severely constrain autonomous decision-making processes at community level (Cumming *et al.*, 2006). Within nation states, these corridors are closely associated with ideological and structural *paradigms* defined by societal worldviews, norms and accumulated institutional and organizational knowledge (Lipietz, 1992). As Davidson (2010, p. 1141) highlighted, "macro-level social structures are seen as providing structural conditions within which micro-level processes unfold". Figure 2.3 in Chapter 2 highlighted that exogenous influences upon community-level decision-making can be scaled up from the individual and down from the global levels, highlighting that transitional corridors can influence decision-making opportunities at regional, national and global levels.

Building on the discussion in Chapters 4 and 5, Figure 6.1 highlights that transitional corridors are based on the assumption that specific pathways of change over space and time are channelled into specific 'corridors' defined by more or less clear decision-making boundaries beyond which decisions are increasingly unlikely (bell-shaped probability of decision-making opportunities centred around middle of the corridor) (see also Figure 5.4). A transitional corridor is the sum total of cumulative actions at macro-scalar levels that influence decisions at community level 'on the ground' (Smit and Wandel, 2006). Community pathways (discussed in Chapter 5) are, therefore, closely aligned with transitional corridors (usually) embedded within 'boundaries of the possible'. By definition, transitional corridors are, thus, *wider* than community-level pathways and embody most (if not all) decision-making opportunities at scales beyond the community level. As Chapter 2 highlighted, these decision-making opportunities (e.g. regionally based norms, national policy, global drivers of change) are ultimately *mediated* by the individual/household within a community and turned into action with tangible effects on resilience/vulnerability 'on the ground'. Figure 2.3 in Chapter 2 highlighted that local communities and individual decision-making pathways are, therefore, embedded in *nested hierarchies* of scales, with transitional corridors representing the sum total of scalar interconnections between the community and the regional, national and global levels.

Similar to notions of path dependency (see Chapter 5), several points are important with regard to the shape and direction of transitional corridors. First, it is important to recognize that the notion of 'transitional corridors' simplifies

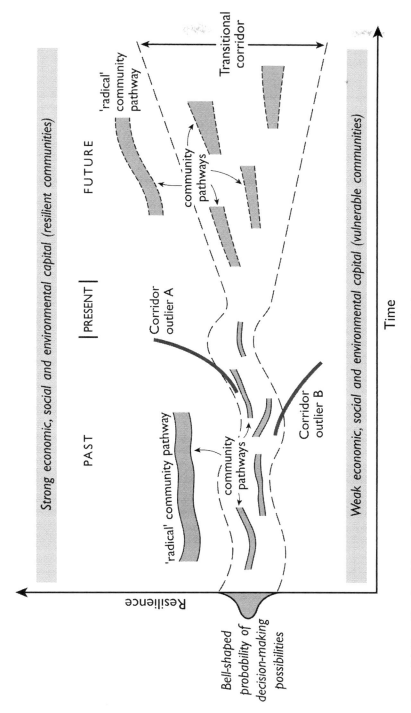

Figure 6.1 Transitional corridors, resilience and community pathways (source: author).

what are complex macro-scalar stakeholder interactions based on power structures within and between nation states. Each corridor is, therefore, comprised of a myriad of different pathways at multiple scales, with multiple and often overlapping path dependencies.

Second, Figure 6.1 shows that, similar to transitional pathways at community level, transitional corridors can be situated along a spectrum from weak to strong resilience. Based on multiple, often overlapping, decision-making structures at regional, national and global level, some transitional corridors will be located close to the vulnerable end of the resilience spectrum, while others will suggest that the 'bundle' of decision-making pathways that make up the transitional corridor will be situated towards the strongly resilient end of the resilience spectrum. As with previous conceptual models of resilience discussed in this book, transitional corridors can never be *fully* resilient and rarely completely vulnerable (the latter would lead to the disappearance of society as a whole). In other words, some decisions among the bundle of decision-making pathways within transitional corridors will inevitably 'pull' the corridor towards either stronger or weaker resilience (see Chapter 7 on the fact that national policies often contradict each other and 'pull' society and communities into different directions). Figure 6.1 suggests a hypothetical example of a transitional corridor situated closer to the vulnerability end of the resilience spectrum, i.e. with bundles of decision-making pathways that have tended to weaken economic, social and environmental capital at community level.

Third, scale is (again) important. As contemporary global societal organization is (still) centred around the nation state (Johnston, 1996), transitional corridors are most frequently conceptualized within the boundaries of nation states. In other words, although the discussion below of various lock-ins highlights that there are multiple transitional corridors that influence community-level decision-making at different temporal and geographical scales, the nation state emerges as a key structural boundary within which political, social and economic decisions are taken that, in turn, 'trickle down' to community level. Cumming *et al.* (2006, p. 8) referred to these scalar interactions as 'scalar mismatches' between different and often conflicting resilience pathways, and argued that "as societies have shifted towards the model of a nation-state with rigid boundaries and a central government, natural resource rights have been increasingly sequestered in the hands of centralized agencies such as government departments". The transitional corridor shown in Figure 6.1, therefore, will most often be closely aligned with a corridor of decision-making and governance bounded by the nation-state level of decision-making (see also Chapter 7).

Fourth, as Figure 6.1 suggests, transitional corridors are rarely static and often fluctuate based on various factors of change at national and supra-national levels (often also influenced by regional or global change). The 'transitional corridor' is thereby defined as the general direction of the corridor trajectory, taking into account upward and downward shifts in macro-scalar decision-making over time. Each community is in some way embedded within wider transitional corridors (i.e. all communities are part of a nation state) and community *autonomy* is largely defined by a community's position within such corridors. This means that a change in the direction of a corridor towards either weaker or stronger resilience will also automatically affect pathways of resilience at community level (e.g. nationally set targets for carbon reduction measures that affect community-level decision-making with regard to implementation of alternative energy pathways). In Figure 6.1 this is shown by individual community pathways generally embedded within the wider transitional corridor. However, as the exact boundaries of transitional corridors often remain vague due to the complex interactions of transitional forces and lock-in mechanisms (see below), the direct impact on communities of their embeddedness in such corridors is not always easy to ascertain. In other words, there are several examples in which communities have gone, or have attempted to go, 'against the grain' of general societal consensus enshrined within the notion of transitional corridors, exemplified by 'radical community pathways' in Figure 6.1 outside the transitional corridor. 'Radicalism' thus implies attempts of communities (with more or less success) to 'break away' from rigid transitional corridor boundaries 'imposed' by macro-structural forces and processes.

Fifth, as with path dependency, understanding the shape and direction of transitional corridors also depends on observational perspectives. Figure 6.1 shows a transitional corridor that is easier to define through backcasting from the present (i.e. known historical shape of decision-making pathways within the corridor), while forecasting the nature and shape of transitional corridors is more uncertain the further into the future one attempts to look (i.e. corridor widens considerably). As with path dependency at community level, the specific location of a transitional corridor on the resilience spectrum will be at its specific starting point in a transition precisely because of the history of decision-making pathways *preceding* that starting point. Transitional corridors also embody the *memory* of a macro-scalar system (e.g. a political or religious system) (Schultz *et al.*, 2000; O'Sullivan, 2004). However, as Section 6.4 will discuss, the direction of transitional corridors is not predetermined, as highlighted by sudden political or economic 'ruptures' (e.g. transition to post-socialism in Eastern European countries in the early 1990s; Stiglitz, 2002). Ruptures are, therefore, possible within macro-scalar transitional corridors, and these ruptures will inevitably also have an effect on community-level resilience.

Sixth, 'learning pathways' are also important for the shape and direction of transitional corridors. However, linked to scale-related lags and the frequent lack of momentum for change (see below), the macro-scalar nature of transitional corridors means that change at the nation-state level or beyond is usually slower than at community level (i.e. societal and nation-state ideology is usually slower to change) (Rotmans *et al.*, 2002; Dahle, 2007). As opposed to community-level path dependencies, transitional corridors can, therefore, not be substantially affected by small effects ('butterfly effect'), but are characterized by much slower 'lethargic' processes of change. This means that the most important catalysts for change in a society are often found at the individual or community level (see, for example, Box 4.6 on the TTM). As the notion of lock-ins discussed in

Chapter 5 implied, this will often mean that 'alternative' pathways leading to a change in the direction of the transitional corridor may not even be considered, and that 'outliers' (e.g. 'radical' thinkers or political groups) will find it difficult to implement pathways of change (e.g. the unlikely corridor outliers A and B in Figure 6.1). As a result, the critical literature often portrays macro-scalar corridors as 'negative' for innovation, as they automatically channel decisions into 'known' and 'already established' pathways, rather than encouraging innovative thinking 'out of the box' (see Tews, 2005, for environmental policy corridors). Seyfang (2009, p. 80), therefore, argued that "while [community] practices where 'the rules are different' have certain strengths, those strengths become barriers when in concerted opposition to incumbent regimes".

As the next section will discuss, lock-in effects associated with transitional corridors are often associated with pathways leading to relatively low resilience, where political and social 'conservatism' and lack of willingness for change may stifle community-level transitional pathways towards increased resilience. Macro-scalar social memory can reinforce path dependency which, in turn, can reinforce the shape and nature of transitional corridors.

6.3 Lock-in effects and transitional corridors

Chapter 5 discussed specific lock-in effects associated with endogenous community-level path dependencies, but lock-in effects also affect transitional corridors, especially lock-ins linked to drivers and forces operating at societal (i.e. national) or supra-national level. These include, in particular, lock-ins associated with political and policy-based decision-making pathways (Section 6.3.1), macro-structural lock-ins (Section 6.3.2), ideological lock-in effects (Section 6.3.3) and macroeconomic lock-ins related to globalization and capitalism (Section 6.3.4).

6.3.1 Political and policy-based lock-ins

'Political and policy-based lock-ins' (governance-related lock-ins) are among the most important macro-scalar lock-ins affecting community resilience and highlight the importance of the state in influencing community-level transitions (Johnston, 1996). Yet, political and policy-related processes are not the only factors affecting transitional corridors, and there are complex interlinkages with other lock-ins discussed below. This means that, whatever the type of political or governance system of a country, policies do not necessarily *control* transitional corridors, they can only *influence* their shape and direction (Martens and Rotmans, 2002). Four key issues are related to macro-scalar political and policy-related lock-in effects: the types of political systems (e.g. democratic versus non-democratic systems; electoral systems; electoral cycles), country-specific governance and geo-political structures (e.g. the political role of the regional or local levels), the orientation of political systems (e.g. conservative versus liberal) and whether and how policy 'trickles down' to community level (implementation gaps and failures).

First, the type of *political system* within which communities are embedded is crucial for shaping transitional corridors and defining decision-making opportunities for community-level resilience (Adger, 2000; Lebel *et al.*, 2006). In *non-democratic* countries, for example, governance structures are often weak and the state assumes a top-down-oriented policy-making structure in which communities may have little say in shaping policies and politics (Johnston, 1996; Wilson and Bryant, 1997). In extreme cases, this may mean that community-level pathways of resilience/vulnerability are *synonymous* with national-level pathways, and that there is little flexibility for communities to 'veer off' established national policy-based transitional corridors (Dryzek, 1997; Lebel *et al.*, 2006). In these situations, communities are often locked into national pathways of change, and local-level decision-making that could improve community resilience is frequently discouraged. The most extreme example of this is currently evident in North Korea where local community action is strictly controlled (Hale, 2005; Woo, 2006), but in other non-democratic countries, such as China, Myanmar, Libya or Uganda (to name but a few), community pathways also continue to be strongly controlled and influenced by national policies and political ideologies. It is also often the case that in non-democratic countries other external drivers such as globalization or the capitalist system may play a lesser role in influencing community-level transitions (e.g. Bhutan where the relative absence of globalization pressures may have increased community-level resilience; see Box 4.2).

There are also substantial differences with regard to political and policy-related lock-ins in *democratic* societies. Indeed, *electoral* and *voting systems* can greatly influence interrelationships between local communities and the national political system (Dobson, 2007). Some systems, such as the Swiss voting system via public referenda, have been described as more 'inclusive' with regard to the empowerment of individuals and communities to shape resilience pathways, compared to electoral systems such as the British 'first past the post' system which can lead to the creation of political barriers (real or perceived) between the political ruling elite and citizens (Dryzek *et al.*, 2003). This can have direct implications for the implementation of policies aiming at raising resilience at community level, especially when voters feel disenfranchised and 'removed' from politics. The fact that many recent elections in the developed world have seen low voter turnouts (at times <50 per cent) suggests that a large proportion of the electorate no longer feel part of political decision-making processes affecting their communities. Political systems can also be linked to short-termism linked to *electoral cycles* (see also Chapter 7). In most democratic countries, electoral cycles range from three to seven years, often giving politicians little options for radical and long-term changes (Dobson, 2007; Wilson and Bryant, 1997). This short-termism at national level means that policy-related transitional corridors often operate on a different timescale to community-level local decision-making pathways (see Figure 6.1). Indeed, long-term plans for raising community resilience at local level may be stifled by changes in government, political ideology and, most importantly, funding for local resilience projects.

Second, *governance and geo-political structures* also affect community resilience. Governance structures, in particular, highlight the political organization of a society with regard to the relationships between different actor groups (from local to national) and the role of institutions in the production of policy outcomes (Rhodes, 1997). Societies with inclusive governance structures usually give voice to marginalized groups (including the community level) and allow 'radical' voices (however defined) to be heard (Murdoch and Marsden, 1995; Goodwin and Painter, 1996). Governance and geo-political structures also influence the roles that local and regional politics play within a nation state. In countries such as Germany or Spain, for example, the *regions* have relatively important political roles which may allow them to implement regional policies independent from national policy. These may be able to more directly affect economic, social and environmental capital at local community level than national policies (Wilson and Wilson, 2001). The south-eastern region of Bavaria in Germany, for example, has some autonomous control over budgets for energy-saving initiatives at local level and, as a result, can provide large subsidies for individual households for installation of photovoltaic cells on house roofs. The result has been a substantial reduction of dependency of Bavarian communities on the national electricity grid, thereby increasing community-level resilience regarding possible future energy shortages (Dryzek *et al.*, 2003; see Allen *et al.*, 2008, for less effective positive opportunities for energy microgeneration in the UK). Similarly, the relative empowerment or disempowerment of local councils/political structures can be a decisive factor regarding the implementation of more resilient pathways at community level. The aforementioned example of the TTM initiative in Totnes (UK) is a case in point, where political backing from the local council has been important for some of the initiatives that have improved community resilience (e.g. allowing the planting of fruit and nut trees on communal spaces and initiatives related to attracting more locally embedded businesses) (Hopkins, 2010). However, entrenched politics at local level can also lead to negative lock-ins for community resilience. In many southern European communities, for example, apathy, corruption and a general lack of institutional expertise and knowledge have led to a worsening of environmental degradation processes such as desertification that are severely reducing environmental capital at community level (soil degradation, salinization, etc.) (Wilson and Juntti, 2005).

Third, entrenched *political ideologies* at national, regional and local levels can also be associated with negative lock-ins affecting community resilience. There is a wide-ranging debate in the literature about the varying impacts of different political ideologies (e.g. socialist, communist, liberal, labour, conservative, etc.) upon local politics, and how such 'lock-ins' can lead to increased or reduced resilience at community level (e.g. Johnston, 1996; Dobson, 2007). While it is generally assumed that liberal political ideologies may offer more flexibility for the implementation of innovations that may raise community resilience (e.g. by providing an enabling environment for alternative energy pathways such as local wind turbines or by implementing more 'radical' relocalized transport policies), evidence suggests that conservative political ideologies may also raise resilience precisely by encouraging conservative values that, at times, may hinder detrimental developments that could lead to increased community-level vulnerability (Burchell, 2002; Tews, 2005). An example of the latter can be found in most European countries, where conservative politics can be associated with a reluctance for further housing development in specific localities (e.g. in the UK a conservative resistance to implement development policies that may tarnish the image of the 'rural idyll'; Woods, 2005; Neal, 2009). Such conservative resistance to change may, simultaneously, help maintain some strongly resilient community attributes linked to established (conservative) actor networks, strong environmental capital (protected by tight legislation aimed at the environmental status quo), and a reluctance to further increase the globalized embeddedness of communities. As with all lock-in factors discussed here, the impact of political ideologies can, therefore, be both 'good' or 'bad' for local community resilience (Martens and Rotmans, 2002; see also Chapter 7).

Fourth, political and policy-based lock-ins can also be associated with *policy implementation gaps and failures*, especially when linked to issues of corruption and unequal power structures. Chapter 5 discussed how the issue of power can have negative effects with regard to endogenous community pathways, and the same is true for the impact of corruption and power at the macro-scalar level. There is much evidence that suggests that policy formulated and developed at the national/regional scale does not always 'trickle down' to communities in the most appropriate way. Commentators such as Winter (1990) and Palumbo and Calista (1990) have highlighted how successful policy implementation can be hampered by different administrative 'layers' in society. These layers usually include the government level (where most policies are formulated), the street-level bureaucratic layer where policies should be transposed into practice, and the local or grassroots layer of the policy recipients. Lipsky (1980) highlighted, in particular, how well-intended national policies (e.g. policies aimed at increasing resilience at community level) can be distorted by street-level bureaucrats who, for reasons often linked to power and/or corruption, transform policies to suit their needs and those of their power networks. A recent EU-level project on desertification, for example, highlighted how many national environmental policies aimed at combating desertification at local community level in Portugal, Spain, Italy and Greece either were never implemented 'on the ground' (implementation gap), with money siphoned off to other policy areas, or where policies have been so distorted that powerful local elites have avoided negative effects of these policies on themselves (e.g. large landowners who could be affected by restrictive irrigation policies) (Wilson and Juntti, 2005).

The latter highlights that there are often disjunctures between the policy needs of a community and the implementation or delivery of policies by national or regional policy actors (Gibbs, 2000). This means that, due to lock-in effects associated with the embeddedness of all communities in national governance and political structures (see above), the best way forward for many communities to improve resilience is to implement their *own* initiatives/policies irrespective of national/regional policy-making structures (Cumming *et al.*, 2006; Kinzig *et al.*, 2006). As Lebel *et al.* (2006) highlighted, in countries with high levels of corruption and non-transparent governance structures this often means that community resilience is improved *despite* government policies and policy-related 'negative' transitional corridors. Similarly, misguided policies, such as planning policies allowing urban encroachment into vulnerable areas such as floodplains or coastal zones threatened by sea-level rise or storm surges, lead to reduced resilience of communities settling in these areas (Bulkeley, 2006; Hastrup, 2009).

6.3.2 Macro-structural lock-ins

Macro-structural lock-ins affecting community resilience are associated with 'structural' processes that often have *negative* effects on community resilience, in particular by constraining the abilities of communities to innovate or implement 'radical' pathways aimed at strengthening community resilience (see Figure 6.1). As a result, macro-structural lock-ins often act as barriers and constraints at national/societal level that influence the implementation of more resilient pathways at community level. As commentators such as Lovins (2003), Seyfang (2006) or Chambers *et al.* (2007) emphasized, these structural barriers are frequently related to transitional corridors associated with technological change, and with the dependency of communities on centralized and globalized energy, transport and food networks. Orr (2009, p. 174), therefore, argued that "critical parts of our infrastructure, including the electric grid, energy systems, food systems, information technologies, and transportation networks, are highly vulnerable".

A century or so ago many communities in both the developed and developing world were relatively self-sufficient with regard to access to specific technologies produced within or near communities (e.g. related to agricultural technologies), and had endogenous knowledge of how to produce and use such technologies. For example, most people involved in agriculture were able to build and/or maintain their agricultural implements/tools. Further, especially in times before electricity, most communities sourced their energy needs (firewood, peat) and building materials (timber, stone) from within their immediate localities, and transport networks were relatively limited (except for the wealthy few) to the community and its immediate vicinity (Seyfang, 2009; Hopkins, 2010).

As much of the critical literature on technological change and globalization has emphasized, globalization processes and technological advances have changed the situation considerably for most communities around the world. The flows of energy, building materials, food and people have become more global, and often communities are increasingly embedded in nationally/internationally centralized macro-structural processes, such as energy grids (national electricity grids/global dependency on oil and gas), global transport networks (motorways, plane travel), national/international food networks (supermarkets), and global technological pathways (e.g. development of new technologies linked to transport, energy, food) (Lovins, 2003; Seyfang, 2009). Pinkerton and Hopkins (2009) and Hopkins (2010) highlighted how these processes have led to a de-skilling of many people (e.g. with regard to local food production) and to a situation where many communities have *lost their autonomy* of decision-making with regard to energy, transport and food matters. Processes of delocalization of energy, transport and food networks are, therefore, restricting decision-making opportunities for communities increasingly embedded within macro-structural transitional corridors (see Figure 6.1) (Mertz *et al.*, 2005; Seyfang, 2006). Orr (2009, p. 42), therefore, argued that

> every increase in local capacity to grow food, generate energy, repair, build and finance will strengthen the capacity to withstand disturbances of all kinds. Distributed energy in the form of widely disbursed solar and wind technology, for example, buffers communities from supply interruptions, failure of the electrical grid, and price shocks. Similarly, a regionally based, solar-powered food system would restore small farms, preserve soil, create local employment, rebuild stable economies, and provide better food while reducing carbon emissions and dependence on long-distance transport from distant suppliers.

Let us look in more detail how these transitional corridors affect community resilience with regard to energy, transport and food in particular.

Discussions on 'peak oil' (see Chapter 2) and increasing dependency of communities on external *energy* sources (oil, gas, nuclear power) beyond community control have highlighted the precarious situation that many communities are facing with regard to their ability to satisfy future energy needs (Heinberg, 2004; Bailey *et al.*, 2010). Especially those advocating the importance of relocalized communities (see Figure 3.6) have recognized how difficult it is for communities to disconnect from national/international energy grids (Hain *et al.*, 2005; Allen *et al.*, 2008). Almost all communities in the developed world, and increasing numbers in the developing world, are closely interlinked with national energy grids associated with state-controlled electricity production, nuclear power plants or oil/gas provision. Although new localized alternative energy technologies, such as small wind generators, household-based photovoltaic cells or ground heat pumps, are beginning to offer some alternatives to national energy providers, in most countries these local initiatives still produce less than 10 per cent (in most cases <3 per cent) of energy used (Barr, 2008; Walker, 2008). In addition, these new technologies are relatively 'technology-heavy' and can most often not be produced locally (i.e. the skills base at community level is usually insufficient to produce or even maintain 'alternative' energy devices). For the past hundred years or so, therefore, most communities have been increasingly locked into transitional corridors linked to national/international energy networks. While at first glance this may not necessarily reduce community resilience, as soon as supplies are threatened (e.g. peak oil debate) resilience of communities may be substantially weakened with no real alternative in sight (Hopkins, 2008, 2010;

Bailey *et al.*, 2010). Yet, despite energy lock-ins at the macro-scalar level, there are indications that some communities are beginning to establish bottom-up energy pathways that are relatively independent of macro-scalar energy networks (Box 6.1).

Box 6.1 Community-based energy initiatives in South Asia: leap-frogging centralized energy grids

Around 1.5 billion people around the world have no access to electricity, about 85 per cent of whom live in small rural communities of the developing world (The Economist Technological Quarterly, 2010). Extending energy grids into these areas is expensive, but new opportunities are becoming available to poor communities to use relatively cheap solar panels or light emitting diodes (LEDs). This may provide opportunities for leap-frogging the need for extending centralized energy grids. At the 'Lighting Africa Conference' (Nairobi, May 2010), for example, projects were proposed to encourage local community-led electricity solutions for poor communities, especially through the use of solar cells for lighting low-energy LEDs. This helps improve economic capital at community level by reducing dependency on expensive kerosene for lighting, as well as improving environmental and social capital by reducing pollution emanating from burning kerosene in closed spaces and by addressing associated health problems. In addition, The Economist Technological Quarterly (2010) reported new initiatives focused on South Asia where about 600 million people in rural areas have no access to electricity. One project in India, for example, focuses on the use of locally available biomass to generate power for village-level electricity micro-grids (supplying *c.*600 families) that can use rice husks (otherwise left to rot) as biomass fuel. It is, therefore, particularly in areas where centralized energy grids have not yet been established (i.e. mainly rural areas in developing countries) that community-based projects may be able to prevent macro-scalar energy lock-ins from the outset.

The situation is equally problematic with regard to structural lock-ins associated with *transport networks* and community resilience (Orr, 2009). In many parts of the world, the past 50 years or so have seen pronounced processes of counter-urbanization, where people working in cities have sought a quieter life in rural settings, but with increasing dependency on cars/public transport for commuting (Woods, 2005). In many ways this has reduced community resilience, as the distances between work and home have continuously increased (see also Section 5.4.2). This has been paralleled by an increased dependency of people on cheap flights (holidays, business) which has, in turn, led to a growing dependency of communities on regional/national airport networks that often have few direct connections with their surrounding communities (Barr, 2008). As with national/international energy grid dependencies, the 'globalization' of transport networks has increased the vulnerability of communities (Cumming *et al.*, 2005; Sheller and Urry, 2006), leading Hopkins (2010, p. 233) to suggest that "most decisions affecting transport provision and use are in the control of local authorities ... rather than community groups". While dependency on cars, planes, transport lorries, trains and oil/petrol has increased, sceptics fear that most communities are not well prepared for the possibility of peak oil and a 'relocalization' of transport to a restrictive radius around the community (Bailey *et al.*, 2010). Indeed, even the most relocalized communities (e.g. the town of Totnes in the UK; see Box 4.6) continue to have a high dependency on car travel for business and holiday, and there is yet no evidence that even the most environmentally conscious citizens are forsaking their holiday travel by plane in order to altruistically strengthen global environmental capital (Barr, 2008). The embeddedness of many communities into national/global transport networks, therefore, forms a key lock-in mechanism shoehorning people into transitional corridors that will be difficult to escape from in the near future.

Some of the most critical discussions about the growing problem of structural lock-ins have revolved around *food* provision at local community level. While in the developed world a hundred years or so ago, most communities grew most of the food consumed within the community locally, today community members (in the developed world at least) are likely to shop for their food in local supermarkets, and many have lost the skills of growing their own food (e.g. vegetables, breeding animals for consumption) (Hopkins, 2010). As many studies have highlighted, the increasing dependency of consumers on globalized agro-commodity chains probably best highlights the growing dependency of many communities on production networks upon which they have little influence (e.g. imports of food from overseas). Lang and Heasman (2004) highlighted that many residents in the developed world no longer know where their food comes from, how it is produced and by whom. Although there are movements attempting to encourage more localized food networks, in the developed world food eaten at home now rarely comes from the locality itself but is instead transported over hundreds if not thousands of kilometres (Goodman, 2004). As with energy and transport, centralization of food processing and sale has increased, epitomized by both the growing power of national/international supermarket chains no longer linked to specific communities, or by the closure of many local abattoirs meaning that animals have to be driven long distances for slaughter (Law, 2006). 'Alternative food networks' – characterized by relocalized production that uses existing agricultural space within or near communities and that encourage people to re-skill with regard to home-grown food production – are beginning to offer some alternatives (see notion of 'foodsheds' shown in Figure 5.2), but overall most of the food consumed in the developed world travels long distances (Lang and Heasman, 2004). The repercussions of these food-related lock-ins are increased vulnerability of many communities with regard to reliance on imported food, a vulnerability towards even short-term breakdowns in global agro-commodity chains and a relative inability of communities to break out of macro-scalar food structures controlled by wealthy and powerful national and multinational businesses (e.g. the big supermarkets such as TESCO or Sainsbury's in the UK, Wal-Mart in the USA, etc.) (Bardhan, 2006; see also Section 6.3.4).

6.3.3 Ideological lock-ins

Ideological lock-ins are among the most challenging and interesting macro-scalar processes affecting community resilience. Ideological lock-ins are closely associated with how societal preferences, fashions, moods and worldviews change over time, and how such macro-scalar changes trickle down to affect decision-making processes in communities. These, in turn, affect the quality of economic, social and environmental capital at community level. Critical social theorists argue that ideological transitional corridors can be seen as the lattice of ideas that permeate society, constituting collective societal consciousness over a specific time (Thompson, 1981; Schama, 1995). Transitional corridors shaped by societal ideologies through religious, moral and other values directly affect local resilience pathways, as it is probably most difficult for communities (and individual citizens) to 'jump over their own shadows' and decide to completely leave behind ideological and social mores exerted by wider society (Schultz *et al.*, 2000). While it may be possible for communities to (at least attempt to) disengage from structural lock-ins related to energy, transport and food (see Section 6.3.2), it is morally and ethically much more difficult for communities to 'go against the grain' of ideological pathways defined by wider society within which these communities are embedded.[1] Communities are, therefore, most often strongly embedded within the *ideological social memory* of wider society of which they are part (notions of 'conformity'), and most citizens are embedded within, or at least affected by, these ideological corridors. Although extreme examples of conformity such as adherence to the Nazi ideology in Germany between 1933 and 1945 or adherence to extreme socialist ideology as in contemporary North Korea are rare, most citizens (long-standing as well as immigrants) adhere to ideological and moral codes exerted by societies in which they live. The close interweaving of societal and community ideologies and norms finds its most succinct expression through the German words of 'Gemeinschaft' (community) and 'Gesellschaft' (society), highlighting how community ideologies and norms are often a subset of societal ideologies and norms (Tönnies, 1963; Neal, 2009). However, critics such as Abercrombie *et al.* (1980), Allen (2003) and Whatmore (2009) have questioned the notion of ideological coherence, integration and stability of societies, and highlighted the complex power relations that underpin ideological dominance of specific stakeholder groups. In addition, the growing multiculturality of most modern societies increasingly blurs the boundaries between national and ethnic/cultural identity (see discussion about exported social memory in Chapter 4) (Langhorne, 2001; Neal, 2009).

Macro-scalar ideological lock-ins are mainly associated with religious and spiritual beliefs, economic ideologies (see Section 6.3.4) and political ideologies (Section 6.3.2). In many cases, communities/community members consciously or subconsciously comply with societal norms, or risk being seen as 'outcasts', 'radical' or 'rebellious', which often sidelines these communities with regard to power and politics within their nation states. There are many examples of communities trying to break free from such societal norms, such as communities based around religious sects (often also attempting to break free from political and structural lock-ins), or communities defining themselves through specific ideological norms (e.g. anthroposophist communities based on ideas developed by Rudolf Steiner that also have a specific 'radical' approach to teaching and education). Yet, in today's globalized world such communities are rare, as it often proves difficult to be in constant opposition to mainstream ideas (Harvey, 1989). While, as highlighted in Chapter 5, almost every community will contain 'non-conformist' and 'radical' or 'rebellious' citizens, most communities will, out of necessity and the need for survival, steer a pathway of compromise usually situated well within the boundaries of ideological transitional corridors. For communities attempting to relocalize, it is probably the fact that they remain closely embedded within ideological transitional corridors at societal level that makes it most difficult to embark on more 'radical' resilience pathways (Hopkins, 2008, 2010). As Macy and Brown (1998, p. 17) emphasized, relocalization "has to be more comprehensive – involving not only the political economy, but the habits and values that foster it".

How do ideological transitional lock-ins affect resilience at community level? First *religious norms and ideologies* at societal level can have a direct impact on environmental attitudes and behaviours (White, 1967; Wade, 2009). Chapter 4 already highlighted how religious beliefs and practices at community level are often closely intertwined with both positive and negative environmental transitions, and are an intrinsic aspect of social memory of a community. Religion can be particularly important in shaping resilience or vulnerability pathways of communities, depending on the specific moral codes enshrined in religious beliefs that may affect community resilience (Schultz *et al.*, 2000). Indeed, religious norms held by individuals can influence how these individuals regard their relationship with the environment, the relative importance they assign to specific actions influencing economic, social and environmental capital at community level, and the moral thresholds individuals use when making decisions directly affecting a community (e.g. the willingness to help neighbours; engagement in community-level social activities) (Greeley, 1993). The Buddhist tendency for encouraging localized and arguably more resilient community pathways predicated on close(r) interconnections between humans and the environment have already been highlighted in Box 4.2 on Bhutan (Bruun and Kalland, 1994). Such religious beliefs at community level are often closely interlinked, or indeed indistinguishable, from religious beliefs in wider society within nation states (e.g. Christian beliefs and ideologies in many Western countries, Islamic ideologies in Middle Eastern countries, Buddhist beliefs in many Asian countries). Although moral codes, traditions and rites can emerge from 'local' structures (i.e. as local processes that may be independent from wider societal processes; see Section 5.3.1), religious lock-ins often show a close intertwining between community and societal level (Schultz *et al.*, 2000). While some remote communities (e.g. subsistence communities in tropical rainforest areas) may have maintained relative religious autonomy from national religious influences (e.g. animist religions surviving among remote tribes in Catholic Brazil or Muslim

Indonesia), macro-structural religious influences will almost always influence moral codes, traditions and rites at community level (Wade, 2009).

Second, Section 6.3.1 already highlighted the importance of *political ideological lock-ins* for community-level resilience pathways. As with societal religious norms, most communities are locked into societal political pathways often predicated on the nation state as the scalar political boundary (Burchell, 2002; Dryzek *et al.*, 2003). Indeed, in democratic systems, local communities themselves influence through the electoral process who will represent them at regional/national political level. Democratic processes themselves, therefore, result in a close intertwining of governance processes between the community and wider society (Rhodes, 1997; Dobson, 2007). As a result, predominant political ideologies at societal/nation-state level shape policies and regulation of decision-making processes at community level. The importance of conservative, liberal or neo-liberal ideologies for community-level resilience pathways was discussed in Chapters 3 and 5, highlighting that autonomous political decision-making is virtually impossible for most local communities in both the developed and developing world. Indeed, the TTM in the UK and beyond, for example, laments the fact that it not only remains locked into macro-structural transitional corridors (see Section 6.3.2), but that it is particularly powerless to implement more 'radical' relocalization structures because it remains firmly embedded within the national political system with all its conservative and constraining influences (Hopkins, 2010; Bailey *et al.*, 2010).

Some authors have also highlighted the importance of political ideologies such as the 'ecological modernization paradigm' or 'market environmentalism' for community-level environmental decision-making. Bailey and Wilson (2009, p. 2325), for example, argued that both ecological modernization (a predominant ideology in the Netherlands and German-speaking countries, for example) and market environmentalism have resulted in market- and technology-led solutions to environmental problems that leave communities little room to manoeuvre, as their "totalizing logic is problematic in the context of developing broad-based and imaginative strategies". As Barry (2003) highlighted, ecological modernization can be seen as an ideology that is essentially 'positive' or 'optimistic' towards community capabilities to deal with environmental problems, although a major role is assigned to the state in solving such problems (rather than the community level). Ecological modernization advocates that tackling environmental problems can be a win-win situation that generates financial profits under the banner of 'prosperity while protecting the environment' (e.g. through implementation of green or alternative energy/technology pathways at community level) (Mol, 2003). Solutions to environmental change are, therefore, seen to be provided through modernization, not reduced economic growth – processes that may, however, ultimately erode social and environmental capital at community level (Bailey and Wilson, 2009). Critics, thus, have argued that communities in countries with strong ecological modernization ideologies may be ill-equipped to deal effectively with social and environmental issues at community level (Liverman, 2004; Bakker, 2005).

Third, *economic ideologies* at societal level have major repercussions for how economic capital at community level is regulated, accumulated and distributed, and for the worldviews of community members. Throughout this book, the importance of ideologies associated with globalization, capitalism and neo-liberalism have been emphasized, and it is probably in this arena that communities have least flexibility for autonomous decision-making. Indeed, globalization means that most communities on Earth are increasingly embedded in complex macroeconomic interlinkages that influence individual decision-making. As the next section will discuss in more detail, such macroeconomic lock-ins often constrain decision-making options, can lead to overexploitation of environmental capital at community level, and may, ultimately, drive communities into much more vulnerable positions.

6.3.4 Macroeconomic lock-ins

Macroeconomic lock-ins are among the most important transitional corridors influencing the implementation of more resilient pathways at community level. These lock-ins are defined by economic values and worldviews at societal/nation-state level, although nation states have begun to lose their autonomy of economic decision-making (e.g. member countries of the Euro zone in the EU, increasing importance of World Trade Organization (WTO) policies on global trade arrangements; see Chapter 7). As Chapter 3 highlighted, macro-economic lock-ins are complex and can raise or reduce resilience at community level. Macroeconomic lock-ins and their impacts on local community resilience revolve in particular around four interconnected processes: economic globalization, the spread of global capitalism, the increasing importance of Anglo-American neo-liberal economic ideologies and the increasingly powerful role of multinational corporations. In the following, each of these will be discussed in detail with regard to how they affect community-level decision-making.

Throughout this book, the importance of globalization processes for community resilience has been highlighted (see Chapters 3 and 5 in particular). As part of these wider influences of globalization, *economic globalization* refers to the increasingly global economic interlinkages between geographical spaces, the embeddedness of (almost all) local communities within complex financial and monetary flows, and processes associated with increasingly uniform patterns of economic interconnectedness and embeddedness across the globe (Jones, 1997; Rofe, 2009). Section 3.3 highlighted that a hundred or so years ago many communities still had some level of economic autonomy – i.e. key decisions affecting economic capital at community level were taken *within* the community itself. Macroeconomic lock-ins of communities in the eighteenth- and nineteenth-century communities were, thus, less pronounced as global economic flows were characterized by internationalization (extension of global economic activities across national boundaries) rather than economic globalization which, since the twentieth century, has meant the economic integration of even the remotest communities into the global economy (Goodman and Watts, 1997). Pre-twentieth century, economic integration of communities was, therefore, more 'shallow' based primarily on arm's-length trade in goods and services, while today's globalized communities are characterized by a much deeper degree of community economic integration – and indeed economic dependency – based upon interconnected configurations of economic production (Gray, 2002; Nederveen Pieterse, 2004).

This suggests that even if communities wish to disengage from global economic flows and retake control over processes related to economic capital at community level, it is increasingly difficult for communities to break free of the shackles of economic globalization (Mander and Goldsmith, 2000; Davidson, 2010). As Jones (1997, p. 47) argued, "communities might thus be developing at a global level, thereby transcending traditional communitarianism and fusing with cosmopolitanism". Examples of community-level attempts to partly disengage from transitional corridors associated with economic globalization – for example, LETS schemes (see Section 5.3.2) – have only partly been successful (relatively low levels of public acceptance). As Bowring (1998) argued, LETS schemes may struggle to compete with the efficiency, choice and global reach of the 'formal' economy, and may be abandoned or never taken up by more mobile and globalized community residents. Alternative economic models at community level can, therefore, not hide the fact that the majority of communities, where these 'alternative currencies' have been used, continue to be firmly embedded ideologically and practically in globalized economic pathways that define the majority of community actions (North, 1999; Winter, 2003). Both Mander and Goldsmith (2000) and Savage *et al.* (2005), therefore, emphasized that, because of economic globalization processes, economic capital at community level is mainly shaped by *exogenous* forces which increasingly shoehorn communities into macroeconomic lock-ins. This suggests that almost all of humanity is now within the same macroeconomic capitalist transitional corridor of economic globalization with all its advantages and disadvantages for raising local community resilience.

As Chapter 3 highlighted, economic globalization is, therefore, closely interlinked with the *spread of global capitalism* during the twentieth century affecting even the remotest communities on the globe. Global capitalism as a macroeconomic lock-in for many communities is closely associated with ideological lock-ins (see Section 6.3.3), especially as capitalism is more than just an economic system or model. Indeed, many argue that capitalism is, first and foremost, an ideology that permeates all aspects of modern life, and that it, with its profit-driven maxim and ideology of continuous expansion and economic growth, influences decision-making at all geographical levels (Harvey, 1989). The downfall of the Soviet empire in 1990 and what some have hailed as the 'ideological victory of the capitalist West' has meant that almost all communities on Earth – increasingly including formerly staunchly socialist countries such as China – are now embedded within transitional corridors defined by global capitalist dictates, with often few economic alternatives (Gray, 2002; Stiglitz, 2002). Yet, as Box 6.2 highlights, the spread of capitalism is by no means uniform. In China, for example, 'islands of capitalism' are surrounded by a 'sea of subsistence' (Cartier, 2001), with local communities facing very different challenges and opportunities. Nonetheless, the global economic crisis of 2008–2011 has only served to highlight how almost all communities on Earth are now affected by similar economic processes that may have, until recently, been perceived to be rather 'distant' from their communities (e.g. the unscrupulous lending of banks leading to the bankruptcy of many community-level businesses).

Box 6.2 'Islands of capitalism' versus 'sea of subsistence': differential impacts of capitalism in Chinese communities

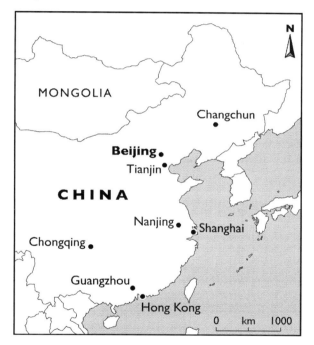

Emerging economies like China are facing geographically very differentiated impacts with regard to the influence of capitalism. While local communities in most urban areas – especially along China's eastern seaboard – have begun to wholeheartedly embrace capitalism (islands of capitalism), communities in rural China – especially in western and north-western areas – still remain largely in a 'sea of subsistence' hardly touched by capitalist thinking and influences (Cartier, 2001; Diamond, 2006). This has pronounced implications for the embeddedness of Chinese communities within capitalist transitional corridors. Communities in urban areas have begun to be locked into capitalist decision-making structures including profit-maximization, greed, belief in private enterprise, and a dramatic move away from past socialist ideologies, with concurrent changes in economic, social and environmental capital at community level (LEDDRA, 2011; see also Section 6.4). Economic capital tends to increase (through vertical rather than horizontal inter-linkages), social capital is gradually eroded (many residents in the rapidly growing Chinese urban areas are migrants from rural areas with little social embeddedness in urban networks) and environmental capital is often reduced (see Chapter 4 on pollution in Chinese cities). Chinese communities in most rural areas, meanwhile, face different challenges. On the one hand, they are still often characterized by strong social networks (although many are losing working-age population who have moved to the cities) and strong environmental capital (China has a relatively well-developed environmental management ethos that can be traced back thousands of years). On the other hand, economic capital is often poorly developed in these rural communities, which provides the main impetus for rural people to seek better opportunities in urban areas (Cartier, 2001; LEDDRA, 2011). The main challenge for countries such as China is, therefore, to reduce the pronounced disparities in community resilience opportunities between capitalist-oriented urban areas and subsistence-oriented rural areas, by providing incentives to raise social and environmental capital in urban communities, and by raising economic capital in rural communities (see Chapter 7).

Community resilience is often negatively affected by the spread of global capitalism, precisely because of the specific attributes associated with capitalism in the form of greed, profit-maximization, selfishness and the increasing need for community members to vertically integrate (i.e. with the global economy) rather than horizontally (i.e. with an emphasis on economic interlinkages within and between the community itself) (Granovetter, 1985; Savage *et al.*, 2005; Davidson, 2010). Aggarwal (2006, p. 1414), therefore, argued that globalization leads to "the breakdown of personal exchange [which] is not just the breakdown of a dense communication network but also the breakdown of communities of common ideologies and of a common set of rules". Indeed, the spread of both global capitalism and economic globalization can be seen as the main reasons why the formerly clearer geographical boundaries of 'communities' have become increasingly blurred and have become more globally than locally oriented. The latter largely also explains why community relocalization movements have, so far, not shown much tangible success, as almost all members of the relocalization process at community level are simultaneously embedded within the global capitalist system through their dependencies on jobs, pensions (especially through globally operating pension funds) and economic exchanges with often global customers, such as internet-based firms/individuals that, although operating from within a geographical 'community', are economically more interlinked with global customers (North, 2010; Bailey *et al.*, 2010). In the absence of an alternative global economic model and ideology (at least for the moment), the transitional corridor 'imposed' by the spread of global capitalism is, therefore, likely to continue to exert a substantial impact on the range of decision-making options available at community level for the foreseeable future.

Economic globalization and the spread of global capitalism are closely associated with the increasing importance of Anglo-American *neo-liberal economic ideologies* which have increasingly shaped global macroeconomic transitional corridors since the 1980s (Castree, 2008b). Chapter 5 already highlighted that neo-liberalism has several characteristics that can lessen community resilience, in particular by encouraging vertical as opposed to horizontal stakeholder interactions (loss of social capital) (Mansfield, 2004), by restructuring local trade flows and exchange of goods based on neo-liberal free market ideals (often exacerbating existing power imbalances within communities) (Harvey, 2005), and by encouraging a mindset that foregrounds the market as the solution to problems as opposed to investments into less economically tangible social capital (Aggarwal, 2006). These processes often lead to the erosion of traditional networks of trust and the neighbourhood characteristic of strong resilience (Heynen *et al.*, 2007; Castree, 2008a). Key for understanding interlinkages between community resilience and neo-liberal transitional corridors and lock-ins is that, in countries where it has become the dominant economic ideology such as the USA and the UK, neo-liberalism has been shown to permeate all layers of society. Every individual – whatever community they feel they belong to – has become 'trapped' by the loss of horizontal stakeholder interactions resulting from neo-liberalization, the profit-driven privatization of former national utilities and services, the relative withdrawal of the state which may have in the past provided some incentives for strengthening community resilience, free market ideals that place profit above strong social capital, and by ideologies of market environmentalism that assume that markets can provide solutions to the loss of community-level environmental capital (Heynen *et al.*, 2007). St Martin (2005), for example, argued that neo-liberal approaches to community fisheries management have overlooked the crucial importance of community cooperation among fishermen with resulting negative impacts for social capital, supported by Mansfield's (2004, 2007) studies that suggested that neo-liberal policies rarely work to strengthen community resilience.

Evidence suggests that neo-liberal lock-in effects may be particularly pronounced in super-globalized communities, where alternative economic pathways are particularly difficult to implement. In addition, with increasing globalization and urbanization, it is likely that lock-ins related to neo-liberal economic ideologies will assume ever greater importance in coming decades across communities in both the developed and developing world (Castree, 2008a). Even where community-level initiatives, such as the TTM (Bailey *et al.*, 2010) or the Italian 'Slow City Movement (CittaSlow)' (Tomlinson, 2007), are trying to break free from neo-liberal ideologies, these communities find it difficult (again) to implement 'pathways of the impossible' or 'radical' community pathways that *completely* break away from underlying neo-liberal pressures and constraints (Hopkins, 2010; see Figure 6.1). The logic and social memory of neo-liberalism, thus, depoliticizes and de-democratizes environmental decision-making through scientific and econocentric discourses that exclude consideration of alternative strategies from the political and social mainstream. Bailey and Wilson (2009, p. 2335), therefore, argued that

> although ... not axiomatically antagonistic to radical ecocentric responses, the neo-liberal ethos underpinning the [global capitalist system] would seem only to accommodate behavioural adjustments that are consistent with other tenets of the paradigm and self-regulating capacity of markets and individual liberty to pursue wealth accumulation.

Yet, for communities to be trapped in neo-liberal transitional corridors may not always be negative for raising community resilience, as some studies suggest that neo-liberalism can also lead to the creation of 'self-sufficient' communities with the cultivation of an ethic that emphasizes less reliance and dependency on state-provided services, with a strong focus on individual communities' rights to maximum freedom and responsibility for their own affairs (see Box 5.1) (Barnett, 2005; Harvey, 2005).

Closely intertwined with these macroeconomic lock-ins is the increasingly powerful role of *large businesses* and *multinational corporations*. While a hundred years ago most businesses would have had some linkages with their local communities (indeed, all multinational corporations once started as locally embedded small businesses), many communities are today served by national or multinational businesses that most often have no link or cultural/social attachment to the communities within which they, their headquarters or their shareholders are located (Korten, 1995; Bardhan, 2006). There are close links with the above discussion on structural lock-ins, in particular with regard to multinational corporations that control food, transport or energy networks. UK communities are a case in point, where a handful of large supermarket chains (e.g. TESCO, Sainsbury's, Morrisons) control a large share of the food market (Marsden, 2003; Lang and Heasman, 2004). Many of these companies now operate as international businesses (e.g. TESCO's recent expansion into the USA and China). A similar trend is evident with regard to energy providers, and the recent acquisition of most of the UK's energy grid and supplies by *Energie de France* emphasizes the increasing geographical disembeddedness of energy suppliers and users (Walker, 2008).

The increasing power and leverage of these companies contributes towards a reduction of community resilience in the following ways. First, the Indonesian case study in Chapter 5 highlighted the often environmentally damaging effects that 'footloose' locally disconnected multinationals can have with regard to preservation of environmental capital (e.g. tropical forest) at community level (Grainger, 2005). Second, multinational corporations or large national businesses often 'crowd out' more locally embedded businesses based on economies of scale and the possibility of competitive price dumping (Bardhan, 2006). Throughout most of the developed world, and increasingly in the developing world, this has meant the gradual death of local businesses which, in turn, has meant the relative loss of business-related localized social and economic networks (loss of social capital) and the disaggregation of horizontal locally oriented economic networks (loss of economic autonomy of communities). This means that economic capital is no longer generated at community level, but benefits far-away shareholders and company managers. Third, the increasing power of multinationals at community level has reduced choice for local costumers, has locked in customers into consumption pathways outside of their control (e.g. dependency on foreign-owned energy providers, dependency on increasingly standardized non-local supermarket brands and levels of choice), and has, ultimately, reduced the ability of communities to increase resilience through the use of local enterprise. The latter suggests that many businesses are no longer directly involved in building local economic capital and in contributing directly towards resilience in a specific locality. Indeed, super-globalized community pathways discussed in Chapter 3 are often predicated on vertical global interlinkages between communities and multinational corporations.

6.4 Macro-level ruptures and transitional corridors

The discussion has thus far assumed that macro-scalar transitional corridors follow relatively smooth and gradual pathways of change. Yet, as with endogenous transitional pathways at community level (Chapter 5), transitional corridors can also be characterized by macro-scalar transitional ruptures. Such ruptures are often associated with large-scale societal disturbances, such as natural catastrophes (e.g. long-scale droughts, earthquakes (e.g. Haiti 2010), volcanic eruptions (e.g. Mt Pinatubo, Philippines, 1998)) or anthropogenic disturbances such as human-induced climate change (e.g. low-lying Pacific island states), recessions or power/governance shifts, or even wars and revolutions (Richards, 2004; Abidi-Habib and Lawrence, 2007) (see Figure 1.1). Macro-scalar transitional ruptures are more usually associated with sudden changes rather than with slow-onset disturbances, although slow-onset disturbances may also lead to sudden ruptures by reaching specific 'tipping points' (Gladwell, 2000), such as climate change (e.g. when sea-level rise reaches destructive levels for low-lying island communities), droughts (e.g. leading to irreversible loss of agricultural production and the decision by people to abandon their communities), or examples of state-led energy transitions discussed in more detail later. However, macro-scalar transitional ruptures do not always have negative outcomes for community resilience. The following discussion will, therefore, assess how macro-scalar transitional ruptures can have *both* positive and negative effects on community resilience (Section 6.4.1). In Section 6.4.2 the complexity of impacts of macro-scalar ruptures on community resilience will then be discussed through the examples of anthropogenic disturbances linked to the post-socialist transition in Eastern Europe, ruptures created during WW2 in countries such as the UK, and ruptures related to shifts in national energy policy with associated impacts on local communities in countries such as China.

6.4.1 Positive and negative impacts of macro-scalar transitional ruptures

Chapter 5 highlighted that transitional ruptures endogenous to communities can have both *positive* and *negative* effects, and the same is true for macro-scalar transitional ruptures. Figure 5.5 already highlighted that, after a disturbance, recovery trajectories at community level can take many different forms. Building on this discussion, Figure 6.2 suggests that a key characteristic of macro-scalar transitional ruptures is the initial loss of resilience within transitional corridors. Sudden disturbances or catastrophes such as floods, tsunamis or earthquakes inevitably lower economic and environmental capital at nation-state level and in communities affected by these disturbances, which, in turn, often leads to a reduction in social capital (Rigg *et al.*, 2005). The discussion below will highlight, however, that complex scalar interactions between different resilience layers in society are at play (see Figure 2.3), and that there is not necessarily a unilinear correlation between national-level disturbances, such as wars or economic recessions, and loss of resilience at community level. Indeed, in some instances, pathways at community level can go against societal transitional corridors ('outliers' shown in Figure 6.1), especially when communities are not well embedded within nation-state politics (e.g. remote communities). Nonetheless, as highlighted in Section 6.3, in most cases communities are closely aligned with regional/national socio-economic and political pathways and ideologies, and are, therefore, often constrained in their resilience actions by the lowering of resilience quality within national transitional corridors, irrespective of whether communities are *immediately* affected by the disturbances causing the transitional rupture. The discussion below assumes, therefore, that community-level responses to macro-scalar ruptures will usually occur within clearly specified corridors of decision-making that define the majority of 'possible' decision-making pathways at community level.

With these caveats in mind, Figure 6.2 suggests three possible long-term *post-rupture pathways* and *recovery trajectories* for transitional corridors. First, macro-scalar transitional ruptures can have a long-term positive impact on resilience building within transitional corridors (Figure 6.2a). Although the disturbance has initially reduced resilience linked to disruptions to economic, social and environmental capital at various geographical scales (e.g. large death tolls, disruption of food and road infrastructure, etc.), more resilient post-rupture transitional pathways may be implemented in the long term. This can be linked to factors such as additional economic resources (including foreign or donor agency aid) allocated to disturbance-affected areas which may not have otherwise received funds, political change sparked by the socio-economic reorientation of disturbance-affected areas, or the building of a new and more efficient post-disturbance housing and road infrastructure. An example may be found in post-tsunami Aceh Province (north-west Sumatra, Indonesia) where the catastrophic event of the 2004 tsunami that killed over 250,000 people led to a large influx of donor money (partly linked to emotional images shown in the world media),

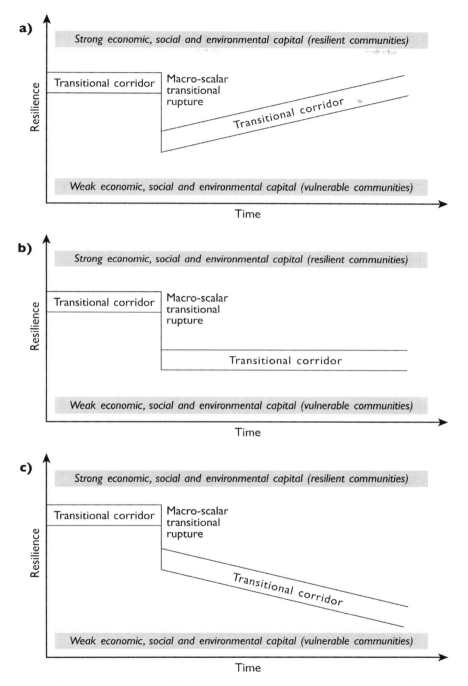

Figure 6.2 Macro-scalar transitional ruptures and post-rupture recovery trajectories (source: author).

thereby enabling relatively rapid rebuilding of local infrastructure and roads. Possibly most importantly, the catastrophe also led to a substantial weakening of the Free Aceh Movement, resulting in improved political stability and associated strengthening of social and economic capital (Miller, 2008) (see also Box 5.4). Despite the large death toll, at the time of writing in 2011, seven years after the catastrophe, it appears that overall resilience in Aceh Province may have increased (for those who survived).

Second, macro-scalar ruptures often lead to long-term reduction in resilience (Figure 6.2b). In these cases, the relative loss of economic, social and environmental capital results in a lowering of adaptive capacity at nation-state level which, in turn, affects many communities irrespective of their own historical resilience trajectories. The *magnitude* of disturbances is of particular importance here. While in the example of Aceh Province above only one region in a large nation state (Indonesia) was affected, long-term reduction of resilience within transitional corridors may occur if an entire nation state or key state institutions (e.g. a state capital or seat of government) are affected by the disturbance. Although possibly too early to fully evaluate at the time of writing (2011), the 2010 earthquake in Haiti may be a case in point. By affecting the capital, Port-au-Prince, and leading to a substantial weakening of social and economic capital, this earthquake directly affected transitional corridors at nation-state level, which, in turn, has affected opportunities for resilience building in almost every Haitian community (see also Box 2.1). The cholera epidemic ravaging many Haitian communities in late 2010 can be seen as a clear indication that communities have not been able (even with international aid) to rebuild environmental capital that would guarantee clean drinking water. A combination of pre-catastrophe low economic and social capital, together with the fact that most Haitian communities have been tied to transitional corridors unable to facilitate a decision-making environment for raising resilience (Diamond, 2006), has meant that high vulnerability transitional corridors are likely to shape development opportunities for some time to come.

Third, in the worst-case scenario macro-scalar ruptures may lead to a lowering of transitional corridors below the thresholds of community survival (Figure 6.2c). Previous chapters have highlighted that examples of this are rare at nation-state level (i.e. some parts of a society or a state tend to survive even the most destructive disturbances, e.g. during the Japanese mega-earthquake in March 2011), but that some examples can be found where weakened economic, social and environmental capital at community level meant that survival was no longer possible (e.g. Easter Island, Anaszasi communities in North America, etc.; see Boxes 4.3 and 5.5). In the case of the latter, community-level vulnerability has usually been synonymous with 'state'-level vulnerability (e.g. Easter Island). *Geographical scale* is, therefore, an important factor in defining whether transitional corridors at nation-state level become so vulnerable that future survival of *all* communities within the nation state is jeopardized. Examples for this, therefore, can only be found in relatively small societies living in a restricted geographical space. Frequently cited examples include the destruction of Minoan society (along the northern shores of Crete, Greece) around 1600 BC in the aftermath of the Santorini volcanic eruption (one of the largest volcanic eruptions in the past 5000 years) which created a tsunami large enough to reduce economic and environmental capital to such an extent that community survival was no longer possible. Other examples include the complete evacuation of the island of Tristan da Cunha (south Atlantic Ocean) in 1961 because of volcanic eruptions (although islanders returned after the eruptions ceased), or the partial evacuation of communities on the island of Montserrat since destructive volcanic activity began in 1995 with severe repercussions for the social, economic and environmental survival of affected communities.

6.4.2 Macro-scalar anthropogenic ruptures and impacts on local community resilience

This section will discuss in more detail the complexity of impacts of macro-scalar ruptures on community resilience through examples of large-scale *anthropogenic* disturbances. As highlighted in Chapter 1, anthropogenic disturbances often are slow-onset disturbances that do not force communities to adjust immediately (i.e. within an instant as is often the case with natural disturbances such as volcanic eruptions or earthquakes). However, as both Brock (2006) and Davidson (2010) emphasized, anthropogenic disturbances such as wars or sudden political changes (e.g. post-socialist transition; see below) can also represent quick-onset ruptures for community resilience as they often affect entire nation states (unlike most natural disturbances) (see also Adger, 2000; Dorfman *et al.*, 2009). Pretty (2007), for example, highlighted how between 1998 and 2004 four million people were killed in internecine warfare in the Congo, with long-lasting repercussions for the survival of many communities in the region. Examples discussed in the following will focus on anthropogenic disturbances to highlight the variety and different challenges faced by communities and will show that macro-scalar anthropogenic ruptures can both increase and reduce community resilience: ruptures linked to the post-socialist transition in Eastern Europe; impacts of WW2 on community resilience in the UK; and shifts in national energy policy and associated impacts on communities.

The post-socialist transition and community resilience

The transition towards post-socialism provides an apt example of a macro-scalar anthropogenic disturbance that has had complex positive and negative repercussions for community resilience. The post-socialist transition is closely associated with the transition from socialism to post-socialism in countries which emerged from the political and economic disintegration of the Soviet Union in 1991 (e.g. Russia, East Germany, Ukraine, Slovakia, Estonia,

Georgia). This transition is seen as one of the classic recent large-scale political and socio-economic transformations of human society (Van Hoven, 2004). The era of socialism is seen to typically involve adoption (forced or voluntary) of state socialist politics and modes of production, with a model of social regulation characterized by a one-party system and top-down economic planning (Pavlinek and Pickles, 2000), or in the words of Przeworski (1995) a system of 'modernization without internationalization'. The most prominent example was the former Soviet Union from 1917 to 1991, but socialism was also imposed onto, or voluntarily adopted by, many other countries that had close ties with the Soviet regime (e.g. Cuba, North Korea, North Vietnam, Albania, etc.) or in countries such as China. The transition to post-socialism occurred through several interlinked processes and socio-economic upheavals (Bradshaw and Stenning, 2001). First, the dismantling of the socialist ideology was made possible by decolonization of former Soviet satellite states in 1991 (e.g. Georgia, Kazakhstan, Uzbekistan). Second, the gradual process of democratization, characterized by a transition from totalitarian to post-totalitarian rule, was crucial for providing a socio-political basis for the transition. Third, economic liberalization ('from Marx to the market') entailed moving from state ownership of the means of production in centrally planned economies to price liberalization, privatization of state-owned enterprises, end of state monopoly over trade and new property rights for citizens. Fourth, globalization enabled the inclusion of newly emerging post-socialist states into the global world economy with modernization via internationalization (Przeworski, 1995). This led to other globalizing forces through inclusion of former socialist countries into the global capitalist system such as free trade, a widening of national and international investment and, arguably, the emergence of more liberal policies in newly formed democratic societies (Stiglitz, 2002; Wilson, 2007). As Van Hoven *et al.* (2004, p. 1) argued,

> transition was a powerful tool, created as an idea largely by neo-liberal economists in North America and Europe. It was eagerly embraced by politicians in Central and Eastern Europe, and was seen by many people living there ... as a remedy for their problems.

Some argue, therefore, that the result of the transition to post-socialism has been a fundamental reorganization of material life within former socialist countries, a transformation of geopolitical relations on a global scale and a major ideological/discursive shift in policy implementation (Pickles and Smith, 1998).

What is interesting in the context of community resilience is the relative pace of the post-socialist transition. On the one hand, some argued that if privatization did not occur rapidly (within a few years), thereby creating stakeholders with a vested interest in capitalism, countries that had been under the influence of the Soviet Union would quickly revert back to socialist ideologies. This school of thought advocated the strategy of *shock therapy* (Sachs,

1992), with a concurrent belief in the stepped transition model as an ideal that would allow communities to quickly move away from socialist structures to be replaced quickly by new (arguably post-socialist) politics and modes of production (Fukuyama, 1992). On the other hand, some argued that if the transition occurred too quickly, the reforms could be disastrous for local communities, resulting in economic failures compounded by political corruption, thereby opening up the way to a backlash from either the extreme left or right (*gradualist approach*) (Stiglitz, 2002). Gradualists believed that the transition would be easier for local communities by moving at a slower and more 'linear' pace. The 'shock therapy' approach was strongly advocated by both the USA and the International Monetary Fund, who provided large sums of money for rapid political and economic restructuring, and was adopted by most countries (e.g. Russia), although some countries such as Poland and China adopted the gradualist approach.

Probably the most dramatic example of 'shock therapy' occurred in former East Germany, which became part of a Western capitalist-oriented enlarged Germany after reunification in 1990 (Stiglitz, 2002). The literature on the impact of German reunification is divided with regard to positive and negative impacts on local community resilience in East Germany (see Pavlinek and Pickles, 2000, and Van Hoven, 2004, for good overviews), but the majority of studies suggest that the main outcome has been an overall loss of resilience (e.g. Weiß, 2006) (Box 6.3). Different impacts of the post-socialist transition on local communities have been described by Fernandez-Gimenez and Batbuyan (2004) for Mongolia, especially with regard to weakening environmental capital. They argued that after 1990 post-socialist Mongolian communities were faced with the dismantling of socialist herding collectives based on low-impact transhumant grazing systems, especially because formal regulatory institutions for allocating pastures which had been in place between 1960 and 1990 vanished. This, combined with increasing loss of economic capital and increasing population pressure in remote rural communities linked to post-1990 urban-rural inmigration, meant that weakened customary institutions were unable to effectively fill the void, leading to a downward spiral of unsustainable grazing practices. Fernandez-Gimenez and Batbuyan (2004, p. 143) thus argued that "once co-ordinated pasture use patterns disintegrated, and grazing patterns [are now] characterized by out-of-season grazing of reserve pastures, concentrations of herds and herding camps near roads, settlements and water points, and decreasing mobility". In this case, therefore, the post-socialist transition has led to the relative loss of environmental capital, with the result that the survival of many local Mongolian communities has been threatened by irreversible land degradation (Fernandez-Gimenez, 2001). Forbes *et al.* (2009) reported similar findings for impacts of the post-socialist transition among Nenets communities on the Yamal Peninsula in arctic Russia, especially with regard to rapid reductions of subsidies leading to a deterioration of grazing vegetation after the collapse of the Soviet Union (see also Adger, 2000, for impacts of the post-socialist transition in Vietnam).

Box 6.3 Post-socialist transitional ruptures and loss of community resilience in East Germany

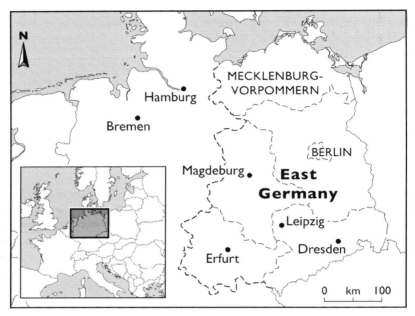

Using the example of several rural communities in Mecklenburg-Vorpommern (former East Germany), Reichert-Schick (2010) referred to 'dying villages' after German reunification. She particularly identified depopulation, loss of transport and service provision, housing issues and degradation of community life as key factors associated with loss of resilience in a post-socialist transition context. While for most communities the socialist era had neglected environmental capital leading to severe issues of air, water and land pollution (Wilson and Wilson, 2001), the socialist regime provided limited but nonetheless predictable security with regard to economic capital. In addition, several studies have highlighted how social capital in Eastern German communities was often relatively well developed during the socialist era, partly because communities were forced to relocalize production (e.g. importance of allotments due to frequent supply shortages), and because neighbours relied on each other for survival in what was often a brutal and controlling regime (Van Hoven, 2004). The situation changed dramatically after German reunification and the concurrent sudden exposure of East German communities to global capitalist market forces. As Reichert-Schick (2010) emphasized, the immediate impact of this was the outmigration of young, active and qualified people, who often moved to former West Germany to find better job opportunities, resulting in a much reduced and less resilient remnant population comprised largely of old people. In some extreme cases, local communities lost over 50 per cent of population between 1990 and 2010, with associated loss in services (schools and shops no longer viable) and transport links (local bus routes no longer commercially viable). A vicious circle of *regressive settlement development* has set in, where loss in services and the gradual dereliction of many properties (a third of the housing stock is empty in some villages; house prices have plummeted) leads to further population loss and further service degradation. As a result, most respondents in Reichert-Schick's (2010) study felt that their communities were not as resilient as they had been before 1990, with many seeing the future for the survival of their villages as bleak. While reunification has brought some improvements to environmental capital in many communities in former East Germany (e.g. tighter policy regime; deindustrialisation), it is evident that in remote rural communities both economic and social capital have been substantially eroded as a result of the macro-scalar rupture of the post-socialist transition.

A different story with regard to environmental capital has been reported by Pavlinek and Pickles (2000) in their study of post-socialist environmental transitions in Central and Eastern Europe. They argued that the transition to post-socialism created a political and policy-based 'positive' rupture that provided an opportunity for a rapid environmental clean-up in Central and Eastern Europe – an area once considered one of the most polluted regions on Earth. This was particularly linked to improved information and service provision to communities with regard to pollution and health, the tightening of environmental policy coupled with enforcement of European pollution and environmental standards, and the rise of environmental non-governmental organizations (NGOs) which lobbied for a rapid improvement of environmental capital at community level. As a result, emission trends in countries such as Slovakia or the Czech Republic declined between 1990 and 2000 by as much as 70 per cent for SO_2 and 40 per cent for CO_2. In this case, therefore, the post-socialist transition appears to have (at least partly) raised community resilience by considerably strengthening environmental capital.

These examples highlight two key issues with regard to community resilience. First, as Figure 6.2 highlighted, it confirms that macro-scalar ruptures can have both positive and negative impacts on community resilience by strengthening or weakening economic, social and environmental capital at community level. Yet, for some communities (e.g. East Germany) evidence suggests that the post-socialist transition has often also led to an overall lowering of resilience, with limited evidence yet that community-level resilience levels have recovered to pre-disturbance levels – akin to corridors shown in Figure 6.2b above. Manser (1993), therefore, applied the notion of 'failed transition' (see Figure 3.3) to the post-socialist transition in Central and Eastern Europe, arguing that none of the transitional pathways used by former socialist countries have necessarily led to a 'new' and 'better' final outcome (see also Dunford, 1998, for the Russian case). Indeed, for many communities, post-socialism has been characterized by economic collapse, an onslaught on labour, and social and political disorientation that has made the contemporary situation worse in economic terms than during the end of the socialist regime (Stiglitz, 2002). Second, the macro-scalar transition towards post-socialism emphasizes the path dependency of transitional corridors at community level linked to the 'legacy' of socialism (e.g. pollution issues) (Grabher and Stark, 1997), as well as the importance of social memory with regard to a frequent idealization of socialist social and economic processes (e.g. reference to strong social networks at community level in the socialist era) (Pickles and Smith, 1998; Van Hoven, 2004). Smith and Swain (1998), therefore, rightly argued that an understanding of the diversity of community responses to the post-socialist transition is partly dependent on the way in which previous legacies of socio-cultural, political and economic relations are 'reworked' within the possible framework of tightly bounded transitional corridors, thereby underlining the three different recovery trajectories of communities to macro-scalar transitional ruptures shown in Figure 6.1 a–c.

The transitional rupture of World War Two: enforced relocalization and the resilience of UK communities

The second example of macro-scalar transitional ruptures focuses on *war* as one of the most frequent and most devastating anthropogenic disturbance. Global conflicts like the First and Second World Wars in the twentieth century have been the most devastating disturbances affecting communities (Beevor, 1999). With over 20 million dead in the First World War (mainly soldiers) and over 60 million dead in WW2 (mainly civilians), these two wars are only overshadowed in terms of catastrophic human death toll by the macro-scalar disturbance of the bubonic plague in twelfth- to fourteenth-century Europe which killed over half of the human population in certain regions (e.g. parts of southern Germany, parts of northern Italy) (Welford and Bossak, 2010). Yet, despite the devastating effects of these wars, the following will highlight that in countries such as the UK, where WW2 killed 'only' about 0.5 million people, transitional ruptures such as WW2 also partly led to a strengthening of community resilience through *enforced relocalization.*[2]

On the one hand, WW2 led to a substantial centralization of decision-making structures in the UK, with more pronounced top-down tendencies in which local communities lost relative autonomy over decision-making. Communities had to 'toe the line', creating new community decision-making pathways with arguably narrower transitional corridors. However, these narrower pathways of decision-making, especially through reduced energy use ('powerdown'), a nationalized and relocalized food economy (push for national food self-reliance and domestic food production) and much more limited transport opportunities, were accepted by most UK citizens under the wartime spirit of 'we are all in it together' that diluted class boundaries, often amplified by highly nationalistic propaganda encouraging people to 'stick together' for the wartime effort (Gardiner, 2004). Chapter 7 will highlight that such pathways were driven by a top-down national policy agenda that helped the relocalization of food (UK food self-sufficiency increased considerably between 1939 and 1944) and the relocalization of transport (by 1942 all individual petrol allocations were abolished leading to a 95 per cent drop in car usage) (Gardiner, 2004). As Simms (2005, p. 156) argued, "recent history demonstrates that whole economies can be re-geared in short periods of time", and asked whether the experience of social and military mobilization in wartime might answer questions associated with community resilience to contemporary disturbances. Intuitively, enforced relocalization during wartime should have reduced community resilience through reduced economic and environmental capital at national level (e.g. reduction in food availability due to the disturbance to global trade flows). However, Hopkins (2010) convincingly argued that enforced relocalization at community level may have led to strengthened resilience, especially as WW2 led to the disruption of negative dependencies between individual communities and wider society. This meant that communities *had to* retrench 'back on themselves' and rely more on harnessing endogenous adaptive capacities (see also Chapter 5). Communities that lagged behind in economic development terms before WW2 thus suddenly had advantages with regard to fostering endogenous resilience pathways, as they could draw on still existing social memory and reserves that were already unavailable to globalized communities more vulnerable to disruptions of energy, food and transport networks.

As part of his research on the Transition Movement in the town of Totnes (UK), Hopkins (2010) analysed in detail the impact of the transitional rupture of WW2 on resilience pathways at community level. Hopkins identified several key aspects that appeared to have strengthened the resilience of Totnes (*c.* 20,000 inhabitants, south-west UK; see Box 4.6) during WW2. For example, residents saw local processing of food increasingly as an integral part of the economy, which also created more local jobs, shortened food chains from production to plate, led to a greater diversity of land uses around the town and created markets that linked local farmers to local consumers. Enforced relocalization also meant that many Totnes households grew their own food, and gardening and small live-stock rearing became (again) a main topic of conversation for the community. This also meant increased urban commercial food production with a small town like Totnes featuring three commercial market gardens. Enforced relocalization also meant a more diverse and higher proportion of locally owned shops, more availability of local casual work, more opportunities for local artisans and builders' yards, and a general need for practical skills and a sense of having to be able to turn one's hand to anything that needed fixing. In addition, despite highly centralized wartime decision-making, Hopkins' Totnes respondents argued that governance structures were much more connected to the community itself. Most crucially, Hopkins (2010) argued, wartime-enforced relocalization in Totnes helped create a cultural ethic of frugality characterized by a revaluation of local food, a recognition of the importance of more sustainably managed local resources and lower expectations with regard to transport needs (little private car use between 1942 and 1945 due to fuel rationing) and thermal comfort. With regard to the latter, one of Hopkins' (2010, p. 311) respondents who lived in Totnes during the 1940s explained that:

from morning to night you were chilled right through the bone. Even coming into the house you got warmer but never really warm. You'd go to bed cold and warm up in bed. You'd have a hot water bottle. It sounds romantically tough, but it was just the way it was, everyone was like that

(see also Dorfman *et al.*, 2009, for similar resilience impacts of WW2 in the USA).

Although enforced relocalization in towns such as Totnes could mean extreme hardship for almost all citizens with regard to heating, provision of diverse types of food and a considerably restricted freedom of movement by rail, bus or private car, Hopkins (2010) argued that enforced relocalization pathways helped increase community resilience by making the town more multifunctional (see also Wilson, 2010). British communities were forced to grow their own food, do their own repairs of broken tools and machinery, rely on local building materials and other resources and – most crucially – re-establish close-knit social networks that helped community residents to survive the hardships of war. Post-WW2 rupture recovery in Totnes may, therefore, be more akin to the transitional corridor shown in Figure 6.2a, where the post-rupture 'quality' of community resilience may have been higher than pre-rupture levels. Hopkins' Totnes respondents, therefore, argued that many elements of relocalization that emerged from the transitional rupture of WW2 could be carried forward into contemporary society to increase Totnes' resilience, especially with regard to changing behaviours associated with energy, food, transport and building materials (see also Chapter 5).

Macro-scalar transitional ruptures induced by the state: shifts in
energy policy, dam building and community resilience

My third example of macro-scalar transitional ruptures is associated with state-induced shifts in energy policy, creating new 'energy corridors' which often affect the resilience of communities in a negative way (Nilsson, 2005). Examples include large-scale dam building (for energy generation) which inevitably weakens economic, social and environmental capital in affected communities through forced relocation and destruction of villages/communities. Jackson and Sleigh (2000) highlighted how most dams are built in the developing world, with an average of two million people a year forced to relocate, often leading to the disintegration of often already vulnerable communities. However, examples of relatively sudden ruptures in state-controlled energy policies also affect communities in the developed world. The political drive away from coal for energy production (both at local and national levels) to natural gas, oil and nuclear power in the UK of the 1980s is a case in point. This rupture – associated with the political goal to 'break up' the union power of left-leaning mining communities by the Thatcherite Government – had large repercussions for economic capital in coal-mining communities of north-eastern England in particular, as community members often found it impossible to find new jobs, to reskill or to find alternative sources of income generation (Hudson, 2005). This, in turn, negatively affected social capital within formerly tight-knit communities, especially through the outmigration of young people, often resulting in reduced community resilience. Half-abandoned villages and boarded-up houses worth very little on the housing market have been the clearest physical evidence of disintegrating communities, while psychological stress and depression has formed less visible, but equally devastating, indicators of weakening resilience (Hudson, 2000) – suggesting community-level post-rupture recovery trajectories akin to Figures 6.2b and c.

The most dramatic ruptures in energy-based transitional corridors occur in non-democratic countries where decisions by the state are not based on democratic processes of compromise that usually dampen impacts on local communities (Dobson, 2007; see also above). One of the most vivid examples can be found in China, where over the past decades top-down state-enforced legislation has led to the building of over a hundred large and medium-sized dams across China's seven major rivers and their tributaries, leading to over 10 million displaced people in numerous communities (Jackson and Sleigh, 2000). Jun (1997, p. 74) argued that for most of these projects "no serious effort was made to respond to local concerns over matters of compensation, community break-up, economic recovery, or social adjustment in the new communities", suggesting that economic and social capital of affected communities were particularly weakened.

The largest of these Chinese dam developments is the Three Gorges Dam, the largest dam on Earth (length of dammed lake 600 km; dam height 185 m; completion of resettlement operations 2009). This led to the enforced destruction of local communities through the flooding of entire valleys, and problematic resettlement programmes that often led to the disintegration of formerly tight-knit communities (Pretty, 2007). 1.3 million citizens have been affected by enforced destruction of their communities through flooding linked to the Three Gorges Dam so far, with another 20 million people indirectly affected upstream and another 300 million downstream (Jackson and Sleigh, 2000; Hwang *et al.*, 2007). The dam has led to loss of substantial areas of fertile agricultural land and the withholding of fertile silt from downstream areas (loss of environmental capital at community level), although the dam has also reduced damaging floods and conserved water on a grand scale that may alleviate local and regional water shortages in the long term (increased environmental capital at community level) (Heggelund, 2006).

There is little debate, however, about the direct negative impact of the flooding of entire valley systems linked to the Three Gorges Dam "for the dispersion and forced settlement of local communities whose plight is the most certain adverse outcome of the dam" (Jackson and Sleigh, 2000, p. 225). The dam has flooded two large cities (Wanxian and Fuling), 11 county towns, 114 smaller towns and thousands of small villages and farms – a transitional rupture through 'indiscriminate relocation' (Hwang *et al.*, 2007) that, inevitably, has led to the complete destruction of these communities with little option for 'positive' post-rupture recovery shown in Figure 6.2a. Most of the critical literature has argued that some resettled communities may never recover socially (e.g. loss of property rights), economically (e.g. lower post-rupture standards of living, loss of agricultural lands with inadequate compensation, loss of employment) or psychologically (Hwang *et al.*, 2007; see Box 6.4), and that displaced villages have been broken up with loss of social capital and the disappearance of long-established tight-knit networks. Hwang *et al.* (2007, p. 1014), therefore, suggested that "relocation not only uproots migrants from their home for many generations, it also tears apart their close-knit social networks". Particularly traumatic has been the fact that many communities refused to move, leading to even more chaotic and rushed decisions for relocation. Thus, "enormous costs [were] forced upon oustees, imposing sacrifices for the community good on people to be relegated to a life of extreme hardship and poverty that may persist for generations" (Jackson and Sleigh, 2000, p. 229). These problems are exacerbated as resettled community residents have been forced to migrate to inhospitable localities (e.g. from farmsteads to high rise tower blocks in cities), live among hostile host populations (particularly problematic for the many displaced minorities like the *Tujia tribal people* dislocated by the dam), be exposed to new disease risks (e.g. new water-borne parasitic diseases such as schistosomiasis or snail fever) and to farm lands that are both less fertile and accessible (Heggelund, 2006). Jackson and Sleigh (2000), therefore, argued that the construction of the Three Gorges Dam has bred untold social discontent and despair among resettled communities, suggesting post-rupture community pathways for affected communities akin to Figure 6.2b or even c.

Box 6.4 Macro-scalar state-induced transitional ruptures: enforced resettlement of communities affected by the Three Gorges Dam, China

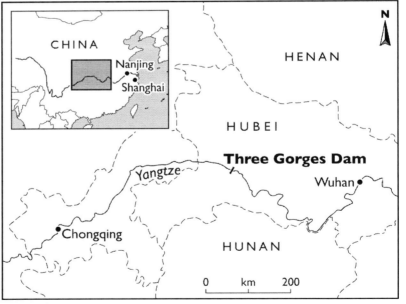

The macro-scalar state-led transitional rupture of the Three Gorges Dam in China (completed in 2009) has led to the forced migration of 1.3 million people from flooded areas (Pretty, 2007). The severe impacts of enforced resettlement with regard to loss of social capital and psychological stress of affected communities have been documented in detail by Hwang *et al*. (2007), who analysed migration stories of about a thousand migrants from the Wanxian region. They highlighted that most affected community residents were farmers who did not all receive compensation lands, but who are also unlikely to be absorbed by non-farm industries. In addition, 99 per cent of residents in the Three Gorges Dam area had never moved before, but most have been forced to live far away from their ancestral lands (loss of social memory) often in unfamiliar urban environments. Hwang *et al*. highlighted that enforced migration has caused large-scale psychological stress with grave social ramifications, especially as relocation destroys migrants' social networks and their sense of self-value and direction. Less educated community members (e.g. farmers), and those with fewer previous political links, appear to have suffered more psychological stress, as have women because of additional gender-induced threats linked to loss of economic capital (fewer opportunities for rural women to find alternative employment). Tan *et al*. (2005) also highlighted how these increasingly unequal gender spaces in resettled communities around the Three Gorges Dam have led to further loss of social capital, weakened resilience and have further contributed to rural migrants' disadvantages. Communities adjacent to flooded and resettled areas have also faced more psychological stress, especially through the Chinese government's imposed sharing of limited resources with their new neighbours – highlighting 'ripple effects' affecting community resilience in the entire Three Gorges Dam region (Hwang *et al*., 2007).

6.5 Conclusions

Chapter 6 focused on the notion of *exogenous* macro-scalar 'transitional corridors' shaped by national and global decision-making processes, and analysed how such corridors influence community resilience. It was argued that the critical literature often portrays macro-scalar corridors as 'negative' for innovation, as they automatically channel decisions into 'known' and 'already established' pathways, rather than encouraging innovative thinking 'out of the box'. The chapter then analysed the importance of macro-scalar lock-in effects external to communities and discussed how these can shape community pathways and resilience in both positive and negative ways. Political and policy-based lock-ins, for example, may raise community resilience but can often also result in increased community vulnerability. Macro-structural lock-ins, meanwhile, are often negative for community resilience and highlight the increasing dependence of communities in both the developed and developing world on consumer goods, energy, food and transport networks exogenous to the immediate sphere of influence of communities. Ideological lock-ins at societal level (e.g. religion, conservatism), on the other hand, can act as both positive or negative processes for community resilience, while macroeconomic lock-ins (e.g. globalization, global capitalism) highlight the increasing embeddedness of communities into global flows of capital, information and cultural exchange, often shoehorning communities into tightly demarcated transitional corridors from which it is difficult to 'escape'. The latter particularly leads to a situation of communities increasingly interconnected and 'sinking or swimming' together. This situation is exacerbated by transitional ruptures influencing macro-scalar transitional corridors, as large-scale ruptures, in particular, can negatively influence community-level attempts to raise resilience. Examples of abrupt changes in political organization of a country (e.g. post-socialist transition) were discussed in the context of positive and negative impacts on community resilience, while severe ruptures caused by wars, dam building or large-scale natural hazards were mentioned as frequently reducing community resilience.

One of the most important macro-scalar transitional corridors to shape community resilience relates to policy corridors. Chapter 7 will, therefore, focus specifically on the role of policy in influencing community resilience, and will highlight how policy can be specifically targeted at community level to increase resilience.

7 Community resilience and the policy challenge

7.1 Introduction

Building on discussions of transitional corridors in Chapter 6, this chapter will focus on the complex interlinkages between community resilience and the policy challenge, with specific emphasis on the importance of *state-led policy corridors*. Section 7.2 will, first, investigate the policy challenge how to make local communities more resilient, with an emphasis on how macro-scalar policy corridors can often stifle 'positive' community-level attempts at strengthening resilient pathways. Section 7.3 then discusses the link between transitional corridors and policy challenges, with specific reference to policy needs of different types of communities. Section 7.4 analyses whether the notion of transitional corridors implies that raising community-level resilience is a zero-sum-game – in other words, whether raising resilience in one locality inevitably leads to increased vulnerability in another. Section 7.5 then discusses how best to 'manage' global resilience transitions and asks specifically which stakeholder groups should be in charge of orchestrating policies encouraging stronger resilience at community level. Concluding remarks are provided in Section 7.6.

7.2 Transitional corridors and policy

This section will investigate in detail the complex interlinkages between policy corridors and community resilience. In contrast to Chapter 5 which discussed 'policy' in the context of endogenous political lock-in effects, policy is understood here as a set of 'formal' rules and regulations largely associated with the state, i.e. policies *exogenous* to communities in the shape of laws and policy documents that set the parameters for human action (Wilson and Bryant, 1997; Martens and Rotmans, 2002). These rules and regulations affect every community within a nation state either directly (by effecting changes in human action at community level) or indirectly by affecting actions of stakeholders and actors at regional/national level which, in turn, influences community-level decision-making pathways (Winter, 1990; Dryzek, 1997). As policy implementation theory emphasizes (Winter, 1990; Sabatier and Jenkins-Smith, 1993), complex scalar processes are at play in policy implementation, but it is at community/household level that policies find their *direct expression* through implementation 'on the ground'. Although many policies developed at national level never reach their recipients (implementation gap), the key for successful national policy implementation is to lead to *tangible action* at community level and to change individuals' environmental attitudes, perceptions and actions with regard to raising community resilience (Söderholm, 2010; Magis, 2010).

The focus in this section is, therefore, on *exogenous* policy trajectories and their influence on community resilience. Three interweaving themes will be explored: Section 7.2.1 will discuss conceptual issues associated with the close interlinkages between transitional and policy corridors. Using examples, Section 7.2.2 will then investigate policies as both malign and benign processes affecting community resilience, while Section 7.2.3 will analyse the policy challenges for raising economic, social and environmental capital for different types of communities.

7.2.1 Policy corridors and community resilience: interlinkages, lock-ins and policy learning

Of all human activities and processes that define macro-scalar transitional corridors shown in Figure 6.1 and discussed in the context of 'lock-in' mechanisms in Section 6.3, state policies are among the most important (Dryzek, 1997; Jordan *et al.*, 2003). The role of policy and other institutional interventions is particularly important in defining, shaping and, at times, distorting, the direction and pace of transitional corridors. Hall (1993) referred to this as 'policy paradigms' that are often difficult to change or overturn, while Bulkeley and Betshill (2003, p. 879) highlighted that policy-making corridors focused on the nation state mean that "the scales of governance remain bounded, and there is little consideration of the possibilities that the governance of global environmental issues might emanate from the 'bottom up'". Almost by definition, state policy-making in the form of economic, social or environmental policies occurs in relatively narrowly defined 'corridors of the possible'. Such policy-related transitional corridors are closely linked to what Rotmans *et al.* (2002) termed 'transition management' through the policy corridor approach. Martens and Rotmans (2002, p. 122) argued that "a policy corridor represents a conceptual space within which policymaking is safe, based on multi-dimensional estimates of economic, socio-cultural and ecological risks". They use the metaphor of the 'safe landing' approach in policy corridors in which an aircraft must approach landing within a well-defined corridor. They argue that the precautionary principle is often applied in these instances, based on the notion that some constraints are necessary to regulate citizens' economic, social and environmental decision-making pathways, but where too many regulations/policies may damage societal economic development.

As Section 6.3.1 highlighted, policy corridors are generally influenced by political systems (e.g. democratic versus conservative politics), societal ideologies influenced by religion and other norms, or by predominant societal economic approaches such as neo-liberalism or socialism (Johnston, 1996). Although such corridors do not emerge in a vacuum and are linked to antecedent social memory (e.g. previous governments or preceding societal ideologies which may differ from current ones), policy learning theory implies that policy corridors are often among the slowest societal processes to change (Hall, 1993; Dolowitz and Marsh, 1996; Bomberg, 2007).[1] As Wilson and Bryant (1997) emphasized, this is often linked to the fact that state bureaucracies (civil servants), who are most commonly in charge of policy formulation, implementation and monitoring, tend to change more slowly than the governments for which they work. Although there is usually some turnover of civil servants after changes in government, in most countries the state policy-making apparatus often shows signs of longevity – suggesting that predominant policy ideologies and approaches that underpin the policy process are slow to change (Sabatier and Jenkins-Smith, 1993). This is particularly the case in non-democratic countries where both government and the civil servant apparatus can stay relatively unchanged (and unchallenged) for decades (e.g. North Korea, China, Myanmar, Cuba, Libya). Entrenched state policy-making bureaucracies are, therefore, one of the key reasons for the sluggishness of change in transitional corridors shown in Figure 6.1 (Hall, 1993).

That policy formulation and implementation occurs often within relatively narrow 'corridors of the possible' has important repercussions for local community resilience and vulnerability. As the discussion on political lock-ins emphasized (see Section 6.3.1), communities can rarely choose to operate outside of the national policy environment, and all communities within a nation state are affected in one way or another (and whether they want it or not) by government policy. Whether communities can develop 'radical' endogenous policy pathways that substantially diverge from these societal policy norms (see Figure 6.1) depends largely on two factors. First, it is contingent upon the level of embeddedness of a community within 'their' nation state, i.e. communities that have not yet been incorporated into the socio-economic and political pathways of their 'host' state (e.g. remote subsistence farming or hunter-gathering communities) may still be able to use their own 'policies', relatively independent from state policy trajectories, in defining their community's transitional pathways (see Chapter 5). Second, in democratic countries, historical evidence suggests that some level of community-based policy autonomy is possible ('radical' pathways in Figure 6.1), such as alternative 'hippie' communities in the 1960s/1970s or the more recent relocalization initiatives (e.g. the TTM discussed). Yet, these communities are only allowed to operate within the state policy framework of 'legality' which, in turn, is directly defined by laws and policies (Sabatier and Jenkins-Smith, 1993). As a result, most governments have been quick to act in disbanding 'illegal' communities, such as radical religious or other sects, in which societal norms and rules linked to child sex abuse or illegal drug taking, for example, have defined some community pathways that have lain well beyond established national law-related corridors.

This highlights that, depending on societal ideologies and norms, the fact that state policy corridors *shoehorn* communities into specific decision-making pathways can have both positive and negative repercussions for raising community resilience. As political scientists and social philosophers emphasize, in theory it should be the state's ultimate aim to help *all* its citizens through the national policy process (Wilson and Bryant, 1997; Abel *et al.*, 2006). Indeed, the abovementioned 'safe landing approach' in state policy-making (Martens and Rotmans, 2002) is based on the assumption that 'safe' decision-making boundaries can be identified within which policy decisions occur, assuming that resulting policies, decided by elected representatives in society, aim for the 'national good' in helping all national citizens to strengthen resilience at community level. However, as political ecologists and critical political scientists, in particular, have emphasized, there is evidence that the state does not always have the interests of all its citizens in mind (Bryant and Bailey, 1997; Forsyth, 2003). Even in democratic settings, there is ample evidence of states 'working against' parts of its citizenry through misguided or wrongly targeted policies, leading to increased vulnerability at community level (e.g. Pavlinek and Pickles, 2000, for the Czech Republic; Hudson, 2005, for north-east England; McCarthy, 2006, for Canada). However, there is particular evidence from non-democratic societies where the state is overtly at war with some of its so-called 'rebel' communities (e.g. Bryant, 2005, for the Philippines; Parnwell, 2007, and Rigg *et al.*, 2008, for Thailand). As emphasized in Chapter 5, in case of the latter it is the state itself which is part of the problem, as it may lead either to substantial reduction of resilience in communities the state does not deem 'fit' for state policy support (e.g. by withholding development funds), or even to outright physical destruction of communities that do not conform with predominant state ideologies and politics. Examples of the latter are plentiful, including the Myanmar military regime fighting Karen 'rebels' on its borders with Thailand (Bryant and Bailey, 1997) or its harsh political clamp-down of political protesters after 'elections' in 2007 and 2010, Saddam Hussein's destruction of ethnic Kurd communities in northern Iraq in the 1980s and 1990s, the Indonesian government fighting Penan hunter-gatherers preventing state-condoned logging operators from entering their ancestral domains (Lebel *et al.*, 2006), the Russian military fighting Chechen 'rebels' within its southern borders in the Caucasus region, or the 2009 annihilation of communities associated with the Tamil Tiger 'rebel' movement in northeastern Sri Lanka.

In the context of democratic societies at least, the critical policy literature suggests that policy corridors can be adjusted through the process of *policy learning*, which may mean that policies can be better targeted to strengthen resilience at community level (Bomberg, 2007; Jazeel and McFarlane, 2010). Policy learning occurs within transitional corridors at multiple scales, ranging from the global (supra-national policies), the national, the regional (e.g. role of street-level bureaucrats as 'gatekeepers' of national policy) to the local level (see Figure 2.3 on the spatial scales of resilience). Hall's (1993) seminal article on policy paradigms, policy learning and the state, highlighted in particular how policy corridors can be adjusted through both learning processes and the shifting of paradigms at different scales. Hall argued that three types of policy changes can be identified, each with an increasing level of change from established policy paradigms. First-order change was termed 'alterations to the calibration of existing instruments', suggesting that only a tinkering with existing state policy-making processes occurs at this stage, which is unlikely to *substantially* alter community resilience. An example could be alterations to existing small business taxation, which may make it more attractive for businesses to locate in remote rural communities, thereby contributing towards increased community-level economic capital. Second-order change he termed 'adoption of new instruments', which suggests some policy innovation which may provide new policy-led opportunities for raising community resilience. An example could be the introduction of *new* policies linked to electricity feed-in tariffs at household level, encouraging communities to shift towards localized alternative energy pathways through photovoltaic cells on roofs or small wind turbines, eventually leading to improved environmental capital at community level (and beyond) (Barr, 2008). The most drastic form of policy learning Hall termed 'goal alteration', which suggests a full paradigmatic strategic shift in both intellectual and ideological frameworks of state policy-making and, potentially, changes in the attitudes and ideological beliefs of wider society. As Jordan *et al.* (2003) emphasized, such third-order changes are paradigm shifts that extend beyond the 'ordinary' policy agenda, and in extreme cases revolutionize the basis and practice of public policy. An example could be societal acceptance of an impending global energy and climate change crisis, with strong policy-led encouragement (including allocation of large budgets) for communities to find ways to relocalize energy production, food production, the sourcing and use of building materials, and transportation (see Chapter 5).

These tensions highlight the complex interlinkages of policy lock-ins straightjacketing communities within specific transitional corridors and the importance of policy learning in altering existing policy paradigms. Policy corridors can have both malign and benign repercussions for community resilience, depending on the willingness and ability of governments to increase community resilience – a key issue that will be investigated in more detail in the following section.

7.2.2 Policy corridors as both malign and benign processes for community resilience

The aim of this section is to illustrate, through specific examples, malign and benign effects state policies can have on community resilience. Again, examples will be selective and the main aim will be to illustrate the wide variety of possible policy effects at community level in different socio-spatial contexts.

Benign policies for community resilience fall under the umbrella of 'adaptive governance' (Anderies *et al.*, 2006) and can be seen as all those national policies specifically targeted at *improving resilience* at community level. These include policies specifically aimed at strengthening economic, social or environmental capital of communities, with the most 'positive' policies targeting all three capitals simultaneously (Magis, 2010). The critical policy literature highlights that two key factors shape the success of policies in raising resilience at community level. First, the most effective policies are usually tailored specifically at the *needs of particular communities* (Ray, 2000; see also below). Such an approach recognizes that individual communities have very specific needs. For example, some communities need policies aimed at strengthening economic capital, while others need more help with improving environmental capital. However, this approach is contingent upon inclusive and flexible – and, as a result, often expensive – policy processes which most countries can ill afford (Wilson and Bryant, 1997). Second, the successful raising of community resilience through state policy is also dependent on the appropriate *timing* of implementation. As policies often require individuals, households or communities to change their actions, community members have to be willing and prepared to take such action in the first place (Granovetter, 1985; Barr, 2008). As Section 5.3.3 highlighted in the context of socio-psychological lock-in effects at community level, the frequent dominance of psychological conservatism (i.e. a tendency to 'leave things as they are') means that policy change induced too early may lead to a rejection of innovative policy ideas by the community, while delayed policy implementation may mean that pathways of vulnerability can no longer be reversed. Recognizing the right timing of policy implementation at community level, therefore, requires relatively intimate knowledge by state policy-makers of targeted communities – knowledge reliant on information often unavailable to ministries hampered by time and budgetary constraints (Swyngedouw, 2001; Sarkissian *et al.*, 2010).

A historic and often cited example of positive state policies aimed at enhancing the resilience of local communities relates to the example of the transitional rupture of WW2 in the UK. In anticipation of possible conflict with Germany, an Act of Parliament in 1936 set up two committees, one commissioned to design and prepare a scheme for food rationing, the other to prioritize the storage of food for 'hard times' to come (Wilt, 2001). This led to the creation of the *Food Defence Plans Department* in the *Board of Trade* which became the key policy framework for preparing communities for war. By 1940, committees had been set up in 476 districts nationwide to coordinate the *enforced relocalization* of agriculture (see also Chapter 6). As well as attempting to increase levels of stored food, increasing community-level production was also heavily promoted (Hopkins, 2010). Wilt (2001) and Gardiner (2004) both suggested that the result was an increase in community resilience, especially as between 1939 and 1944 the amount of land under cultivation increased from five to eight million ha, with the result that dependency on food imports halved as British communities were now able to feed themselves for 160 days rather than just 120 days/year. As a result of the policy drive for enforced relocalization, local authorities set up horticultural committees to advise people to grow food, complemented by a large-scale programme of promoting virtues of thrift and economy, as well as teaching practical skills for resilience (Hopkins, 2010). Cities like Bristol, for example, had 150,000 allotments by 1942, and over half of the UK's manual workers had access to an allotment or garden, producing about 10 per cent of the nation's food (Gardiner, 2004). This example shows that at times of extreme disturbance (war), it is possible for a top-down policy-led approach to guide relocalization pathways, at times with positive outcomes for community resilience (Wilt, 2001; Hopkins, 2010; see also example of Totnes discussed in Chapter 6). Simms (2005, p. 156), therefore, argued that "when governments really want to, they can do almost anything, including good things". Similarly, Brown (2006, p. 206) argued that on the basis of the historical example of attempting to increase the resilience of local communities in the USA at the beginning of WW2, the "mobilization of resources within a matter of months demonstrates that a country and, indeed, the world, can restructure its economy quickly if it is convinced of the need to do so".

Another classic and much written-about example of a suite of policies aiming to enhance resilience at community level can be found in EU agri-environmental policies. These policies are linked to both supra-national and national policy initiatives that aim at providing 'green subsidies' for farming communities (Buller *et al.*, 2000). Although closely associated with EU policy corridors and agendas, the principle of subsidiarity enshrined in these policies means that EU member states have substantial latitude in implementing agri-environmental policies targeted towards specific needs of their rural communities (Robinson, 2008). Agri-environmental policies have two complementary goals. First, they provide financial payments to farmers for environmental management services such as hedgerow maintenance, sustainable water and forest management, or agricultural extensification measures (Wilson, 2007). Most importantly, they encourage farming communities to maintain traditional farming practices that are usually beneficial for environmental capital at community level. Second, agri-environmental payments have also been interpreted as a 'backdoor subsidy' that provides cash-stricken rural communities with vital payments that may help with long-term economic survival, irrespective of environmental benefits they may incur (Dibden and Cocklin, 2009; Wilson, 2010).

There is a plethora of studies that have analysed the impacts of agri-environmental policies on environmental capital at community level, and although results are at times ambiguous (see Buller *et al.*, 2000, for a comprehensive review), there is general consensus that, in the context of the EU, these policies have helped prevent intensification, reduced applications of polluting fertilizers, pesticides and herbicides, and, in some cases, have led to improved sustainable environmental management of the countryside (Robinson, 2004, 2008; Woods, 2005; Box 7.1). However, the situation with regard to impacts of agri-environmental policies has been complex, and wholly positive results with regard to raising community resilience are rare. Box 5.3 already highlighted that the predominant psychological conservatism of many farming communities has often led to resistance with regard to the implementation of non-productivist agri-environmental policies, in particular as these policies often force farmers to change their identities away from food and fibre production towards becoming 'landscape gardeners' (Wilson and Hart, 2000; Burton and Wilson, 2006).

Indeed, the voluntary nature of many agri-environmental policies has meant that farming communities are often split into adopters and non-adopters, which can lead to social and psychological frictions and possible weakening of social capital in formerly tight-knit communities (Wilson, 2007, 2010).

Box 7.1 Agri-environmental policies and the strengthening of environmental capital at community level

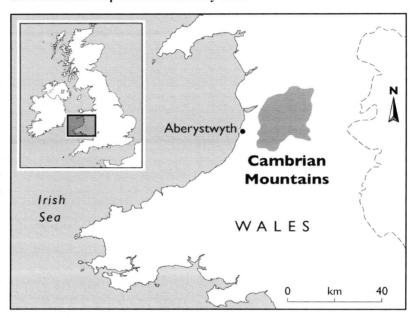

An extensive analysis of whether and how agri-environmental policies contributed towards strengthening environmental capital at community level was conducted during the 1990s in the Cambrian Mountains (Central Wales, UK) by this author (Wilson, 1997). This area had been designated as part of the UK Environmentally Sensitive Areas (ESA) Scheme within which farmers were eligible to apply for agri-environmental payments. A complete census survey found that on large farms, in particular, the ESA scheme had positive outcomes through the prevention of intensi-fication. This resulted in the maintenance of a traditional farming landscape based on extensively used semi-natural rough grazing areas, traditional hay meadows and sus-tainably managed remnant oak woodlands. These remnant habitats were highly valued by tourists who, in turn, helped maintain/improve economic capital in com-munities located within the ESA. However, the study also highlighted that not all farmers within the ESA were able to benefit from participation in the ESA scheme, especially those with small farms with little room to manoeuvre. This led to psycho-logical and social tensions in local communities, and an associated weakening of social capital (see also Meert *et al.*, 2005, for the Netherlands).

More tangible evidence of beneficial impacts of policies at community level has arguably come through rural development policies associated with the EU LEADER programme (Liaisons Entre Actions de Développement de l'Economie Rurale). LEADER projects are focused specifically on providing financial assistance for small projects at community level. LEADER contains support actions which focus on support for bottom-up community development, i.e. engendering *endogenous* development potential of communities, and support for better networking and communication between rural communities (Woods, 2005). By 2007, LEADER was delivered through over 1200 local action groups in the EU's 27 member states, with funds in the order of €7 billion available between 2000 and 2007 alone (Wilson, 2007). Ray (2000) emphasized the relative success of LEADER as a policy that has generally helped raise community resilience (win-win situation), especially as implemented LEADER projects have been firmly rooted in bottom-up approaches that have involved targeted communities in decision-making processes about how projects should be implemented in order to benefit the community (Box 7.2).

Malign state policies for community resilience, meanwhile, are particularly evident when the state overtly acts *against* the interests of its citizens and local communities (Abel *et al.*, 2006; Kelkar *et al.*, 2008). Malign policies predominate in nation states with internecine struggles over territory and power, in which 'rebel' communities are perceived as enemies to the national interest (see examples mentioned above). As the critical political science literature emphasizes, such *dissonances* between state and community interests are not restricted to the developing world, as policy implementation gaps, as well as policies acting against the best interest of communities, are evident in almost all nation states (Rhodes, 1997; Jordan, 2005). Although policy dissonances usually refer to the lack of policies addressing issues linked to community needs, they can also be interpreted as gaps linked to insufficient policy learning between the state and communities (Dolowitz and Marsh, 1996; Bomberg, 2007; see also Kelkar *et al.*, 2008, for policy dissonances between the state and local communities in India). In the worst-case-scenarios, policy dissonances are a result of the state using its coercive power to implement policies *against* the will of communities – policies that can be outright damaging or lethal for communities (Grainger, 2005; Bardhan, 2006). The most prominent examples can be found in the context of autocratic one-party states, e.g. the imposition of policies upon local communities associated with the 'great leap forward' in Maoist China in the 1960s, the building of large dams (e.g. Three Gorges Dam in China, Narmada Dam in India; see Box 6.4), or the imposition of (often impossible-to-meet) agricultural production targets at village level in North Korea (Woo, 2006; Hwang *et al.*, 2007). The example of national nuclear power policies in the developed world also highlights that state coercive power can be used to override serious (and largely justified) concerns about health- and security-related issues linked to the location of nuclear power plants and nuclear waste storage sites near communities (Jordan, 2005; Pretty, 2007) (Box 7.3).

Box 7.2 The EU LEADER programme as a positive policy for raising community resilience

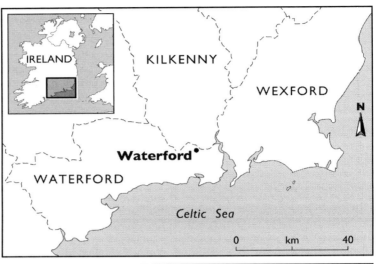

The LEADER programme is a community-driven, territorially focused policy that maximizes the retention of benefits within the local territory by valorising and exploiting both physical and human local resources. Most LEADER projects have targeted specific needs of communities, such as strengthening community-level economic capital through the promotion of rural tourism (*c.*30 per cent of LEADER projects EU-wide), by adding value to agricultural production through local branding initiatives or other initiatives emphasizing the value of locally pro-duced food (*c.*15 per cent of projects), or by supporting small firms and craft industries already located in rural communities (*c*.12 per cent of projects). In addition, some LEADER projects have focused on strengthening social capital at community level by focusing on training and human development initiatives (*c*.10 per cent of projects). Most projects have jointly targeted the strengthening of economic and environmental capital, such as the introduction of green forestry engineering techniques based on the use of endogenous resources and natural materials to help revitalize local forestry cooperatives (e.g. village of Garfagnana, Italy). Apart from improving environmental capital by encouraging the planting of local species (e.g. improvements in local biodiversity levels), the Garfagnana LEADER project also helped create 120 jobs, further strengthening economic capital of the community. Similarly, in the rural town of Waterford (Ireland), a LEADER project has led to the establishment of wetlands for cleaning dirty water from farmyards, as well as newly created lagoons planted with vegetation and stocked with fish. Apart from improving local environmental capital (improved water quality, improvement of biodiversity, flood protection), these schemes have also acted as a magnet for tourism, thereby simultaneously strengthening economic capital of the community (Woods, 2005).

Box 7.3 Malign state policies and the designation of nuclear waste storage sites in former West Germany

In the late 1970s, policy-makers in former West Germany were facing increasing problems with the storage of nuclear waste from German nuclear power plants. In 1977 a decision was taken to store nuclear waste in a disused salt mine near the village of Gorleben in the county of Lüchow-Dannenberg. Several factors contributed to the selection of this location. First, this county was located at the border to former East Germany (part of the Soviet power bloc at the time), which meant that any accidental nuclear fallout would most likely be blown eastwards over foreign territory (due to prevailing westerly winds). Second, due to its marginal geographical location near East Germany, the Bezirk Lüchow-Dannenberg was one of the poorest in former West Germany, and communities such as the village of Gorleben had little economic and political power to resist aggressive top-down state policies. Third, disused salt mines were, at the time, seen as ideal places to store nuclear waste due to their perceived geological stability and safety with regard to water seepages. Although there continues to be substantial debate about the advantages and disadvantages of different geological sites for nuclear waste storage, the 'malign' nature of nuclear waste policies of the German state became rapidly obvious as the salt mine later proved inadequate for the storage of highly radioactive waste, with substantial pollution and health hazards for local communities related to water seepage into and out of the nuclear waste dump since the 1980s. Not only did this lead to substantial psychological and health-related stress in affected communities (loss of environmental capital), but it also led to accelerating outmigration of community members able to find jobs elsewhere, loss of local services and the stigmatization of the entire Bezirk Lüchow-Dannenberg as a 'condemned' place (loss of social and economic capital). House prices have plummeted, and formerly close-knit (largely rural) communities have been severely negatively affected. As a result, Gorleben has become the centre of regular mass protests against the 'bullying policies' of the German state, with frequent disruption of nuclear waste transport by activists, and (so far fruitless) attempts to close the nuclear waste storage site (www.castor.de/diskus/sonst/lambke. htm; last accessed 1 February 2011).

Classic examples of confrontation and policy dissonance between negative policy corridors engendered by the state and vulnerable stakeholder groups, such as subsistence farming or hunter-gathering communities, can be found in many tropical rainforest areas (Grainger, 2005; Pretty, 2007). Chapter 5 already highlighted the example of path dependencies and political lock-ins of a hypothetical Indonesian village community, severely affected by a powerful coalition between the Indonesian state and multinational logging companies intent on profit maximization (see Section 5.4.1). In such instances forest policies linked to tax and other revenue for the state and policy officials (including payments for often corrupt state employees), as well as profits from sale of timber for the multinational company, override any local community needs (e.g. maintenance of relatively intact community forest) resulting in increased community vulnerability (Bardhan, 2006). Indeed, many instances of tropical deforestation can be interpreted as a result of malign policy corridors associated with state coercive, political and economic power used to take control over poorly mapped and legally often insecure resources located within ancestral domains of relatively powerless grassroots actors (Abel *et al.*, 2006; Lebel *et al.*, 2006).

Another example of malign policy corridors comes from a relatively unsuspecting policy domain, namely that of the EU's Common Agricultural Policy (CAP). This example of a supra-national policy corridor shows the complex interplay between supra-national, national, regional and local policy levels and associated responses by affected stakeholder groups. Evidence from a large EU-funded project into the effects of desertification processes on the survival of rural communities in northern Mediterranean countries indicated that CAP-related policies have led to substantial intensification of agriculture (see also Box 4.4). Although initially intended to help communities through the raising of economic capital (e.g. through farm modernization grants or livestock subsidies) the result has often been a substantial loss of environmental capital (desertification) through overintensive use of soils linked to policy-encouraged mechanization and overstocking. Due to inadequate understanding of local needs and local environmental conditions by policy-makers situated in far-away Brussels (where CAP policies are formulated), these policies, therefore, became malign policies for many communities, often resulting in reduced resilience based on often irreversible soil degradation and loss (Wilson and Juntti, 2005).

The latter example particularly highlights that malign policy corridors need not be *intentionally* malign, but that poorly managed policy formulation and implementation processes can turn policies formulated with good intentions into policies with negative repercussions for local community resilience (e.g. Kelkar *et al.*, 2008, for northern India; Forbes *et al.*, 2009, for arctic Russia). As a result, Aggarwal (2006, p. 1415) argued that "it is often the case that a policy change ... increases productivity of a single resource but decreases the resilience of the ecosystem in which it is embedded". Yet, the fact that many communities are often locked into specific policy corridors (see Figure 6.1) means that even if such negative effects of macro-scalar policies are becoming apparent, it may be very difficult for communities to disengage from these policy corridors (e.g. agricultural subsidy dependency of many rural actors in above CAP policy example). At times, accepting that macro-scalar policies may reduce community resilience may be a better option for a community than to 'opt out' completely from established policy corridors ('radical' community pathways outside of policy corridors shown in Figure 6.1) – actions that, ultimately, may have much worse repercussions for long-term resilience of the community.

7.3 Transitional corridors and policy challenges

This section will focus on the interlinkages between communities' policy needs and options for the state to provide such policy help. Throughout this book, it has become evident that there are complex interrelationships between community resilience predicated on well-developed economic, social and environmental capital, with the exogenous policy environment (i.e. state policies) as an enabling or disenabling process (see Section 7.2). Based on the normative approach used in this book predicated on notions of strong and weak community resilience, policy should be seen as a particularly potent mechanism for raising

resilience, especially as policy corridors can greatly contribute towards influencing – and indeed shaping – transitional pathways at community level. How can
states develop policies that help strengthen community resilience, i.e. identify
'positive' policies for community resilience?

Building on Figure 3.6 (Chapter 3), which showed challenges faced by different types of communities over space and time, Figure 7.1 highlights where and
how different exogenous policy actions may help raise community resilience.
Figure 3.6 highlighted complex transitions with regard to the gradual loss, and
possible rediscovery, of strongly resilient community pathways. These highly
differentiated processes necessitate equally differentiated policy responses. As
Chapters 4 and 5 emphasized, communities may be more or less well prepared to
address loss of resilience – in other words, resilient adaptive capacity to respond
and 'bounce back' will vary based on the severity of propelling forces and the
strength of communities' economic, social and environmental capital. While
Chapter 5 highlighted that community resilience can often be harnessed through
endogenous forces emanating from the community itself (Pretty, 1995), often
there are substantial limits as to how the local level can shape and influence
resilience trajectories. This suggests that regulation external to the community
level (usually in the shape of national policies) is often crucial in helping communities to raise resilience (Ray, 2000), although – as Section 7.2 highlighted –
the regulatory environment can both lead to increased and reduced community
resilience (Wilson, 2007, 2010). If we accept both the *normative* and *moral* goals
of increasing community resilience, several ways in which policy can be used to
influence resilience trajectories can be conceptualized. Building on Wilson
(2010), Figure 7.1 highlights that varied and often individually tailored policy
action is necessary to raise the resilience of different types of communities.

While *subsistence farming communities* show wide levels of resilience
ranging from weak to strong resilience (see Chapter 3), most subsistence farming
communities have relatively poorly developed economic capital and would often
benefit from policies aimed at enhancing such capital (i.e. financial poverty is
often the key issue) (Rigg, 2006). Ideal policy implementation in this context
would mean the development of policies that have real impact on the ground and
that do not result in weakening social and environmental capital. For many commentators, raising resilience in subsistence farming communities is largely a
response to poverty, where only complex multiple strategies will enable households and communities to survive (Parnwell, 2007). Indeed, as Chapter 3 highlighted, many subsistence farming communities would most likely be willing to
weaken social and environmental capital for the sake of increasing economic
capital in an increasingly globalized world in which monetary signifiers assume
ever more importance – processes that, as this book has highlighted in several
places, are currently leading to the rapid loss of social and environmental capital
in many 'traditional' communities. Rigg (2006, p. 195), therefore, questioned
whether policies should "be aimed at oiling and assisting the process of transformation of farmers into non-farmers, and rural people into urbanites, rather than
shoring up the livelihoods of smallholders through agricultural subsidies, land

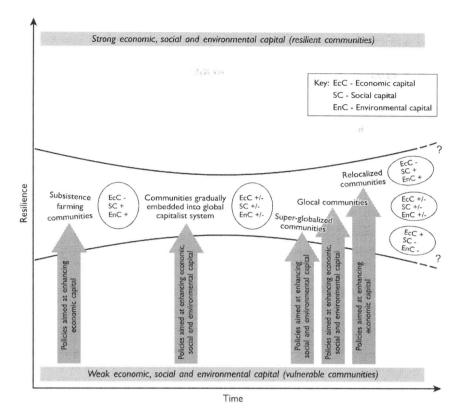

Figure 7.1 State policy and community resilience (source: author; after Wilson, 2010).

reforms, and piecemeal employment schemes"? Although asked in the context of communities in South East Asia, these questions are equally pertinent in the global North. Although the answer depends on the circumstances of individual communities, what is important is that strongly resilient pathways are becoming increasingly divorced from agricultural production in many parts of the world. While this process began in the 1950s (or earlier) in many rural districts in developed countries, Rigg (2006) has highlighted how processes of deagrarianization in the South are also increasingly calling for *more differentiated policy responses* aimed at engendering stronger resilience. Rigg *et al.* (2008) particularly argued that policies endowing rural people in the South with skills so that they can escape from farming and the countryside may be the best way forward. Community resilience in this context can be interpreted as a form of 'resistance' and coping strategy (McCarthy, 2006), where increasing *economic capital* is the ultimate goal in the first instance (Wilson, 2010). This means that opportunities need to be provided to help rural stakeholders in the global South to leave the poverty trap (especially through improved education/skills/gender roles; see Chapter 5) without jeopardizing existing resilience attributes, especially where social and environmental capital are still well developed. Yet, many of the two billion subsistence and small-scale farmers on Earth simply do not have the option to change resilience pathways and to diversify income streams away from agriculture (Pretty, 2007). Although many of these systems have retained elements of strong resilience, the policy challenge is particularly evident for these communities with regard to striking the *right balance* between economic, social and environmental capital.

Communities gradually embedded into the global capitalist system, meanwhile, will most often benefit from policies aimed at strengthening all three forms of capital (economic, social and environmental) (see Figure 7.1). The key issue for these communities is that the transitional corridor is often narrowing due to the globalization 'bottleneck' (see Chapter 3) which leads to different pressures on communities depending on historical pathways of change (see Chapter 5). For communities that have raised economic capital by being more firmly embedded into the global capitalist system, policies have to target possible loss of social and environmental capital (see case study example of Indonesia in Chapter 5). Other communities, meanwhile, may have improved environmental and social capital through globalization processes, but will need policy help to raise economic capital. 'Ideal' policy scenarios for communities gradually embedded into the global capitalist system should, therefore, mean providing help for resilience pathways away from overdependence on monofunctional production pathways (e.g. often engendered by increased dependency on external agents such as multinational corporations). In other words, state-led policy corridors for 'managed globalization' could ensure a smooth(er) transition of these communities towards (re)discovery of strong resilience (Bardhan, 2006).

Required policy action is even more complex for hybrid community pathways on the right-hand side of Figure 7.1. Here, state policies should be particularly concerned with helping to increase resilience in *super-globalized communities* by enhancing social and environmental capital (e.g. through targeted social and conservation policies). Cynics would argue, however, that the dominance of both neo-liberal mindsets and globalized lifestyles in these communities makes it difficult for state policy to effect large changes in people's actions (Barr, 2008). For *glocal communities*, meanwhile, all three forms of capital may need support. Some commentators argue that glocal communities may be the most interesting in the context of policy corridors, as policy action may have the most pronounced effects in these communities as only relatively 'small' changes in the direction and shape of policy corridors may have large impacts in these communities (e.g. policies aimed at reinvigoration of economic capital after loss of agricultural base, or strengthening social capital in peri-urban counter-urbanized commuter settlements). Many *relocalized communities*, on the other hand, will already be on endogenous pathways of 'rediscovery' of environmental and social capital (see Chapter 5), but may need policy help with (re)invigorating economic capital. However, as endogenous resilience pathways are usually well developed in these communities (see Chapters 4 and 5), commentators have argued that it may be more difficult for these communities to accept the need for external policy influence, even if such policies aim at enhancing community resilience (Bailey *et al.*, 2010).

The policy situation is further complicated by the fact that a complex 'geography of policy corridors' exists in which certain communities will have more opportunities to implement strongly resilient pathways than others. For example, policy-makers will find it easier to implement targeted policies aimed at raising economic and environmental capital in communities in scenically attractive areas (e.g. EU LEADER programme; see above) (Clark, 2006; Wilson, 2007). Similarly, more policy opportunities for raising economic and social capital usually exist in communities in the peri-urban fringe (Vandermeulen *et al.*, 2006). Super-globalized communities caught in the capitalist treadmill, meanwhile, often have more limited access to policies aimed at raising resilience, exacerbated by the fact that neo-liberal agendas often dictate economic processes in these communities and tend to favour market rather than policy solutions (Castree, 2008a, 2008b). This suggests the existence of a *vicious circle* where communities with already stronger resilience (e.g. in tourist areas) usually have access to more policy opportunities to increase resilience than vulnerable communities who often only have the option of further reinforcing monofunctional super-globalized pathways (Marsden, 2003; Wilson, 2010). This highlights that understanding the synergies between policy corridors and communities is key to understanding the interaction between policy opportunities and community resilience.

It is also evident that the debate about the need for targeted policy corridors for community resilience increasingly transcends boundaries between the global North and South. Rigg *et al.* (2008), in particular, have shown through their case study of deagrarianized (glocal) communities in South East Asia that the differentiation between policy needs of communities in the North and South is increasingly artificial, and that resilience transitions are converging across the world. The temporal coexistence of super-globalized and relocalized communities, in particular, suggests that policy corridors have to widen at global level to address complex and multiple needs of highly varied communities with regard to strengthening economic, social and environmental capital. This is particularly true with regard to simultaneous policy needs of communities characterized by environmentally and socio-culturally problematic deepening of vulnerability pathways (e.g. super-globalized communities) and the fostering of concurrent new opportunities for the 'rediscovery' of strongly resilient pathways in *both* the global North and South.

The nature and shape of policy corridors influencing resilience of diverse communities is, ultimately, also linked to *moral* judgements about the importance of state policies in shaping human action (Dryzek, 1997). While normative judgements about community resilience pathways can form important baselines for defining the shape and nature of such policy corridors, the situation is complicated by the fact that the 'right balance' between economic, social and environmental capital will mean different things to different people (and especially to policy-makers), and that the notion of resilience is closely associated with notions of *power* within and beyond communities (see Chapter 5). While neo-liberals would argue for less impact of policies and that communities should use endogenous capacities to raise resilience, those believing that the state has a role to play in shaping individual behaviour will place greater emphasis on policy corridors as key influences for raising community resilience, in turn affecting policy-makers' perceptions of core social and political values (Jones, 1997). The final outcome with regard to the impacts of the embeddedness of communities within policy corridors defined by state policy will, therefore, depend on issues of governance, transparency, corruption and the willingness of both policy-makers and community members to work together for 'the greater good' of raising community resilience.

7.4 Policies for community resilience as a win-win situation or zero-sum-game?

This chapter has so far highlighted the importance of policy corridors for shaping resilience at community level. It has also highlighted that state policies can have both positive and negative effects for community resilience, and that many state policies may not always aim at improving levels of resilience for all its citizens (especially in non-democratic countries) (Johnston, 1996). However, Section 7.3 also highlighted that in most countries the assumption underlying state policy goals has to be that there is an intrinsic interest by the state to help its citizens to strengthen economic, social and environmental capital (Hall, 1993; Dryzek, 1997). If we accept this moral assumption, is it possible for state policy to raise resilience of all communities simultaneously (win-win situation), or is the raising of resilience levels in some communities predicated on loss of resilience in others (zero-sum-game)? This section will analyse whether it is possible for all societies to improve resilience levels, or whether trade-offs have to be made accepting that the concurrent weakening of some capitals is inevitable. The focus throughout will be on different (and similar) challenges faced by communities in the global North and South. Section 7.4.1 will ask whether resilience pathways can be seen as a global win-win scenario, while Section 7.4.2 will analyse policy and common drivers influencing community resilience at global level.

7.4.1 Resilience pathways as a global win-win scenario?

The previous chapters highlighted that the increasing embeddedness of most communities into the global capitalist system may make it difficult for communities to simultaneously strengthen economic, social and environmental capital. Indeed, the complex interplay of strengthening and weakening capitals at community levels discussed throughout this book already emphasized that the strengthening of one capital (e.g. economic) may be at the expense of weakening another (e.g. environmental; see Chapter 5). *Globalization*, in particular, was identified as often strengthening economic capital while, on the other hand, weakening social and environmental capital (see Figures 3.6 and 7.1). Globaliza-tion may, therefore, amplify resilience processes leading to a zero-sum-game in which 'global average resilience' (if this could be estimated) remains broadly at the same level. Chapters 5 and 6 also highlighted that *relocalized* resilience path-ways may also not necessarily produce a win-win situation, as the strengthening of social and environmental capital in these communities is often undertaken at the expense of economic capital (Hopkins, 2008; Bailey *et al.*, 2010). This begs the question whether achieving a global-level win-win situation with regard to raising community resilience is at all possible.

The previous chapters have also emphasized that strengthening community resilience is highly scale-dependent. Chapters 4 and 5, in particular, highlighted that it may be easier to strengthen community resilience at the local and regional levels, while the discussion of transitional corridors in Chapter 6 suggested that trade-offs become inevitable at national, let alone supra-national levels. The more 'open' a system under investigation, therefore, the less likely it will be that community resilience can be raised across the board (Cutter *et al.*, 2008). Yet, as Section 7.2 emphasized, it is at the national and supra-national levels that state policy corridors become particularly important, either as enabling or disenabling forces. This makes it more likely that national state policy corridors result in a zero-sum-game situation – or even worse, lead to a gradual loss of community resilience through misguided policies – than would locally targeted policies.

These questions assume particular relevance if we consider potential differ-ences in community resilience potentials between the global North and South. Does strengthening resilience in communities of the developed world rely on weakening resilience in communities of the developing world? In other words, is the raising of economic, social and environmental capital in communities of the global North dependent on a weakening of these capitals in the context of the global South through overexploitation of resources, abuse of unequal North–South power relations, and neo-colonial tendencies predicated on the continuing assumption that the global North has a 'moral right' to exploit people and resources in the South? Are transitional corridors in the global South, therefore, different from those in the North? If the latter was the case, who should manage a policy-led transition towards stronger resilience in *both* the North and South (see Section 7.5.2)? Considering the weak power of the UN and the absence of a global Leviathan directing global policies (Johnston, 1996; Wilson and Bryant, 1997), is national policy robust enough to address issues of unequal resilience opportunities (zero-sum-game) across the globe?

Two key state-led policy corridors may be particularly relevant in this context. First, as Section 7.3 highlighted, policies in the global South may have to focus on *preventing* further loss of resilience at community level, especially in communities gradually embedded into the global capitalist system and increas-ingly 'squeezed' in their decision-making options through globalization proc-esses. Second, policies in the developed world may have to focus more on the *rediscovery* of strongly resilient pathways. As both Figures 3.6 and 7.1

highlighted, more options within transitional corridors may be available in the future for both the North and South because of widening future decision-making opportunities that may include many different resilience pathways. However, we also need to acknowledge that this may occur on the back of relatively *narrow* transitional potential at present, as increasing numbers of communities are caught in the globalization treadmill. The widening of the transitional corridor in future may, therefore, herald a *rediscovery* of strong(er) resilience based on a win-win situation, depending on how and by whom these new transitional opportunities are 'managed' (see below).

Most crucially, developed and developing countries may still be at different temporal points in transitional corridors affecting resilience. Most communities in the global South may have, so far, only undergone the first part of the transitional pathway highlighted in Figure 7.1 and are heading for the 'globalization squeeze' in the near future. Most communities in advanced economies, meanwhile, have been affected by globalization processes for much longer and are now beginning to re-evaluate policy (and community-based) approaches for raising community resilience (see Section 7.3). This suggests that there may also be an inherent temporality in the question whether strengthening community resilience based on a win-win scenario is possible at global level, especially considering the still pronounced differences in resilience pathways between communities in the North and the South. Davidson (2010, p. 1143), therefore, argued that "a given social system can purposefully postpone the effects of ecological disruption to itself either in space or in time, leading to greater disruption being imposed on people elsewhere or elsewhen". This is further complicated by the fact that it will also be difficult to identify appropriate policy corridors at global level that help create more *open-minded societies* that see the strengthening of community-level resilience as key for future survival at a time of complex and accelerating environmental transitions. This is particularly problematic as many communities in the global South still aim to 'catch up' with wealthier communities in the North, and do not currently foresee the importance of resilience-enhancing processes such as relocalization (e.g. China) (Diamond, 2006). This means that few societies have yet made the *mental* adjustments towards recognizing the need for stronger resilience (Wilson, 2008, 2010).

However, it would be problematic to imply that communities in the developing world *inevitably* follow resilience transitions observed in the developed world. While some of the temporal characteristics between the developed and developing world share commonalities (with growing similarities due to globalization processes; see Chapters 3 and 5), differences in political and regulatory environments guiding resilience pathways (e.g. stronger role of policy in the developed world), differing moral and ideological values, differing governance and social structures, and varying environmental capital facilitating/hindering community development processes, also mean that the nature and shape of community transitions in the developing world will often take a different pathway (Rigg, 2006; Parnwell, 2007). This means that the possible gap between the *appearance* of different community-level resilience transitions, and the underpinning *ideology* or *mindset* between North and South need to be considered. Policy-led strongly resilient community pathways in a Northern country may mirror resilience appearances in a community of the South in terms of empirics, but the logics that produce these systems may be inherently different. This suggests that 'new' or 'rediscovered' resilience in the South is often different not only in terms of propelling or moulding forces, but also in terms of the logics that underpin emerging systems (Wilson, 2008). It is, therefore, not clear yet whether new, qualitatively different, resilience pathways may emerge in communities of the global South. However, what is less contested is that the key resilience trajectories in today's (and tomorrow's) world are largely associated with *developing* countries, as it is here that we find the majority of the world's agricultural population (over two billion overall) living in communities whose resilience characteristics are currently undergoing the most rapid changes. While loss of resilience equally impacts all communities in the world, the potential (further) loss of resilience in communities in the developing world will affect many more people and their adaptive capacity to deal with external disturbances (Pretty, 1995, 2002).

7.4.2 Policy and common drivers influencing community resilience at global level

Socio-political developments over the past few decades have highlighted that, increasingly, global-level resilience drivers need to be taken into account that may impact *equally* on both communities in the North and South. In this section I wish to explore whether we can identify common drivers for change in raising community resilience at global level and whether policy can help achieve global-level strongly resilient communities based on a win-win situation.

Any discussion of global-level community resilience pathways needs to take into account *resilience interdependencies* between countries and territories. Although the nation state still provides the platform for implementation of policy corridors affecting community resilience in both North and South (see Section 7.2), national-level resilience is highly dependent on the movement of energy and goods in and out of a country. This can be referred to as the *global spatiality* of resilience processes, highlighting the importance of conceiving community-level resilience pathways as composed of all individual parts of a wider system, including globalized flows of energy and goods. Chapter 5 already discussed the interlinkages between food dependency and community resilience (e.g. in the context of the TTM), and food policy provides a good example to highlight issues related to resilience as either a zero-sum-game or a win-win situation, especially in the context of environmental capital at community level. Indeed, the import of food from another country may reduce resilience in the exporting country as cash crops produced for the global market may displace local foods and thereby reduce local resilience by weakening environmental capital (Marsden, 2003; Aggarwal, 2006). Although interactions between territories will often be complex (i.e. cash crop production may also increase economic capital of the exporting community, thereby raising resilience levels), these global inter-actions may mean that a community may be able to maintain relatively strong levels of resilience (e.g. well-developed local environmental capital not predi-cated on productivist farming) because policies encourage the import of food and fibre from less resilient productivist communities. Indeed, exporting produc-tivist communities may follow a pathway of weaker resilience precisely because their agricultural systems are predicated on intensive export-oriented food and fibre production, making them more vulnerable to the vicissitudes of global agri-cultural markets (Wilson, 2007, 2008). As a consequence, the reduction in agri-cultural productivity in one community can be *neutralized* through increased imports of food from elsewhere.

Communities in the UK (usually not self-sufficient) and Kenya (food exporter) may be interesting examples to invoke in this context. The former communities have often been able to maintain strong environmental capital through extensification of agricultural production (especially in upland and agri-culturally more marginal areas), while the latter has been characterized by com-munities increasingly embedded into globalized agro-commodity chains predicated on mass-produced and often environmentally harmful production of specific products (e.g. 'mange-tout') for the European market (Barrett *et al.*, 1999; Mertz *et al.*, 2005). Relatively high levels of resilience predicated on strong environmental capital in communities in the UK may only have been pos-sible due to policies enabling food imports from countries such as Kenya that may have weakening environmental capital as a result. Another example relates to Japan's role as an 'ecopredator', whereby many Japanese communities have managed to maintain strong environmental capital (Japan has over 60 per cent forest cover) based on overexploitation of forest resources elsewhere in the world (Turner *et al.*, 1990) (see also Chapter 2). In these specific contexts, global community resilience may, therefore, only be a *zero-sum-game*, characterized by 'resilience competition' in which strongly and weakly resilient territories 'balance each other out', rather than a win-win scenario in which all communi-ties can simultaneously move towards stronger resilience. This suggests that it may only be possible to implement strongly resilient pathways in one commu-nity *at the expense* of other territories.

It is evident, however, that global-level influences on community resilience cannot be fully understood without considering the rising importance of macro-scalar policy corridors emanating from supra-national decision-making frame-works that increasingly influence community resilience constraints and opportunities. As Potter and Tilzey (2005) argued, the role of the state as a 'pro-tector' of national interests is increasingly undermined by neo-liberal globaliza-tion. Two policy arenas are particularly interesting in this context: the rising importance of WTO policies and policies associated with climate change.

The rising importance of WTO discussions needs to be particularly acknowl-edged, as these debates are increasingly shaping ideological and practical approaches of national policies shaping community-level resilience. The WTO aims to regulate global trade flows through policy decisions affecting specific goods and specific countries (i.e. regulations on the flow of products across nation-state boundaries). WTO negotiations influence policy decisions at the nation-state level (e.g. in the context of agricultural products in recent CAP reforms, agricultural pathways within Cairns Group countries) which, in turn, influence decision-making pathways at community level (Potter and Burney, 2002). Yet, many commentators have highlighted the continuing lack of a 'global Leviathan' that dictates what nation states should do (Wilson and Bryant, 1997). This makes it difficult to conceptualize resilience needs at the global level, as it continues to be unclear *whose* resilience is advocated in these policies (e.g. that of the EU, the Cairns Group, the WTO, the United Nations, or even just the G8 countries?). The influence of the supra-national level of decision-making influencing community-level resilience at national level is, therefore, highly complex and influence will vary greatly depending on specific policy contexts (e.g. whether suggested policy change 'fits' broadly with national policy goals), the coercive powers underlying supra-national policy suggestions, and the general willingness and approach of a nation state to work towards 'the greater good' (i.e. by adopting policies encouraging more strongly resilient community-level pathways) beyond narrow needs and expectations of the nation state and its citizens (Bardhan, 2006). There is increasing evidence that WTO policies have a highly differential impact upon community resilience, for example by favouring certain trade arrangements over others, and by being highly dependent on power balances within WTO trading networks (Aggarwal, 2006). Potter and Burney (2002) and Potter and Tilzey (2005) have particularly emphasized that WTO trade agreements often have negative impacts for poorer communities in the global South, while communities in the North have often benefited from targeted policies favouring trading needs of industrialized countries (zero-sum-game).

As Adger (2003) highlighted, the situation is even more complex with regard to how local communities are affected by climate change policies. Again, evidence tends to suggest that the notion of zero-sum-game is a more apt description of the current situation, and that a win-win scenario is still a far away goal (e.g. Kelkar *et al.*, 2008, for Indian communities). The failure of the *Intergovernmental Panel on Climate Change* Copenhagen (2009) and Cancun (2010) summits has highlighted the continuing rift both between and within countries in the North and South, the predominance of selfish national interests and the lack of willingness for compromise that may jeopardize economic capital at nation-state level. The unfortunate outcome for the most vulnerable communities on the globe, such as low-lying coral atolls or communities threatened by more severe freak weather events (see Chapter 3), is that the global-level policy corridor shaped through international treaties and conventions is insufficient to safeguard their survival.

In view of the fact that global resilience transitions appear to be shaped more by a zero-sum-game scenario than by a win-win situation, how can resilience at community level be best managed at global level? The assumption underlying the normative resilience spectrum (see Chapter 2) is that strong community resilience should be seen as the 'ultimate goal' at global level, as this model can be seen as the most *moral* and *qualitatively best* type of community development (Wilson, 2010). Any discussion about managing global resilience transitions needs to be based on the assumption that the ultimate aim of any policy-maker is to either *maintain* strong resilience or to move away from weak resilience/ vulnerability towards 'rediscovery' of strong resilience. Empirical support can be given to the need for strong resilience by studies that have highlighted that if communities fail to adopt at least *some* aspects of strong resilience, their survival may be severely jeopardized (Diamond, 1998, 2006). Yet, as this section has highlighted it is far from established whether resilience transitions are a zero-sum-game or whether there is a possibility for global-level strong resilience based on a win-win situation in which *all* communities may be able to adopt strongly resilient pathways. As Marsden (2003, p. 27) emphasized,

> it would seem that valued consumption spaces need to continuously devalue other spaces in order to reproduce more sensitive capital accumulation ... In this sense globalization and deregulation tend to redistribute risks and power, making it easier in one place to extract value only at the expense of other places.

A headlong rush towards strong global resilience may not only be unrealistic, but may defy complex social systems of self-organization within often only *gradually* changing equilibriums. Echoing Beck (1992), achieving global-level strong resilience at community level may only be possible through a combination of social iteration, pragmatism and, above all, reflexive policies across the resilience/vulnerability spectrum.

7.5 Managing global resilience transitions

Section 7.4 has highlighted the importance of understanding whether resilience pathways can be conceived of as global win-win scenarios, and how policy corridors are interrelated with common drivers influencing community resilience at global level. Building on these discussions, the aim of Section 7.5 is two-fold: first, it will analyse in more detail the role of policy in the global resilience transition (Section 7.5.1) and, second, it will ask who should orchestrate this global resilience transition (Section 7.5.2) – questions inevitably interlinked with complex moral, ideological and normative standpoints that are key to understanding the barriers for raising resilience at community level.

7.5.1 The role of policy in the global resilience transition

This book has emphasized throughout that global resilience trajectories are often on a *downward* trend. How can the transition from weak to moderate to strong resilience be encouraged and what should be the role of policy in this transition? There are two key problems associated with the management of global resilience transitions. First, in areas where policy can actively shape the direction of transitional pathways, a key issue revolves around the definition of the 'correct' direction of policy corridors. In particular, *who* is to be in charge of defining the boundaries of the policy corridor? As Section 7.2 highlighted, most state-led policies affecting resilience (in both developed and developing countries) have tended to operate within relatively narrow margins of transitional potential, and state policy in advanced economies has often encouraged weak resilience. Policy formulated and implemented by state-related actors has often been a key driver for weak resilience pathways at community level, rather than a solution for the rediscovery or maintenance of strong resilience (e.g. Wilson and Juntti, 2005, for the Southern European context).

Second, as Section 7.4 highlighted, many of the resilience transitions conceptualized from a Northern-centric viewpoint do not necessarily resonate well with the experience in the South (Wilson and Rigg, 2003). As highlighted in Chapters 4 and 5, in many regions of the developing world, strongly resilient community pathways have evolved independently of external policies or actors, often predicated on the embeddedness of community members within almost exclusively local networks. Yet, with the increasing importance of state regulation influencing community resilience in even the most remote areas of the globe, resilience in many communities is increasingly shaped by external forces. Achieving strong resilience will, therefore, only be possible through a complete re-thinking of state-community interactions. In the North and, increasingly, in many communities of the South such re-thinking will need to be based on policy corridors facilitating *relocalization* of decision-making pathways. As Chapter 3 emphasized, relocalization will particularly help contribute towards increased socioeconomic 'retention capacity' of communities based on strong social and environmental capital (Bailey *et al.*, 2010) and will also counteract increasing 'place neutrality' engendered by globalized pathways of change – strongly resilient characteristics still evident in many communities of the developing world that have not yet been impelled to 'delocalize' (Wilson, 2008). Clark (2006) termed such relocalization processes 'neo-endogenous' developments that mobilize local social and economic capital, closely associated with Marsden's (2003) notion of the 'new associationalism' that emphasizes the (re)connection of local stakeholders with their local/regional communities, and linked to potential for rediscovery of (an often lost) 'cultural repertoire' (Pretty, 1995, 2002). In many regions of the developing world, these neo-endogenous developments should be associated with changes in governance structures that enable local self-organizing systems – referred to as 'adaptive governance' by Folke (2006). Such developments are already encouraged in some regions through international institutions and national or international environmental NGOs (Pretty, 1995), and may be indicative of a win-win situation with regard to a large-scale strengthening of community-level resilience (see Section 7.4).

In the context of food dependencies and resilience, the notion of relocalization is also closely associated with the idea of 'foodsheds' based on sustainable agro-food systems within bioregions (see Figure 5.2), i.e. self-reliant, locally or regionally based food systems comprised of diversified farms using sustainable practices to supply healthier food to small-scale locally embedded processors and consumers to whom producers are linked by the bonds of community as well as economy (Hopkins, 2008; Robinson, 2008). In this context, policy corridors should encourage the emergence of more diverse commercial opportunities in communities in both the developing and developed world derived from urban and some international markets, for example through certification, branding, payments for ecosystem services or diversification in demand for indigenous products (Barrett *et al.*, 1999; Pretty, 2002). All of these can help engender (more) strongly resilient community pathways, which suggests that, in theory, the evolution of relocalized strongly resilient systems should not only be possible in marginal areas distant from major population centres, but also in agricultural foodsheds close to large conurbations. But, as Chapter 5 highlighted, relocalization should also go well beyond mere shortening of food chains and should also include the spatial and social *reconnection* between agricultural and rural/urban activities, communities and food consumers. In this way, relocalization processes may hold the potential to reinforce social and environmental interactions within communities as major agents in sustaining economy and culture. However, the notion of strongly resilient communities predicated on relocalization processes is not synonymous with *reification* of the 'local' as a spatial configuration that is ontologically given, but is rather a contingent outcome of dynamic processes of socio-spatial change necessary for a shift (back) towards/ or maintenance of strongly resilient community pathways (Winter, 2003; DuPuis and Goodman, 2005). Caution is, therefore, needed about assuming that relocalization is necessarily associated with 'positive' outcomes and the global with the often 'negative' universal.

It is also evident that the encouragement of relocalization does not resonate so obviously with many communities in the South – as the discussion in Section 7.3 of how to 'target' policies at specific types of communities has highlighted. It could be argued, for example, that there needs to be considerable demographic turbulence and livelihood transition in poor districts before transitions towards, or regulated maintenance of, relocalized pathways are possible. At the moment, the South is, in large part, agrarian and there needs to be the absorption of 'surplus' rural populations into urban/industrial sectors and spaces before the rural population that remain can entertain such a relocalized reconnection with their environment, social networks and local foodsheds (Parnwell, 2007). In this context, Rigg (2006) suggested that the richer 'developing' countries of East Asia (particularly South Korea and Taiwan) could provide interesting case studies in the future where such processes may be possible without substantial implications for livelihoods and associated potential loss of community resilience.

Bearing these important caveats in mind, it is, nonetheless, evident that a new contract between the state (and associated state-led policy corridors) and communities may have to be established or, as Goodman and Watts (1997) suggested, new forms of institutionalization, regulation and spatialization become significant in the uneven development of spaces of resilience. Bryant's (2005) notion of 'moral capital' is particularly relevant for the latter, as is the concept of a 'moral contract' guiding wider community development issues (Neal, 2009). Indeed, the rediscovery of strong resilience has to be an inherently *moral process*. Only if the moral capital of a community, region or country is such that envisioning strong resilience becomes a tangible goal, is it likely that policy action for the implementation of strong resilience will follow at *both* local and national level. As various studies have highlighted, identification of 'best practice' through mutual community visits, for example, may be one way to strengthen the moral capital of a community, as it is here that actors see positive examples of how strongly resilient pathways have been adopted by their neighbours (also across the North–South divide). Indeed, various commentators have highlighted how many communities have much to learn from (still) strongly resilient communities in the developing world in which strong local embeddedness and horizontal communication flows within community members are key ingredients for survival and sustainable environmental management (Pretty, 1995, 2002; see Figure 7.1). It is through these processes that a possible 'snowballing' of moral values underpinning strong resilience may be most effectively promulgated. Managing the transition towards strong(er) resilience, therefore, relies on a series of *interconnected actions* that, due to their complexity regarding temporal characteristics, spatial and scale-dependent processes and multilayered actor levels, will be difficult to implement.

7.5.2   *Who should orchestrate the global resilience transition?*

Above discussion has highlighted that the final key question is whether policy corridors associated with state-led policy regulation of resilience transitions are the best approach, or whether other stakeholders and different forms of transition management and governance need to be found to implement strongly resilient processes? Further, can and should strong resilience be *orchestrated* at all (e.g. through appropriate state-led policy corridors) or should resilience transitions have a life of their own? In other words, should the state (and its associated polices and institutions) be alone in its role of managing resilience transitions (Pretty, 2007)? These questions are particularly important in communities of the developing world in which the state has traditionally played a limited role (or none at all) in shaping resilience pathways (see Section 7.2). As Marsden and Sonnino (2005, p. 29; original emphasis) rightly argued in the context of rural community resilience, there is an inherent risk that current academic thinking has "led social science researchers into an implicit belief that the state *can* be conducive and empowering with regard to rural development". Indeed, where the state has had large influence over community resilience, Section 7.2 highlighted that the outcome has often been a weakening of resilience with often disastrous consequences for economic, social and environmental capital (e.g. Woo, 2006; Hwang *et al.*, 2007). However, as Chapters 4 and 5 highlighted, building strong community resilience is often an *endogenous* process linked to local customs that, at times, may operate, change and influence decision-making outside of the state policy realm and that builds on existing customary policy-independent strong resilience pathways.

But can community-level actors be left alone to guide their own resilience pathways without interference from the state? In many instances (especially in the developed world) the answer would be negative, as individuals will often tend to put personal profit before adoption of strongly resilient pathways for 'the greater good' (Granovetter, 1985; see case study examples in Chapter 5). Yet, as Figure 7.1 (above) highlighted, localized communities in the South, operating largely independently from exogenous forces and actors, have also often led to strongly resilient pathways. There may, thus, be clear differences between the role of policy in networked and policy-led resilience transitions in the North and in the more 'nucleated' resilience networks in the South. Clark's (2006) study is enigmatic of policy processes in the developed world by highlighting the complexity of actor groups involved in implementing policies encouraging community-level resilience pathways at the regional level (his list of actors for a region in the UK covers two entire pages!) and, linked to political and knowledge barriers, the often contradictory goals pursued by individual stakeholder groups and the marginalization of what he termed 'peripheral organizations' (see also Wilson and Juntti, 2005, for similar patterns in Southern Europe).

Yet, it is becoming increasingly evident that adoption of strong resilience pathways by individual stakeholders would almost always imply a reduction in personal wealth – or, in the case of developing countries, the forsaking of potential increased wealth associated with adoption of weak(er) resilience pathways predicated on increased embeddedness into global capitalist development pathways (Wilson, 2008). Is it, therefore, possible that individuals would be willing to altruistically adopt (or maintain) strongly resilient pathways for the sake of their wider community if they had the option to increase personal profits by lowering community-level resilience (e.g. by overexploiting community-level environmental capital)? Current evidence would suggest that this is not the case as, given the opportunity, individuals often choose trajectories that take them away from strong resilience (e.g. Barr, 2008). Clark (2006) further emphasized that some stakeholder groups have clear vested interests that make them actively support weakly resilient strategies, which may be particularly true for the growing global power of corporate retailers or multinational corporations who increasingly influence and shape consumer demand, purchasing powers and, ultimately, many community development pathways around the globe. Irrespective of initiatives such as the TTM and other relocalization attempts (see Chapters 4 and 5), increasing intensification and globalization of individual life, and associated economic pressures for households to seek maximum profits, tends to suggest that non-state-led individual transition management towards strong resilience is unlikely (Turner, 2009).

As Lebel *et al.* (2006) argued, this suggests that some external regulation of resilience transitions may be needed and that the state has to play at least *some* role in guiding and influencing the transition towards strong community resilience. In the developed world this would usually mean a *continuing* role for state policy, while in many developing world countries this may mean a *new* role for policy to prevent loss of community resilience. Calls for strong state support have not only come from anti-neo-liberalist authors such as Losch (2004), but also from those advocating strong locally grounded sustainability pathways (e.g. Pretty, 1995). Yet, as Clark (2006) emphasized with reference to regional-level resilience, a combination between state- and grassroots-led approaches appears to offer the best solution, in particular as a much wider range of actors is now involved in interpreting and producing resilient pathways at community level in both the developed and developing world. This is important regarding the definition of the shape and direction of policy corridors (see Figure 6.1). Identification of external boundaries of policy corridors and the general direction of this corridor should not be left to state-related actors alone, but should also include non-state actors – especially if these actors have encouraged and implemented strongly resilient pathways independent of regulatory policies and state interference in the past. Indeed, and as Cumming *et al.* (2006, pp. 8–9) argued, "centralized institutions frequently lack the necessary multiscale outlook and associated flexibility to solve ... problems ... that occur at scales that they are not used to considering [e.g. community-level scale]". In return, grassroots actors should not be the only ones defining transitional trajectories for their localities, but should coordinate their actions and aspirations with the needs of wider society. This means that the governance of resilience pathways should be *inclusive, deliberative* and *open*, involving as many actors and stakeholders in society as possible. Pretty (1995) emphasized the importance of 'trust' in such transitional processes, both within communities and between different segments of society. Yet, the problem with much community-level research is that it has often poorly understood the nature of 'indigenous' and local people's knowledge (see Rival, 2009, for a good discussion). This means that local (or relocalized) processes are still often associated by many in the scientific community with notions of 'primitive' and 'unscientific'.

Ideally, and as advocates of ecological modernization tend to argue (e.g. Mol, 2003), policy should help in guiding individual actions within agreed transitional corridors, and should act as a facilitator of strongly resilient pathways at different spatial scales, rather than as a strongly regulatory framework that, through its lack of inclusivity, has often engendered weak(er) resilience based on crude 'one-size-fits-all' approaches. Thus, "resilience-based approaches to the development of management solutions offer an important alternative to 'command and control'" (Cumming *et al.*, 2005, p. 985). In other words, resilience is not 'made' and does not emerge out of a vacuum, but it is transferred through complex processes of policy and other exchanges between communities and wider society. A highly differentiated policy approach for resilience transitions will, therefore, be needed (Wilson, 2010). In some societies, more grassroots-led initiatives may continue to work well (especially where local resilience processes predominate), while in more networked and globalized communities more regulatory approaches may be needed. The latter will be particularly important if there is evidence of autochthonous state-independent processes towards weaker resilience trajectories. This may, for example, be the case in some Mediterranean countries (Wilson and Juntti, 2005), in some developing countries at the cusp of full integration into the global capitalist market (e.g. China, Malaysia, Brazil) with concurrent threatened loss of community resilience (Cartier, 2001; Chakrabarti and Cullenberg, 2003) or in Eastern Europe where commentators have highlighted the inability of the state to fully control societal transitional processes (e.g. Pavlinek and Pickles, 2000; Stiglitz, 2002). More regulatory approaches will also be important in countries with weak governance structures (e.g. current Iraq, Haiti, Libya) or where specific elites control most of the local decision-making powers often in close symbiosis with 'governmental' interests (e.g. North Korea, Myanmar, Syria) (Wilson and Bryant, 1997; Forsyth, 2003).

7.6 Conclusions

This chapter has discussed the complex interlinkages between community resilience and the policy challenge, linked especially to the notion of state-led policy corridors. It was highlighted that macro-scalar policy corridors can often stifle 'positive' community-level attempts at strengthening resilient pathways, although state policy can act as both a benign and malign force for community resilience. The situation is further complicated by the fact that different types of communities have very different policy needs for raising community resilience, and these needs are not always compatible between communities in the global North and South. Policy-led resilience transitions may, therefore, result in a global zero-sum-game rather than a win-win situation, and it appears unlikely that it will be possible to raise resilience of all communities at global level simultaneously in the near future. Indeed, in many instances, raising resilience in one locality inevitably leads to increased vulnerability in another. Moral questions were, therefore, raised as to who should be in charge of managing the global resilience transition. It was highlighted throughout that cultural, political and economic differences between nation states and between communities themselves makes it difficult to identify 'appropriate' stakeholder groups who should be in charge of orchestrating policies encouraging stronger resilience at community level.

8 Conclusions

The rationale for this book was based on current gaps in our knowledge about resilience, especially linked to limited work on *social resilience* at *community level* (i.e. geographically bounded communities) which formed the scalar focus of the book. Indeed, many have argued that it is important to understand resilience at the local level first, before scaling up to regional, national and global environmental decision-making levels. The book was also based on the premise that there is insufficient understanding of interlinkages between resilience and anthropogenic slow-onset hazards such as socio-political or economic change, and a lack of information about the complex interplay between community resilience and different forms of economic, social and environmental capital. As a result, the book provided a novel analytical framework for assessing community resilience and environmental transitions based on notions of economic, social and environmental capital and how these may help conceptualize social resilience at community level. Different characteristics of community resilience and vulnerability were discussed, and the complexity of interactions of different characteristics that make up a resilient community were highlighted. In particular, the complex interlinkages between economic, social and environmental characteristics were discussed as a basis for understanding environmental transitions over time, and scalar issues for understanding community resilience were analysed, especially in the context of communities as relatively 'open' systems. The book also provided a critical discussion of possible methodologies to assess community resilience, highlighting that multi-method approaches that combine quantitative and qualitative approaches are best to assess the complex interlinkages between resilience and community-level decision-making.

The book argued that due to the relative novelty of the research field of social resilience, theoretical discussions about processes, drivers and indicators of social resilience are not yet fully developed (Adger, 2000; Davidson, 2010). The aim of the book was, therefore, to apply a transition theory approach to understand community resilience, whereby the community level was seen as the key scalar dimension enabling detailed investigation of processes affecting social resilience. The book argued that transition theory forms a useful theoretical framework for understanding how environmental pathways at community level evolve, and how resilience and vulnerability of communities change over time. Different transitional models were discussed, highlighting the complex nature of community transitions and the spatial and temporal heterogeneity associated with transitional pathways. The main argument was based on the assumption that, over time, many communities around the world have lost resilience and that many have adopted transitional pathways that take them close to, or indeed beyond, resilience thresholds and tipping points. Indeed, in some cases community-based adaptive capacity to 'rebound' has been insufficiently developed due to loss of economic, social and/or environmental capital. Recently we have witnessed a bifurcation and hybridization of community development pathways, with super-globalized communities often showing low levels of resilience on the one hand, and relocalized communities attempting to re-engage with environmental practices that have raised community resilience (to some extent) on the other. Theoretical and conceptual issues linked to these complex questions will be discussed in the following section, while Section 8.2 will conclude this book by discussing opportunities for future research on community resilience.

8.1 Theoretical and conceptual considerations

Transition theory formed the conceptual framework for analysis of three interlinked transitional processes affecting community resilience: social memory, path dependency and transitional corridors. Focusing on social memory enabled a better understanding of the importance of community learning, tradition and stakeholder networks for community resilience. The book argued that all communities have specific inherent qualities shaped by the 'memory' contained within the system which may be linked to individuals and/or stakeholder groups within a community. 'Acquired memory' (how memory and learning are passed on from generation to generation to improve resilience) and 'communal memory' were identified as particularly important as the sum total of learning processes embedded in communities in the form of traditions, rites and local policies often passed on informally and orally. Yet, it was also recognized that social memory can act both as a benign and malign force in shaping community resilience.

The book argued that social memory forms a key characteristic of path dependencies influencing community resilience – endogenous pathways determining actions of the 'possible' and 'impossible' affecting community resilience. Path dependencies, therefore, often stifle the implementation of innovative pathways. In particular endogenous 'lock-in' effects at community level (structural, endogenous economic and socio-psychological lock-ins), that make certain community pathways unthinkable and impossible to implement, can be severe hindrances for raising community resilience. The book, therefore, suggested that although many communities would like to change their development trajectories and levels of resilience, they are often impeded of doing so because of path dependencies inherent in the community itself through factors such as entrenched customs, habits, conservatism, negative attitudes or lethargic behaviour. The situation is often exacerbated by the fact that transitional pathways at community level are often characterized by 'transitional ruptures' (natural catastrophes, wars, revolutions) usually associated with negative pathways (i.e. loss of resilience).

Exogenous macro-scalar 'transitional corridors', meanwhile, are shaped by national and global decision-making processes which are often negative for innovation as they automatically channel decisions into 'known' and 'already established' pathways, rather than encouraging innovative thinking 'out of the box'. The book analysed in detail the importance of macro-scalar lock-in effects external to communities and discussed how these can shape community pathways and resilience in both positive and negative ways. It was argued, for example, that political and policy-based lock-ins can raise community resilience, but can also result in increased community vulnerability. Macro-structural lock-ins, meanwhile, were described as often negative for community resilience and highlight the increasing dependence of communities in both the developed and developing world on consumer goods, energy, food and transport networks exogenous to the immediate sphere of influence of communities. Ideological lock-ins at societal level (e.g. religion, conservatism), on the other hand, were seen to act as both positive or negative processes for community resilience, while macroeconomic lock-ins (e.g. globalization, global capitalism) highlighted the increasing embeddedness of communities into global flows of capital, information and cultural exchange, often shoehorning communities into tightly demarcated transitional corridors from which it is difficult to 'escape'. This situation is exacerbated by transitional ruptures influencing macro-scalar transitional corridors (e.g. wars, energy transitions or socio-political transitions such as the post-socialist transition) and large-scale ruptures, in particular, can negatively influence community-level attempts to raise resilience.

The book then analysed the complex interlinkages between community resilience and the policy challenge. It was highlighted that macro-scalar policy corridors can often stifle 'positive' community-level attempts at strengthening resilient pathways, although state policy can act as both a benign and malign force for community resilience. The book highlighted that the situation is further complicated by the fact that different types of communities have very different policy needs for raising community resilience, and that these needs are not always compatible between communities in the global North and South. It was argued that policy-led resilience transitions may, therefore, result in a global zero-sum-game rather than a win-win situation, and that it appears unlikely that it will be possible to raise resilience of all communities at global level simultaneously in the near future. Indeed, in many instances, raising resilience in one locality may lead to increased vulnerability in another. Moral questions were, therefore, raised as to who should be in charge of managing the global resilience transition. It was highlighted throughout that cultural, political and economic differences between nation states and between communities themselves make it difficult to identify 'appropriate' stakeholder groups who should be in charge of orchestrating policies encouraging stronger resilience at community level.

Based on these approaches, the book can be seen to differ in two distinctive ways from much of the existing literature on resilience. First, the book forms a critique of often simplistic assumptions formulated in the natural science dominated literature on resilience that assumes that human systems respond in similar ways to natural systems. Instead, the book agrees with the notion that the delineation between social and environmental systems is artificial (e.g. Adger, 2003; Forbes *et al.*, 2009; Davidson, 2010) and that human systems are inherently complex, non-linear, dynamic, and often unpredictable in their quest for strengthened resilience. Most importantly, due to processes of social learning human systems can never 'return' to their initial starting point.

Second, the book used a normative and openly subjective assessment of 'good' and 'bad' community pathways. Although this subjectivity can be questioned for being 'unscientific', this approach not only helped to develop a conceptual model for understanding community resilience from an innovative angle, but also provided an explanatory tool and a normative ideal for environmental transitions at community level. The book argued that the strong resilience model is the *qualitatively* best and most *moral* model based on synergistic mutual benefits – a model that all societies should strive to rediscover (in vulnerable communities) or maintain (in resilient communities). This means that the ultimate aim of any community should be to 'move' towards or maintain strong resilience. In the long term, economic efficiency and survival of communities around the world will be *predicated* on more strongly resilient pathways – especially in view of increasingly challenging disturbances affecting communities linked to accelerating climate change and deepening globalization processes (Kelkar *et al.*, 2008; Davidson, 2010). Indeed, it could be argued that if communities fail to adopt at least *some* aspects of strong resilience, then the social and economic survival of these communities may be severely jeopardized.

However, it was also acknowledged throughout that any normative assessment of community resilience is imbued with pitfalls linked to cultural preferences, researcher embeddedness and positionalities about what constitutes 'good' or 'bad' community pathways. This was particularly acknowledged with regard to arguments linked to impacts of globalization and the global capitalist system on community pathways, as this book overtly formed a critique of how the contemporary global capitalist system and globalization processes often *negatively* affect community resilience. The book acknowledged, however, that economic productivity is not necessarily incompatible with most of the indicators that characterize strongly resilient communities, and that key to successful implementation of strongly resilient community pathways has to be striking the right balance between change that is *desirable* from a community resilience perspective and change that is realistically *feasible* from a local/regional development trajectory perspective.

Issues of positionality were particularly acute as this book (at least partly) has acted as a plaidoyer for *relocalized* strongly resilient communities. Although it was argued that relocalization can help re-empower local actors to take more control of resilient transitional corridors, it was also acknowledged that full relocalization is almost impossible in a world where most citizens are embedded globally into complex energy, food, transport and pension networks predicated on globalized flows and exchanges. Issues of positionality further became apparent in my choice of case study examples to illustrate issues of community resilience, including case studies from my own PhD conducted in New Zealand, frequent reference to the burgeoning literature on the 'Transition Town Movement' (the initiator of which was one of my PhD students) or examples taken from European projects (e.g. LEDDRA, 2011) in which I have been involved over the years. This has meant that case studies were selective and reflected my own research background, networks, research project interlinkages and personal preferences. Inevitably, this also meant that the focus of the book was more on rural than urban communities and focused more on the developed than the developing world. Nonetheless, normative judgements resulting from this approach can form important baselines for policy action, despite the fact that community resilience will mean different things to different people. Some readers will quite rightly point towards other examples and case studies that may lead to different conclusions – a process which I invite and encourage as part of using this book as a platform for further critical studies on questions surrounding environmental/societal transitions and community resilience.

8.2 Opportunities for future research on community resilience

It is evident, therefore, that further work is needed to fully unravel the intricacies of community resilience. What specific research questions, therefore, are particularly important for future researchers? In my view, there are nine arenas of research that warrant closer scrutiny.

First, echoing Adger (2000), Folke (2006) and Davidson (2010), more dialogue is needed between social and natural scientists working on questions of resilience. Indeed, resilience provides a fertile ground for interdisciplinary work, and is an ideal opportunity for researchers to leave their often discipline-specific 'silo mentality' (Brand and Jax, 2007). As Folke (2006, p. 260) highlighted, "the resilience approach provides ... for generating integrative science and interdisciplinary collaboration on issues of fundamental importance". Yet, although innovative approaches exist that attempt to bridge the chasm between natural and social research on resilience (e.g. Gunderson and Holling, 2002; Chaskin, 2008; Cutter *et al.*, 2008; Thomalla and Klocker Larsen, 2010), many attempts to understand resilience processes by natural scientists are often too reductionist and deterministic for application to human systems (Davidson, 2010). This has led some commentators (e.g. Brand and Jax, 2007, p. 10) to argue that "the original ecological dimension of resilience is about to vanish. Our impression is that recent studies increasingly stress the social, political, and institutional dimensions of resilience." Adger (2000, p. 347) further highlighted that "it is not clear whether resilient ecosystems enable resilient communities", while Davidson (2010, p. 1145) argued that "socio-ecological analyses that ignore agency ... are woefully insufficient". In particular, more work is needed that challenges the assumption that human communities move through adaptive cycles in the same way as ecological systems do – i.e. as this book has highlighted, more research is needed that focuses specifically on the importance of social memory and social learning, and that highlights that resilience in human systems is usually characterized by non-linearity, heterogeneity, multiple parallel evolutionary pathways and, at times, chaotic and unpredictable behaviour. In short, resilience work is needed that accepts that human nature can, at times, not be scientifically assessed and that resilience solutions may not always be possible (Hopkins, 2008; Demeritt, 2009).

Second, while this book has extended existing work that has attempted to conceptualize environmental/societal transitions and social resilience at the local community scale, it could not engage much with questions of regional, national or, indeed, supra-national resilience. The justification was that it is at the *local community* that resilient pathways are implemented 'on the ground' with specific and tangible resilience actions that can be methodologically assessed (with more or less success). However, scale issues were important throughout this book as communities can be conceptually treated as 'more closed' systems than analysis of regional-, national- or global-level resilience processes would permit. A key question is, for example, whether large cities with several million inhabitants can strengthen resilience across their varied urban communities characterized by large income disparities, multiculturalism and multi-ethnicity, complex resilience expectations and large scalar issues of urban transport, food and energy provision (Bulkeley and Betshill, 2003; Pelling, 2003; Thrift, 2005). Indeed, large-scale open systems have more 'escape values' with regard to both in- and outflow of people/resources, which makes analysis of the characteristics of resilience and environmental transitions increasingly complex the larger the scale of investigation – the reason why hardly any studies have attempted to analyse resilience beyond the regional level (Adger, 2000; Folke, 2006). Yet, if we want to address issues about the management of global resilience transitions addressed in Chapter 7 in more detail, inevitably future studies will have to engage more with 'larger' scales related to the nested hierarchies of resilience highlighted in Figure 2.3, although methodological and positional challenges are immense.

Third, the impact of globalization on community resilience was highlighted throughout this book. However, it was also acknowledged that answers related to the specific impacts of globalization inevitably remain incomplete, as interpretation of globalization processes is a highly subjective issue depending on the positionality and cultural embeddedness of commentators (e.g. Langhorne, 2001; Bhagwati, 2004; Read, 2004; Harvey, 2005; Aggarwal, 2006; Leichenko and O'Brien, 2008). Although globalization means more options for strengthening community resilience, interconnectedness of communities means less isolation than in the past, and communities affected by disturbances can be helped more easily from 'outside' than in the past, this book has also highlighted that disentangling the complex interlinkages between globalization processes and community-level resilience pathways is difficult. As a result, this book should be seen as a platform for further work on interconnections between globalization and community resilience in a rapidly changing world. In my view, a particularly interesting question relates to how the resilience of communities in transition economies such as China, India, Brazil or Russia will be affected by the rapid socio-economic (and possibly political) changes expected in these countries over the next decades.

Fourth, the importance of power between members of communities and between communities and other societal layers of decision-making for understanding opportunities for community resilience has been highlighted throughout. Yet, as Allen (2003) emphasized, power is relational and, therefore, a highly subjective notion whose importance and extent varies considerably within/ between communities and between nation states. As a result, many studies on resilience have shied away from in-depth analysis of interlinkages between power and resilience, and this book may be no exception although I have attempted to interweave notions of power wherever possible in the various discussions about community resilience. Further work is, therefore, particularly needed with regard to the implications of power imbalances and adaptive capacity within communities (including more in-depth historical analyses of changes in configurations of power and resilience), as well as more complex studies about how power exogenous to the community affects specific community-level resilience pathways (Swyngedouw, 2001; Derkzen *et al.*, 2008).

Fifth, the book also argued that there are differences between resilience pathways in developing and developed countries, in particular with regard to nucleated versus networked resilience processes and the potential role of policy in shaping community transitions (albeit with increasing similarities). As a result, *one* approach towards strong resilience is unlikely to be successful to address transitional issues in highly geographically, culturally, economically and historically different areas. This means that more *geographically nuanced* research is needed across the global North/South divide in future, in particular if the strengthening of resilience in some areas may engender vulnerability in others.

Sixth, the book also analysed in detail *who* should be in charge of managing the transition towards stronger community resilience. Each region and community will have different governance structures with differing opportunities for policy to act as a trigger for strengthened resilience. The solution for finding the best pathway towards stronger resilience will, therefore, be to accept that different governance structures exist, and that not one specific transitional strategy can be developed that would suit all multilayered actor spaces and power structures. This means that more work is needed on understanding such differences. Future research should particularly focus on the question whether state-led policy should act as a *facilitator*, rather than as an *orchestrator*, in resilience processes. Indeed, in many developed countries further encouragement of strong resilience may have to be predicated on strengthening and clarifying the role of *subnational* actors and organizations, while in the developing world strengthening policy interactions between the *grassroots* and *state levels* may be key to successful implementation (or maintenance) of strongly resilient community pathways. This means that more research will be needed that unravels these complex scalar problems as a basis for implementation of tangible resilience action on the ground in culturally and politically different domains.

Seventh, the book has highlighted that the ultimate aim has to be to make communities more resilient. As Magis (2010, p. 413) highlighted, "a community's resilience will influence its ability to successfully respond to … change, thus making resilience critically important to community and social sustainability". However, as highlighted, this may only be possible with radical rethinking and restructuring of social processes (Pretty, 2007). Although the argument in this book was based on the assumption that the globalized capitalist system is often a root cause of loss of community resilience, questions still remain whether *relocalized* community pathways provide the best solution for raising resilience – in other words whether reification of the 'local' is inevitably the appropriate way forward (Agrawal and Gibson, 1999; Hinrichs, 2003; Hopkins, 2008; Bailey *et al.*, 2010). While authors such as Kunstler (2005, p. 239) have argued that the future "will be increasingly and intensively local and smaller in scale", Haxeltine and Seyfang (2009, p. 14) warned of the dangers of "relying heavily on equating resilience with a relocalization of production-consumption patterns" (see also Beckerman, 1995). Most importantly, it is also recognized that relocalization can never fully eliminate vulnerability, and Hopkins (2010, p. 316) – one of the key initiators behind the now global TTM – warned that "it is easy to look back historically in the search for models of a resilient society, and to view a more localized world through a romantic lens". Hopkins has particularly argued that the challenge for initiatives such as the TTM is how to replicate effective but restricted local efforts to enable change which impacts upon poverty and resource degradation at supra-national and even global scales. As a result, more work is needed on the complex interplay between relocalization initiatives and community resilience in different geographical settings and, in particular, whether relocalization could form a global solution for addressing loss of resilience.

Eighth, reconceptualizing the notion of community resilience into a normative concept that can also be applied in a developing world context is one thing, but it is quite another challenge to *operationalize* and *implement* strongly resilient community pathways in practice. As Seyfang (2009) emphasized, building resilience is ultimately a political process that relies on complex methodologies and processes. Readers should, therefore, see this book as an initial (hopefully thought-provoking) conceptualization that awaits further *empirical refinement*. Indeed, more studies are now needed to test the robustness of the resilience spectrum suggested here in different geographical and cultural contexts.

Finally, it is evident that meeting these future challenges also means further refinement of methodologies to assess community resilience. In particular, more critical analysis of the applicability of different 'indicators' is necessary. Indeed, both the Resilience Alliance (2007) and Cutter *et al.* (2008) emphasized that such indicators should be sensitive to issues of validity, sensitivity, robustness, reproducibility, scope, availability, affordability, simplicity and relevance and, most importantly, that these indicators should be culturally as neutral as possible to allow global comparisons of resilience levels across different societies and communities. This book should, therefore, also be seen as a basis for further development of methodologies to assess community resilience.

This book has not provided specific answers about how to strengthen community resilience. Indeed, the future may just mean going back to what communities have (relatively successfully) done for thousands of years of moderate/strong resilience (otherwise we would not be here!), but without losing sight of positive lessons that have emerged from more recent globalized pathways of change such as improved interconnectedness within and between communities. The advantage that current communities may have for strengthening resilience is that the in-built memory of social systems should ensure that future development pathways will be qualitatively, economically and socio-politically different – and, therefore, possibly more resilient – than past and current pathways of change.

Notes

1 Introduction

1 Bryant (2005) suggested that social and cultural capital should also incorporate 'moral' capital – i.e. the ability of a community or society to agree on basic components seen as essential for a 'good' and 'moral' society.
2 'Environmental capital' is also often referred to as 'natural capital' (Costanza *et al.*, 1997; Millennium Ecosystem Assessment, 2005).

2 Towards a framework for understanding community resilience

1 As Cutter *et al.* (2008) have highlighted, most assessment techniques for community resilience have been quantitative and have been based on selected indicators or variables. These indicators are then used as 'proxies', since it is often difficult to quantify resilience in absolute terms without any commonly agreed external reference with which to validate the quantitative assessments (see also Section 2.5).
2 I will return to Easter Island in Box 4.3 as an example of a self-imposed destructive environmental transition at community level, leading to the near extermination of Eastern Island society by about AD 1700 (i.e. an example of extreme community vulnerability linked to endogenous degradation of environmental and social capital).
3 This was forcefully highlighted during the political uprising in the Arab world in early 2011 (especially in Egypt and Tunisia) where the internet acted as a powerful tool to bypass national government restrictions and for organizing community-level activism.

3 Transition theory: pathways of change and resilient communities

1 Chapter 5 will discuss in more detail how these 'pathways of the possible' are synonymous with notions of 'path dependency' – i.e. a transitional realm beyond which 'radical' action against prevailing norms and values is difficult to implement.
2 Backcasting can be associated with the problem of 'presentism' which suggests that we often re-interpret the past through a contemporary lens, thereby potentially changing the 'reality' and 'meaning' of past transitions.
3 Critical literature on impacts of climate change on communities also highlights potential benefits in some areas through increased agricultural productivity and poleward shift of agricultural zones (e.g. Cline, 2007; Chaskin, 2008).
4 The evolution from one type of community to another is not necessarily linear, as all community structures shown in the figure continue to coexist simultaneously (i.e. subsistence farming systems still exist alongside super-globalized communities) (Wilson, 2007).
5 'Glocalization' suggests that some geographical spaces are influenced by hybrid pathways that involve both local and global influences (Swyngedouw, 1997, 2001).

6 Today, only a few 'non-globalized' societies remain including in particular North Korea as the last bastion of entrenched state socialism, reclusive military dictatorships such as Myanmar, or a few countries that have actively chosen to resist globalization pressures (with more or less success) such as Bhutan.

7 This may be most evident in the rapidly rising importance of web-based games in which individuals are immersing themselves in 'fantasy communities', where the use of 'avatars' (virtual alter-egos) emphasizes the increasing importance of internet-based virtual communities that no longer comprise 'real' people or geographical spaces.

8 Parnwell (2007) also refers to these systems as 'neo-localized'.

9 See Hines (2000), Winter (2003), North (2010) and Bailey *et al.* (2010) for detailed discussions of the terminologies associated with 'localism', 'localization' and 're-localization'. In these studies, localism is primarily concerned with the devolution of governance, while localization is seen as a wider more far-reaching adjustment of economic focus from the global to the local, which carries within it an inherent social justice and resource-focused critique of globalization.

10 A particularly problematic issue in this context – conceptually as well as morally – is the need to acknowledge that relocalized communities, despite all their positive attributes regarding community resilience based on strong social and environmental capital, may not be able to feed a growing world population (see Wilson's, 2008, notion of 'zero-sum-game' in global agricultural transitions).

4 Social memory: community learning, tradition, stakeholder networks and community resilience

1 The original Polynesian population (the Maori) had settled New Zealand about AD 1000 and, over time, cleared about 60,000 km^2 of native forest (25–30 per cent of pre-human forests) in the most accessible and warmer northern regions (Wilson and Bryant, 1997).

2 In New Zealand, this persisted to the 1920s and 1930s with vast forest plantations of Monterey Pine (*Pinus radiata*) – a fast-growing softwood originally from California – planted on areas that had been cleared of native forest.

5 Path dependency: 'lock-in' mechanisms, power structures and pathways of the (im)possible at community level

1 Castree (2008a) rightly argued that 'neo-liberalism' is largely an academic and critics' term, rather than a 'real' term used by decision-makers, and that it is specific to an international group of leftists (an epistemic-political community of the like-minded) who are largely opposed to free market capitalist ideologies.

2 Again, we need to remember that in most communities within democratic structures resilience pathways are made up of the 'sum total' of political views in a community, usually comprised of a multitude of different views along a spectrum ranging from liberal to conservative. However, as various political studies have emphasized, it is nonetheless possible to 'label' communities (and entire electoral districts) as having one predominant political view (see also the second case study discussed in Section 5.4) (Forrest, 2001; Dobson, 2007).

3 The globalized dependency of almost all European communities on imported fresh fruit and vegetables (mainly flown in by airplane to central hubs and then distributed by lorry) was brought into sharp focus during the Icelandic volcanic eruption in April 2010 which brought all European flights to a standstill for nearly a week, leading to food supply shortages within a short amount of time.

4 The notion of *ancestral domains* challenges state claims to control *all* the national territory, and provides a framework for indigenous people to assert legal rights over 'their' lands with associated autonomy in environmental decision-making (often through 'community mapping' of tribal domains) (Peluso, 1992, 1995; Bryant, 2005).

5 Notions of power are, again, important in this respect, as in some communities (e.g. in autocratic or non-democratic contexts) ruling minority elites may be able to impose specific community development pathways over alternative pathways that may be supported by the majority.

6 Examples are related to situations where natural catastrophes/disturbances can result in a strengthening of community-level environmental capital, for example through the sudden depositing of fertile soils after floods or volcanic eruptions (although negative factors would usually outweigh the few positive outcomes).

6 Transitional corridors: macro-structural influences and community resilience

1 Exceptions would be 'closed' communities that have no or little interlinkages with the nation state within which they are embedded (e.g. remote subsistence or hunter-gatherer communities) (see Section 2.4).

2 'Enforced relocalization' is not only related to transitional ruptures associated with wars. Goldsworthy (2010, p. 351), in his historical analysis of the decline of the western Roman empire, for example, argued that enforced relocalization also occurred after the decline of Roman influence in communities in Britain, where in the fifth century AD "everything, including power, trade and warfare, became far more local than had been true under the Romans".

7 Community resilience and the policy challenge

1 Exceptions are sudden political upheavals – transitional ruptures – discussed in Section 6.4 and socio-political disturbances such as wars or revolutions (see Figure 1.1).

Bibliography

Aage, H. (ed.) (1998) *Environmental Transition in Nordic and Baltic Countries*, CABI, Wallingford

Abdallah, S., Thompson, S., Michaelson, J., Marks, N. and Steuer, N. (2009) *The Unhappy Planet Index 2.0: Why Good Lives Don't Have to Cost the Earth*, New Economics Foundation, London

Abdel-Fadil, M. (1989) 'Colonialism', in J. Eatwell, M. Milgate and P. Newmans (eds) *Economic Development*, Blackwell, Oxford, pp. 61–67

Abel, N., Cumming, D.H. and Anderies, J.M. (2006) 'Collapse and reorganization in social-ecological systems: questions, some ideas, and policy implications', *Ecology and Society*, vol. 11, no. 1, article no. 17 (online) www.ecologyandsociety.org/vol. 11/iss1/art17/

Abercrombie, N., Hill, T. and Turner, B.S. (1980) *The Dominant Ideology Thesis*, Allen and Unwin, London

Abidi-Habib, M. and Lawrence, A. (2007) 'Revolt and remember: how the Shimshal Nature Trust develops and sustains social-ecological resilience in Northern Pakistan', *Ecology and Society*, vol. 12, no. 2, article no. 35 (online) www.ecologyandsociety. org/vol. 12/iss2/art35/

Adams, W.M. (1990) *Green Development: Environment and Sustainability in the Third World*, Routledge, London

Adger, W.N. (2000) 'Social and ecological resilience: are they related?', *Progress in Human Geography*, vol. 24, no. 3, pp. 347–364

Adger, W.N. (2003) 'Social capital, collective action and adaptation to climate change', *Economic Geography*, vol. 79, pp. 387–404

Adger, W.N. (2006) 'Vulnerability', *Global Environmental Change*, vol. 16, no. 3, pp. 268–281

Adger, W.N., Arnell, N.W. and Tompkins, E.L. (2005a) 'Successful adaptation to climate change across scales', *Global Environmental Change*, vol. 15, no. 2, pp. 77–86

Adger, W.N., Hughes, T.P., Folke, C., Carpenter, S.R. and Rockstrom, J. (2005b) 'Social-ecological resilience to coastal disasters', *Science*, vol. 309, pp. 1036–1039

Adger, W.N., Huq, S., Brown, K., Conway, D. and Hulme, M. (2003) 'Adaption to climate change in the developing world', *Progress in Development Studies*, vol. 3, pp. 179–195

Adger, W.N., Kelly, P.M., Winkels, A., Huy, L.Q. and Locke, C. (2002) 'Migration, remittances, livelihood trajectories and social resilience', *Ambio*, vol. 31, no. 4, pp. 237–251

Aggarwal, R.M. (2006) 'Globalization, local ecosystems, and the rural poor', *World Development*, vol. 34, no. 8, pp. 1405–1418

Agrawal, A. and Gibson, C.C. (1999) 'Enchantment and disenchantment: the role of community in natural resource conservation', *World Development*, vol. 27, no. 4, pp. 629–649

Allen, J. (1997) 'Economies of power and space', in R. Lee and J. Wills (eds) *Geographies of Economies*, Arnold, London, pp. 59–70

Allen, J. (2003) *Lost Geographies of Power*, Wiley-Blackwell, Oxford

Allen, P. (1993) 'Connecting the social and the ecological in sustainable agriculture', in P. Allen (ed.) *Food for the Future: Conditions and Contradictions of Sustainability*, Wiley, New York, pp. 1–16

Allen, S., Hammond, G. and McManus, M. (2008) 'Prospects for and barriers to domestic micro-generation: a UK perspective', *Applied Energy*, vol. 85, pp. 528–544

Amin, S. (1990) *Delinking: Towards a Polycentric World*, Zed Books, London

Anderies, J.M., Walker, B.H. and Kinzig, A.P. (2006) 'Fifteen weddings and a funeral: case studies and resilience-based management', *Ecology and Society*, vol. 11, no. 1, article no. 21 (online) www.ecologyandsociety.org/vol.11/iss1/art21

Anielski, M. (2007) *The Economics of Happiness: Building Genuine Wealth*, New Society Publishers, Gabriola Island

Appadurai, A. (1996) *Modernity at Large*, University of Minnesota Press, Minneapolis

Bailey, I. and Wilson, G.A. (2009) 'Theorising pathways in response to climate change: technocentrism, ecocentrism, and the carbon economy', *Environment and Planning A*, vol. 41, pp. 2324–2341

Bailey, I., Hopkins, R. and Wilson, G.A. (2010) 'Some things old, some things new: the spatial representations and politics of change of the peak oil relocalisation movement', *Geoforum*, vol. 41, no. 4, pp. 595–605

Bakker, K. (2005) 'Neoliberalizing nature? Market environmentalism in water supply in England and Wales', *Annals of the Association of American Geographers*, vol. 95, pp. 542–565

Bardhan, P. (2006) 'Globalization and rural poverty', *World Development*, vol. 34. no. 8, pp. 1393–1404

Barnett, C. (2005) 'The consolations of neoliberalism', *Geoforum*, vol. 36, no. 1, pp. 7–12

Barnett, J. and Adger, W.N. (2003) 'Climate dangers and atoll countries', *Climatic Change*, vol. 61, no. 3, pp. 321–337

Barr, S. (2008) *Environment and Society: Sustainability, Policy and the Citizen*, Ashgate, Aldershot

Barrett, H.R., Ilbery, B., Browne, A.W. and Binns, T. (1999) 'Globalisation and the changing networks of food supply: the importation of fresh horticultural produce from Kenya into the UK', *Transactions of the Institute of British Geographers*, vol. 24, no. 2, pp. 159–174

Barry, J. (2003) 'Ecological modernisation', in E. Page and J. Proops (eds) *Environmental Thought*, Edward Elgar, Cheltenham, pp. 191–213

Bebbington, A. and Perrault, T. (1999) 'Social capital, development and access to resources in highland Ecuador', *Economic Geography*, vol. 75, pp. 395–418

Beck, U. (1992) *Risk Society*, Sage, London

Beckerman, W. (1995) *Small is Stupid: Blowing the Whistle on the Greens*, Duckworth, London

Beevor, A. (1999) *Stalingrad*, Penguin, London

Beierle, T.C. and Cayford, J. (2002) *Democracy in Practice: Public Participation in Environmental Decisions*, Earthscan, London

Beit-Hallahmi, B. and Argyle, M. (1997) *The Psychology of Religious Behaviour, Belief and Experience*, Routledge, London

Bell, M.M. (2004) *Farming For Us All: Practical Agriculture and the Cultivation of Sustainability*, Pennsylvania State University Press, University Park (Penn.).

Bellaigue, M. (1999) 'Globalisation and memory', *International Journal of Heritage Studies*, vol. 5, no. 1, pp. 35–43

Berkes, F. (1999) *Sacred Ecology: Traditional Ecological Knowledge and Management Systems*, Taylor & Francis, London

Berkes, F., Colding, J. and Folke, C. (eds) (2003) *Navigating Social-Ecological Systems: Building Resilience for Complexity and Change*, CUP, Cambridge

Bhagwati, J. (2004) *In Defence of Globalization*, OUP, Oxford

Black, J. (1970) *The Dominion of Man: the Search for Ecological Responsibility*, Edinburgh University Press, Edinburgh

Blaikie, P.M. and Brookfield, H. (1987) *Land Degradation and Society*, Methuen, London

Bodin, Ö. and Crona, B.I. (2008) 'Management of natural resources at the community level: exploring the role of social capital and leadership in a rural fishing community', *World Development*, vol. 36, no. 12, pp. 2763–2779

Bohnet, I., Potter, C. and Simmons, E. (2003) 'Landscape change in the multi-functional countryside: a biographical analysis of farmer decision making in the English Weald', *Landscape Research*, vol. 28, no. 4, pp. 349–364

Bomberg, E. (2007) 'Policy learning in an enlarged European Union: environmental NGOs and new policy instruments', *Journal of European Public Policy*, vol. 14, no. 2, pp. 248–268

Bonnano, G.A. (2004) 'Have we underestimated the human capacity to thrive after extremely adverse events?', *American Psychologist*, vol. 59, no. 1, pp. 20–28

Bourdieu, P. (1987) 'What makes a social class? On the theoretical and practical existence of groups', *Berkeley Journal of Sociology*, vol. 32, pp. 1–18

Bowring, F. (1998) 'LETS: an eco-socialist initiative?' *New Left Review*, vol. 232, pp. 91–111

Bradshaw, M. and Stenning, A. (eds) (2001) *The Transition Economies of East Central Europe and the Former Soviet Union*, Addison Wesley Longman, London

Brand, F.S. and Jax, K. (2007) 'Focusing the meaning(s) of resilience: resilience as a descriptive concept and a boundary object', *Ecology and Society*, vol. 12, no. 1, article no. 23 (online) www.ecologyandsociety.org/vol. 12/iss1/art 23/.

Briassoulis, H. (ed.) (2005) *Policy Integration for Complex Environmental Problems: the Example of Mediterranean Desertification*, Ashgate, Aldershot

Brierley, G.J. (2010) 'Landscape memory: the imprint of the past on contemporary landscape forms and processes', *Area*, vol. 42, no. 1, pp. 76–85

Briguglio, L. (1995) 'Small island developing states and their economic vulnerabilities', *World Development*, vol. 23, no. 9, pp. 1615–1632

Brock, W.A. (2006) 'Tipping points, abrupt opinion changes, and punctuated policy change', in R. Repetto (ed.) *Punctuated Equilibrium and the Dynamics of US Environmental Policy*, Yale University Press, New Haven (Conn.)

Brown, L.R. (2006) *Plan B: Rescuing a Planet Under Stress and a Civilization in Trouble*, Norton, London

Brunk, G.G. (2002) 'Why do societies collapse? A theory based on self-organized criticality', *Journal of Theoretical Politics*, vol. 14, no. 2, pp. 195–230

Bruun, O. and Kalland, A. (eds) (1994) *Asian Perspectives of Nature: a Critical Approach*, Curzon Press, London

Bryant, R.L. (2005) *Nongovernmental Organizations in Environmental Struggles:*

Politics and the Making of Moral Capital in the Philippines, Yale University Press, New Haven (Conn.)

Bryant, R.L. and Bailey, S. (1997) *Third World Political Ecology*, Routledge, London

Bryceson, D.F. (2002) 'The scramble in Africa: reorienting rural livelihoods', *World Development*, vol. 30, no. 5, pp. 725–739

Bulkeley, H. (2006) 'Urban sustainability: learning from best practice?' *Environment and Planning A*, vol. 38, pp. 1029–1044

Bulkeley, H. and Betshill, M. (2003) *Cities and Climate Change: Urban Sustainability and Global Environmental Governance*, Routledge, London

Buller, H., Wilson, G.A. and Höll, A. (eds) (2000) *Agri-Environmental Policy in the European Union*, Ashgate, Aldershot

Bumpus, A. and Liverman, D. (2008) 'Accumulation by decarbonisation and the governance of carbon offsets', *Economic Geography*, vol. 84, pp. 127–156

Burchell, J. (2002) *The Evolution of Green Politics: Development and Change within European Green Parties*, Earthscan, London

Burton, R.J. and Wilson, G.A. (2006) 'Injecting social psychology theory into conceptualisations of agricultural agency: towards a post-productivist farmer self-identity?' *Journal of Rural Studies*, vol. 22, pp. 95–115

Burton, R.J., Kuczera, C. and Schwarz, G. (2008) 'Exploring farmers' cultural resistance to voluntary agri-environmental schemes', *Sociologia Ruralis*, vol. 48, no. 1, pp. 16–37

Cahn, E. (1999) 'Time dollars, work and community: from "why" to "why not"?' *Futures*, vol. 31, pp. 499–509

Callicot, J.B. and Ames, R.T. (1989) *Nature in Asian Traditions of Thought*, Suny Press, Albany (N.Y.)

Caraveli, H. (2000) 'A comparative analysis on intensification and extensification in Mediterranean agriculture: dilemmas for LFAs policy', *Journal of Rural Studies*, vol. 16, pp. 231–242

Carrier, J.G. (ed.) (2004) *Confronting Environments: Local Understanding in a Globalizing World*, AltaMira Press, Oxford

Cartier, C. (2001) *Globalizing South China*, Wiley-Blackwell, Chichester

Castells, M. (1996) *The Rise of the Network Society*, Blackwell, Oxford

Castree, N. (2008a) 'Neoliberalising nature: the logics of deregulation and reregulation', *Environment and Planning A*, vol. 40, pp. 131–152

Castree, N. (2008b) 'Neoliberalising nature: processes, effects, and evaluations', *Environment and Planning A*, vol. 40, pp. 153–173

Chakrabarti, A. and Cullenberg, S. (2003) *Transition and Development in India*, Routledge, London

Chambers, S., Lobb, A., Butler, L., Harvey, K. and Traill, W.B. (2007) 'Local, national and imported foods: a qualitative study', *Appetite*, vol. 49, pp. 208–213

Chaskin, R.J. (2008) 'Resilience, community, and resilient communities: conditioning contexts and collective action', *Child Care in Practice*, vol. 14, no. 1, pp. 65–74

Chester, D., Duncan, A. and Dibben, C. (2008) 'The importance of religion in shaping volcanic risk perception in Italy, with special reference to Vesuvius', *Journal of Volcanology and Geothermal Research*, vol. 172, pp. 216–228

Childs, P. and Williams, W. (1997) *An Introduction to Post-Colonial Theory*, Prentice Hall, London

Clapp, J. (2005) 'The political economy of food aid in an era of agricultural biotechnology', *Global Governance*, vol. 11, pp. 467–485

Clark, J. (2006) 'The institutional limits to multifunctional agriculture: subnational governance and regional systems of innovation', *Environment and Planning C: Government and Policy*, vol. 24, pp. 331–349

Clerveaux, W. (2010) 'Aftermath of category 4 hurricane (Ike) in the Turks and Caicos Islands', Paper presented at the Hazards Mitigation Workshop, 13–15 October 2010, University of Plymouth, UK

Cline, W. (2007) *Global Warming and Agriculture: Impact Estimates by Country*, Peterson Institute, Washington (D.C.)

Coleman, J.S. (1988) 'Social capital in the creation of human capital', *American Journal of Sociology*, vol. 94, pp. 95–120

Costanza, R. (1992) 'Natural capital and sustainable development', *Conservation Biology*, vol. 6, pp. 37–46

Costanza, R., D'Arge, R., De Groot, R., Farber, S., Grasso, M., Hannon, B., Limburg, K., Naeem, S., O'Neill, R.V., Paruelo, J., Raskin, R.G., Sutton, P. and Van den Belt, M. (1997) 'The value of the world's ecosystem services and natural capital', *Nature*, vol. 387, pp. 253–260

CPRC (Cancer Prevention Research Centre) (2006) 'Detailed overview of the transtheoretical model', www.uri.edu/research/cprc/TTM/detailedoverview.htm

Cumming, G.S., Barnes, G., Perz, S., Schmink, M., Sieving, K.E., Southworth J., Binford, M., Holt, R.D., Stickler, C. and Van Holt, T. (2005) 'An exploratory framework for the empirical measurement of resilience', *Ecosystems*, vol. 8, pp. 975–987

Cumming, G.S., Cumming, D.H. and Redman, C.L. (2006) 'Scale mismatches in social-ecological systems: causes, consequences, and solutions', *Ecology and Society*, vol. 11, no. 1, article no. 14 (online) www.ecologyandsociety.org/vol.11/iss1/art14/

Curry, G.N. and Koczberski, G. (2009) 'Finding common ground: relational concepts of land tenure and economy in the oil palm frontier of Papua New Guinea', *The Geographical Journal*, vol. 175, no. 2, pp. 98–111

Cutter, S.L., Barnes, L., Berry, M., Burton, C., Evans, E., Tate, E. and Webb, J. (2008) 'A place-based model for understanding community resilience to natural disasters', *Global Environmental Change*, vol. 18, pp. 598–606

Dahle, K. (2007) 'When do transformative initiatives really transform? A typology of different paths for transition to a sustainable economy', *Futures*, vol. 39, pp. 487–504

Davidson, D.J. (2010) 'The applicability of the concept of resilience to social systems: some sources of optimism and nagging doubts', *Society and Natural Resources*, vol. 23, pp. 1135–1149

Davies, P. (1995) *About Time*, Penguin, London

Davis, D.S. (ed.) (2000) *Consumer Revolution in Urban China*, University of California Press, Berkeley (Cal.)

Davis, M. (2004) *Victorian Holocaust*, Verso, London

Dawkins, R. (2006) *The God Delusion*, Black Swan, London

Deffeyes, K.S. (2001) *Hubbert's Peak: the Impending World Oil Shortage*, Princeton University Press, New York

Demeritt, D. (2009) 'From externality to inputs and interference: framing environmental research in geography', *Transactions of the Institute of British Geographers*, vol. 34, no. 1, pp. 3–11

Dennett, D.C. (2006) *Breaking the Spell: Religion as a Natural Phenomenon*, Viking, London

Derkzen, P., Franklin, A. and Bock, B. (2008) 'Examining power struggles as a signifier of successful partnership working: a case study of partnership dynamics', *Journal of Rural Studies*, vol. 24, no. 4, pp. 458–466

Devine-Wright, P. (2009) 'NIMBYism: the role of place attachment and place identity in explaining place-protective action', *Journal of Community and Applied Social Psychology*, vol. 19, pp. 426–441

Diamond, J. (1998) *Guns, Germs and Steel: a Short History of Everybody for the Last 13,000 Years*, Vintage, London

Diamond, J. (2006) *Collapse: How Societies Choose to Fail or Survive*, Penguin, London

Dibden, J. and Cocklin, C. (2009) ' "Multifunctionality": trade protectionism or a new way forward?', *Environment and Planning A*, vol. 41, pp. 163–182

Dicken, P. (1998) *Global Shift: Transforming the World Economy* (3rd edn), Paul Chapman, London

DiClemente, C.C. (2003) *Addiction and Change: How Addictions Develop and Addicted People Recover*, Guilford Press, New York

Dobson, A. (2007) *Green Political Thought*, Routledge, London

Dolowitz, D. and Marsh, D. (1996) 'Who learns what from who? A review of the policy transfer literature', *Political Studies*, vol. 44, no. 2, pp. 343–357

Donovan, K. (2010) 'Doing social volcanology: exploring volcanic culture in Indonesia', *Area*, vol. 42, no. 1, pp. 117–126

Dorfman, L.T., Mendez, E.C. and Osterhaus, J.K. (2009) 'Stress and resilience in the oral histories of rural older women', *Journal of Women and Aging*, vol. 21, pp. 303–316

Dryzek, J.S. (1997) *The Politics of the Earth*, OUP, Oxford

Dryzek, J.S. (2001) 'Resistance is fertile', *Global Environmental Politics*, vol. 1, pp. 11–17

Dryzek, J.S., Downs, D., Hernes, H.-K. and Schlosberg, D. (2003) *Green States and Social Movements: Environmentalism in the United States, United Kingdom, Germany and Norway*, OUP, Oxford

Dudley, W., Goff, J., Chagué-Goff, C. and Johnston, J. (2009) 'Capturing the next generation of cultural memories: the process of video interviewing tsunami survivors', *Science of Tsunami Hazards*, vol. 28, no. 3, pp. 154–170

Dunford, M. (1998) 'Differential development, institutions, modes of regulation and comparative transitions to capitalism: Russia, the Commonwealth of Independent States and the former German Democratic Republic', in A. Pickles and A. Smith (eds) *Theorising Transition: the Political Economy of Post-Communist Transformations*, Routledge, London, pp. 76–114

DuPuis, E.M. and Goodman, D. (2005) 'Should we go "home" to eat? Towards a reflexive politics of localism', *Journal of Rural Studies*, vol. 21, pp. 359–371

Earle, A., Jägerskog, A. and Öjendal, J. (eds) (2010) *Transboundary Water Management: Principles and Practice*, Earthscan, London

Ekins, P., Simon, S., Deutsch, L., Folke, C. and De Groot, R. (2003) 'A framework for the practical application of the concepts of critical natural capital and strong sustainability', *Ecological Economics*, vol. 44, pp. 165–185

Featherstone, M. (1995) *Undoing Culture: Globalization, Postmodernism and Identity*, Sage, London

Fernandez-Gimenez, M.E. (2001) 'The effects of livestock privatization on pastoral land use and land tenure in post-socialist Mongolia', *Nomadic Peoples*, vol. 5, no. 2, pp. 49–66

Fernandez-Gimenez, M.E. and Batbuyan, B. (2004) 'Law and disorder: local implementation of Mongolia's Land Law', *Development and Change*, vol. 35, no. 1, pp. 141–165

Fine, B. (2001) *Social Capital Versus Social Theory*, Routledge, London

Flenley, J. and Bahn, P. (2003) *The Enigmas of Easter Island*, OUP, New York

Folke, C. (2006) 'Resilience: the emergence of a perspective for social-ecological system analyses', *Global Environmental Change*, vol. 16, no. 3, pp. 253–267

Forbes, B.B., Stammler, F., Kumpula, T., Meschtyb, N., Pajunen, A. and Kaarlejärvi, E. (2009) 'High resilience in the Yamal-Nenets social-ecological system, West Siberian Arctic, Russia', *Proceedings of the National Academy of Sciences of the USA*, vol. 106, pp. 22041–22048

Ford, J. and Smit, B. (2004) 'A framework for assessing the vulnerability of communities in the Canadian Arctic to risks associated with climate change', *Arctic*, vol. 57, pp. 389–400

Forrest, R. (2001) 'Social cohesion, social capital and the neighbourhood', *Urban Studies*, vol. 38, no. 12, pp. 2125–2143

Forsyth, T. (2003) *Critical Political Ecology: the Politics of Environmental Science*, Routledge, London

Frigg, R. (2003) 'Self-organized criticality: what it is and what it isn't', *Studies in History and Philosophy of Science A*, vol. 34, pp. 613–632

Fukuyama, F. (1992) *The End of History and the Last Man*, Free Press, New York

Gahin, R., Veleva, V. and Hart, M. (2003) 'Do indicators help create sustainable communities?', *Local Environment*, vol. 8, no. 6, pp. 661–666

Gaillard, J.C., Clare, E., Ocean, V., Azhari, D., Denain, J.C., Efendi, Y., Grancher, D., Liamzon, C.C., Sari, D.R. and Setiwan, R. (2008) 'Ethnic groups' response to the 26 December 2004 eruption and tsunami in Aceh, Indonesia', *Natural Hazards*, vol. 47, pp. 17–38

Gale, D. (1996) 'What have we learned from social learning?', *European Economic Review*, vol. 40, pp. 617–628

Gallopin, G.C. (2006) 'Linkages between vulnerability, resilience, and adaptive capacity', *Global Environmental Change*, vol. 16, pp. 293–303

Gammage, B. (2008) 'Plain facts: Tasmania under Aboriginal management', *Landscape Research*, vol. 33, no. 2, pp. 241–254

Gardiner, J. (2004) *Wartime Britain 1939–1945*, Headline Book Publishing, London

Geddes, M. Davies, J. and Fuller, C. (2007) 'Evaluating local strategic partnerships: theory and practice of change', *Local Government Studies*, vol. 33, no. 1, pp. 97–116

Gibbs, D. (2000) 'Ecological modernization, regional economic development and regional development agencies', *Geoforum*, vol. 31, pp. 9–19

Giddens, A. (1984) *The Constitution of Society: Outline of the Theory of Structuration*, Polity Press, Cambridge

Giddens, A. (1990) *The Consequences of Modernity*, Polity Press, Cambridge

Gladwell, M. (2000) *The Tipping Point: How Little Things Can Make a Big Difference*, Little Brown, New York

Goldsworthy, A. (2010) *The Fall of the West: the Death of the Roman Superpower*, Phoenix, London

Goodman, D. (2004) 'Rural Europe redux? Reflections on alternative agro-food networks and paradigm change', *Sociologia Ruralis*, vol. 44, pp. 3–16

Goodman, D. and Watts, M. (1997) *Globalising Food: Agrarian Questions and Global Restructuring*, Routledge, London

Goodwin, M. and Painter, J. (1996) 'Local governance, the crises of Fordism and the changing geographies of regulation', *Transactions of the Institute of British Geographers*, vol. 21, no. 4, pp. 635–648

Goss, J. and Burch, D. (2001) 'From agricultural modernisation to agri-food globalisation: the waning of national development in Thailand', *Third World Quarterly*, vol. 22, no. 6, pp. 969–986

Gow, K. and Paton, D. (eds) (2008) *Phoenix of Natural Disasters: Community Resilience*, Nova Science, New York

Grabher, G. and. Stark, D. (eds) (1997) *Restructuring Networks in Post-Socialism: Legacies, Linkages and Localities*, OUP, Oxford

Graham, S. (1998) 'The end of geography or the explosion of place? Conceptualising space, place and information technology', *Progress in Human Geography*, vol. 22, no. 2, pp. 165–185

Grainger, A. (2005) 'Environmental globalization and tropical forests', *Globalizations*, vol. 2, no. 3, pp. 335–348

Granovetter, M. (1985) 'Economic action and social structure: the problem of embeddedness', *American Journal of Sociology*, vol. 91, no. 3, pp. 481–510

Gray, J. (2002) *False Dawn: the Delusions of Global Capitalism* (2nd edn), Granta Books, London

Greeley, A. (1993) 'Religion and attitudes toward the environment', *Journal for the Scientific Study of Religion*, vol. 32, pp. 19–28

Grêt-Regamey, A., Walz, A. and Bebi, P. (2008) 'Valuing ecosystem services for sustainable landscape planning in Alpine regions', *Mountain Research and Development*, vol. 28, pp. 156–165

Gunderson, L.H. and Holling, C.S. (eds) (2002) *Panarchy: Understanding Transformations in Human and Natural Systems*, Island Press, Washington (D.C.)

Hain, J., Ault, G., Galloway, S., Cruden, A. and McDonald, J. (2005) 'Additional renewable energy growth through small scale community orientated energy policies', *Energy Policy*, vol. 33, pp. 1199–1212

Hale, C.D. (2005) 'Real reform in North Korea? The aftermath of the July 2002 economic measures', *Asian Survey*, vol. 45, no. 6, pp. 823–842

Halfacree, K.H. (1999) 'A new space or spatial effacement? Alternative futures for the post-productivist countryside', in N. Walford, J. Everitt and D. Napton (eds) *Reshaping the Countryside: Perceptions and Processes of Rural Change*, CABI, Wallingford, pp. 67–76

Hall, P. (1993) 'Policy paradigms, social learning and the state: the case of economic policy-making in Britain', *Comparative Politics*, vol. 25, pp. 275–296

Hall, P. (2002) *Urban and Regional Planning* (4th edn), Routledge, London

Hamilton, L.C., Colocousis, C.R. and Johansen, T.R. (2004) 'Migration from resource depletion: the case of the Faroe islands', *Society and Natural Resources*, vol. 17, no. 5, pp. 443–453

Harte, M.J. (1995) 'Ecology, sustainability and environmental capital', *Ecological Economics*, vol. 15, pp. 157–164

Harvey, D. (1989) *The Condition of Postmodernity: an Enquiry Into the Origins of Cultural Change*, Blackwell, Oxford

Harvey, D. (1996) *Justice, Nature and the Geography of Difference*, Blackwell, Oxford

Harvey, D. (2005) *A Brief History of Neoliberalism*, OUP, Oxford

Harvey, D. (2006) *The Limits to Capital*, Verso, London

Hastrup, K. (2009) 'Waterworlds: framing the question of social resilience', in K. Hastrup (ed.) *The Question of Resilience: Social Responses to Climate Change*, Det Kongelige Danske Videnskabernes Selskab, Viborg (DK), pp. 11–30

Haxeltine, A. and Seyfang, G. (2009) 'Transitions for the people: theory and practice of "transition" and "resilience" in the UK's transition movement', Tyndall Centre for Climate Change Research, Working paper 134

Head, L. (1989) 'Prehistoric Aboriginal impacts on Australian vegetation: an assessment of the evidence', *Australian Geographer*, vol. 20, pp. 37–46

Head, L. (1993) 'Unearthing prehistoric cultural landscapes: a view from Australia', *Transactions of the Institute of British Geographers*, vol. 18, no. 4, pp. 481–499

Heggelund, G. (2006) 'Resettlement programmes and environmental capacity in the Three Gorges Dam Project', *Development and Change*, vol. 37, no. 1, pp. 179–199

Heinberg, R. (2004) *Powerdown: Options and Actions for a Post-Carbon World*, New Society Publishers, Gabriola Island

Held, D., McGrew, A., Goldblatt, D. and Perraton, J. (1999) *Global Transformations: Politics, Economics and Culture*, Polity Press, Cambridge

Heynen, N., McCarthy, J., Prudham, S. and Robbins, P. (eds) (2007) *Neoliberal Environments*, Routledge, London

Hines, C. (2000) *Localisation: a Global Manifesto*, Earthscan, London

Hinrichs, C.C. (2003) 'The practice and politics of food system relocalisation', *Journal of Rural Studies*, vol. 19, pp. 33–45

Hirst, P. and Thompson, G. (1996) *Globalization in Question*, Polity Press, Cambridge

Holling, C.S. (1973) 'Resilience and stability of ecological systems', *Annual Review of Ecology and Systematics*, vol. 4, pp. 1–23

Holmes, J. (2006) 'Impulses towards a multifunctional transition in rural Australia: gaps in the research agenda', *Journal of Rural Studies*, vol. 22, pp. 142–160

Homer-Dixon, T. (2008) *The Up-Side of Down: Catastrophe, Creativity, and the Renewal of Civilization*, Island Press, Washington (D.C.)

Hopkins, R. (2008) *The Transition Handbook: From Oil Dependency to Local Resilience*, Green Books, Dartington

Hopkins, R. (2010) 'Localisation and resilience at the local level: the case of Transition Town Totnes (Devon, UK)', PhD thesis, School of Geography, Earth and Environmental Sciences, University of Plymouth, UK

Hudson, R. (2000) *Production, Places and Environment: Changing Perspectives in Economic Geography*, Prentice Hall, London

Hudson, R. (2005) 'Rethinking change in old industrial regions: reflecting on the experiences of North East England', *Environment and Planning A*, vol. 37, pp. 581–596

Hwang, S.S., Xi, J., Cao, Y., Feng, X. and Qiao, X. (2007) 'Anticipation of migration and psychological stress and the Three Gorges Dam Project, China', *Social Science and Medicine*, vol. 65, pp. 1012–1024

Jackson, S. and Sleigh, A. (2000) 'Resettlement for China's Three Gorges Dam: socio-economic impact and institutional tensions', *Communist and Post-Communist Studies*, vol. 33, pp. 223–241

Jackson, T. (2009) *Prosperity Without Growth: Economics for a Finite Planet*, Earthscan, London

Janssens, W. (2010) 'Women's empowerment and the creation of social capital in Indian villages', *World Development*, vol. 38, no. 7, pp. 974–988

Jazeel, T. and McFarlane, C. (2010) 'The limits of responsibility: a postcolonial politics of academic knowledge production', *Transactions of the Institute of British Geographers*, vol. 35, no. 1, pp. 109–124

Johnston, R.J. (1996) *Nature, State and Economy: a Political Economy of the Environment* (2nd edn), Wiley, Chichester

Jones, R.J. (1997) 'Globalisation versus community', *New Political Economy*, vol. 2, no. 1, pp. 39–51

Jordan, A. (2005) *Environmental Policy in the European Union*, Earthscan, London

Jordan, A., Wurzel, R. and Zito, A. (eds) (2003) *'New' Instruments of Environmental Governance? National Experiences and Prospects*, Frank Cass, London

Jun, J. (1997) 'Rural resettlement: past lessons for the Three Gorges project', *The China Journal*, vol. 38, pp. 65–92

Kaplinsky, R. and Messner, D. (2008) 'The impact of Asian drivers on the developing world', *World Development*, vol. 36, no. 2, pp. 197–209

Kawharu, M. (2000) 'Kaitiakitanga: a Maori anthropological perspective of the Maori socio-environmental ethic of resource management', *Journal of the Polynesian Society*, vol. 109, pp. 349–370

Keen, M., Brown, V.A. and Dyball, R. (eds) (2005) *Social Learning in Environmental Management*, Earthscan, London

Kelkar, U., Narula, K.K., Sharma, V.P. and Chandna, U. (2008) 'Vulnerability and adaptation to climate variability and water stress in Uttarkhand State, India', *Global Environmental Change*, vol. 18, pp. 564–574

Kinsella, J., Wilson, S., De Jong., F. and Renting, H. (2000) 'Pluriactivity as a livelihood strategy in Irish farm households and its role in rural development', *Sociologia Ruralis*, vol. 40, no. 4, pp. 481–496

Kinzig, A.P., Ryan, P., Etienne, M., Allison, H., Elmqvist, T. and Walker, B.H. (2006) 'Resilience and regime shifts: assessing cascading effects', *Ecology and Society*, vol. 11, no. 1, article no. 20 (online) www.ecologyandsociety.org/vol. 11/iss1/art20

Knox, P. and Pinch, S. (2006) *Urban Social Geography: an Introduction* (5th edn), Verso, London

Korten, D.C. (1995) *When Corporations Rule the World*, Earthscan, London

Kumar, C. (2005) 'Revisiting "community" in community-based natural resource management', *Community Development Journal*, vol. 40, no. 3, pp. 275–285

Kunstler, J.H. (2005) *The Long Emergency: Surviving the Converging Catastrophes of the 21st Century*, Atlantic Monthly Press, New York

Lambek, M. (1992) 'Taboo as cultural practice among Malagasy speakers', *Man*, vol. 27, pp. 245–266

Lang, T. (1999) 'The complexities of globalisation: the UK as a case study of tensions within the food supply system and the challenge to food policy', *Agriculture and Human Values*, vol. 16, pp. 169–185

Lang, T. and Heasman, M. (2004) *Food Wars: the Global Battle for Mouths, Minds and Markets*, Earthscan, London

Langhorne, R. (2001) *The Coming of Globalization: its Evolution and Contemporary Consequences*, Palgrave, Basingstoke

Larner, W. (2003) 'Neoliberalism?' *Environment and Planning D: Society and Space*, vol. 21, no. 4, pp. 509–512

Latour, B. (1993) *We Have Never Been Modern*, Prentice Hall, London

Law, J. (2006) 'Disaster in agriculture: or foot and mouth mobilities', *Environment and Planning A*, vol. 38, pp. 227–239

Lebel, L., Anderies, J.M., Campbell, B., Folke, C., Hatfield-Dodds, S., Hughes, T.P. and Wilson, J. (2006) 'Governance and the capacity to manage resilience in regional social-ecological systems', *Ecology and Society*, vol. 11, no. 1, article no. 19 (online) www.ecologyandsociety.org/vol. 11/iss1/art19/

LEDDRA (Land and Ecosystem Degradation and Desertification: Response Assemblages)

(2011) 'Theory of responses to land and ecosystem degradation and desertification in croplands/grazing lands/forests (WP4: UK team)', European Commission, Brussels

Leichenko, R. and O'Brien, K. (2008) *Environmental Change and Globalization: Double Exposures*, OUP, Oxford

Liepins, R. (1998) 'The gendering of farming and agricultural policies: a matter of discourse and power', *Australian Geographer*, vol. 29, pp. 371–388

Lipietz, A. (1987) *Mirages and Miracles: the Crises of Global Fordism*, Verso, London

Lipietz, A. (1992) *Towards a New Economic Order: Postfordism, Ecology and Democracy*, OUP, New York

Lipsky, M. (1980) *Street-Level Bureaucracy: Dilemmas of the Individual in Public Services*, Russell Sage Foundation, New York

Liverman, D. (2004) 'Who governs, at what scale and at what price? Geography, environmental governance, and the commodification of nature', *Annals of the Association of American Geographers*, vol. 94, pp. 734–738

Locke, C., Adger, W.N. and Kelly. P. (2000) 'Changing places: migration's social and environmental consequences', *Environment*, vol. 42, pp. 24–35

Losch, B. (2004) 'Debating the multifunctionality of agriculture: from trade negotiation to development policies by the South', *Journal of Agrarian Change*, vol. 4, no. 3, pp. 336–360

Lovins, A. (2003) *Small is Profitable: the Hidden Economic Benefits of Making Electrical Resources the Right Size*, Earthscan, London

Macleod, D. (2002) 'Disappearing culture? Globalisation and a Canary Island fishing community', *History and Anthropology*, vol. 13, no. 1, pp. 53–67

Macnaughten, P. and Urry, J. (1998) *Contested Natures*, Sage, London

Macy, J. and Brown, M.Y. (1998) *Coming Back to Life: Practices to Reconnect our Lives, our World*, New Society Publishers, Gabriola Island

Madaleno, I.M. (2010) 'No fear: Tuvalu islanders and the rising Pacific waters', Paper presented at the RGS/IBG Conference, 1–3 September 2010, RGS London, UK

Magis, K. (2010) 'Community resilience: an indicator of social sustainability', *Society and Natural Resources*, vol. 23, pp. 401–416

Mander, J. and Goldsmith, E. (eds) (2000) *The Case Against the Global Economy and for Local Self-Reliance*, Earthscan, London

Manser, R. (1993) *Failed Transitions: the Eastern European Economy and Environment Since the Fall of Communism*, New Press, New York

Mansfield, B. (2004) 'Neoliberalism in the oceans: "rationalisation", property rights, and the commons question', *Geoforum*, vol. 35, no. 3, pp. 313–326

Mansfield, B. (2007) 'Property, markets and dispossession', *Antipode*, vol. 39, no. 3, pp. 479–499

Marsden, T.K. (1999) 'Rural futures: the consumption of the countryside and its regulation', *Sociologia Ruralis*, vol. 39, pp. 501–520

Marsden, T.K. (2003) *The Condition of Rural Sustainability*, Van Gorcum, Assen (NL)

Marsden, T.K. and Smith, E. (2005) 'Ecological entrepreneurship: sustainable development in local communities through quality food production and local branding' *Geoforum*, vol. 36, pp. 440–451

Marsden, T.K. and Sonnino, R. (2005) 'Setting up and management of public policies with multifunctional purpose: connecting agriculture with new markets and services and rural SMEs (UK national report (WP5), EU Multagri Project)', Cardiff University, Cardiff

Marsh, G.P. (1864) *Man and Nature*, Harvard University Press, Cambridge (Mass.)

Martens, P. and Rotmans, J. (eds) (2002) *Transitions in a Globalising World*, Swets and Zeitlinger, Lisse (NL)

Maslow, A.H. (1943) 'A theory of human motivation', *Psychological Review*, vol. 50, no. 4, pp. 370–396

Massey, D. and Jess. P. (eds) (1995) *A Place in the World? Places, Cultures and Globalization*, OUP, Oxford

Masten, A.S. and Obradovic, J. (2008) 'Disaster preparation and recovery: lessons from research on resilience in human development', *Ecology and Society*, vol. 13, no. 1, article no. 9 (online) www.ecologyandsociety.org/vol. 13/iss1/art9

Mazmanian, D. and Kraft, M.E. (eds) (2009) *Toward Sustainable Communities: Transition and Transformations in Environmental Policy*, MIT Press, London

McCarthy, J. (2006) 'Neoliberalism and the politics of alternatives: community forestry in British Columbia and the United States', *Annals of the Association of American Geographers*, vol. 96, no. 1, pp. 84–104

McCaskill, L.W. (1973) *Hold This Land*, Reed, Wellington (NZ)

McGregor, R.K. (1988) 'Changing technologies and forest consumption in the Upper Delaware Valley, 1790–1880', *Journal of Forest History*, vol. 32, pp. 69–81

McMichael, P. (ed.) (1995) *The Global Restructuring of Agro-Food Systems*, Cornell University Press, Ithaca (N.Y.)

Meert, H., Van Huylenbroek, G., Vernimmen, T., Bourgeois, M. and Van Hecke, E. (2005) 'Farm household survival strategies and diversification on marginal farms', *Journal of Rural Studies*, vol. 21, pp. 81–97

Merrett, C.D. (2001) 'Understanding local responses to globalisation: the production of geographical scale and political identity', *National Identities*, vol. 3, no. 1, pp. 69–87

Mertz, O., Wadley, R.L. and Christensen, A.E. (2005) 'Local land use strategies in a globalizing world: subsistence farming, cash crops and income diversification', *Agricultural Systems*, vol. 85, pp. 209–215

Mestre-Sanchis, F. and Feijoo-Bello, M.L. (2009) 'Climate change and its marginalizing effect on agriculture', *Ecological Economics*, vol. 68, pp. 896–904

Michie, J. and Grieve-Smith, J. (eds) (1995) *Managing the Global Economy*, OUP, Oxford

Millennium Ecosystem Assessment (2005) *Millennium Ecosystem Assessment: Ecosystems and Human Well-Being, Volume 1: Current State and Trends*, Island Press. Washington (D.C.)

Miller, M.A. (2008) *Rebellion and Reform in Indonesia: Jakarta's Security and Autonomy Policies in Aceh*, Routledge, London

Mol, A. (2003) *Globalization and Environmental Reform: the Ecological Modernisation of the Global Economy*, MIT Press, Cambridge (Mass.)

Murdoch, J. and Marsden, T.K. (1995) 'The spatialisation of politics: local and national actor-spaces in environmental conflict', *Transactions of the Institute of British Geographers*, vol. 20, pp. 368–380

Neal, S. (2009) *Rural Identities: Ethnicity and Community in the Contemporary English Countryside*, Ashgate, Aldershot

Nederveen Pieterse, J. (2004) *Globalization and Culture: Global Mélange*, Rowman and Littlefield, New York

Nilsson, M. (2005) 'Learning, frames, and environmental policy integration: the case of Swedish energy policy', *Environment and Planning C: Government and Policy*, vol. 23, pp. 207–226

Noe, E., Fjelsted, A.H. and Langvad, A.M. (2008) 'A polyocular framework for research on multifunctional farming and rural development', *Sociologia Ruralis*, vol. 48, no. 1, pp. 1–15

Norberg-Hodge, H. (2003) 'Globalisation: use it or lose it', *The Ecologist*, vol. 33, no. 7, pp. 23–25

Norgaard, R.B. (1994) *Development Betrayed: the End of Progress and a Coevolutionary Revisioning of the Future*, Routledge, London

North, P. (1999) 'Explorations in heterotopias: local exchange trading schemes (LETS) and the micro-politics of money and livelihood', *Environment and Planning D: Society and Space*, vol. 17, pp. 69–86

North, P. (2010) 'Eco-localisation as a progressive response to peak oil and climate change: a sympathetic critique', *Geoforum*, vol. 41, no. 4, pp. 585–594

Nurul Islam, G.M., Yew, T.S., Abdullah, N.M. and Viswanathan, K.K. (2011) 'Social capital, community based management, and fishers' livelihood in Bangladesh', *Ocean and Coastal Management*, vol. 54, pp. 173–180

Olick, J.K. and Robbins, J. (1998) 'Social memory studies: from "collective memory" to historical sociology of mnemonic practices', *Annual Review of Sociology*, vol. 24, pp. 105–140

Oostindie, H., Roep, D. and Renting, H. (2006) 'Definitions, references and interpretations of the concept of multifunctionality in the Netherlands', *European Series on Multifunctionality*, vol. 10, pp. 41–81

O'Riordan, T. (ed.) (2001) *Globalism, Localism and Identity: Fresh Perspectives on the Transition to Sustainability*, Earthscan, London

Orr, D. (2009) *Down to the Wire: Confronting Climate Collapse*, OUP, Oxford

Osborne, M., Sankey, K. and Wilson, B. (2007) *Social Capital, Lifelong Learning and the Management of Place*, Routledge, London

Ostrom, E. (2009) 'A general framework for analyzing sustainability of social-ecological systems', *Science*, vol. 325, pp. 419–422

O'Sullivan, D. (2004) 'Complexity science and human geography', *Transactions of the Institute of British Geographers*, vol. 29, no. 3, pp. 282–295

Oudenhoven, F.J., Mijatovic, D. and Eyzaguirre, P.B. (2010) 'Social-ecological indicators of resilience in agrarian and natural landscapes', *Management of Environmental Quality*, vol. 22, no. 2, pp. 154–173

Paagman, A., Strijker, D. and Haartsen, T. (2010) 'Zoutkamp: fishing village forever? Senses of places in transition', Paper presented at the RGS/IBG Conference, 1–3 September 2010, RGS London, UK

Palumbo, D.J. and Calista, D. (eds) (1990) *Implementation and the Policy Process: Opening Up the Black Box*, Greenwood Press, Westport (Conn.)

Park, G. (1995) *Nga Uruora: Ecology and History in a New Zealand Landscape*, Victoria University Press, Wellington (NZ)

Parnwell, M.J. (2007) 'Neolocalism and renascent social capital in northeast Thailand', *Environment and Planning D: Society and Space*, vol. 25, pp. 990–1014

Passmore, J. (1980) *Man's Responsibility to Nature* (2nd edn), Duckworth, London

Paton, D., Millar, M. and Johnston, D. (2001) 'Community resilience to volcanic hazard consequences', *Natural Hazards*, vol. 40, pp. 157–169

Pavlinek, P. and Pickles, J. (2000) *Environmental Transitions: Transformation and Ecological Defence in Central and Eastern Europe*, Routledge, London

Pelling, M. (2003) *The Vulnerability of Cities: Natural Disasters and Social Resilience*, Earthscan, London

Peluso, N.L. (1992) *Rich Forests, Poor People: Resource Control and Resistance in Java*, University of California Press, Berkeley (Cal.)

Peluso, N.L. (1995) 'Whose woods are these? Counter-mapping forest territories in Kalimantan, Indonesia', *Antipode*, vol. 27, no. 4, pp. 383–406

Peterson, G. (2000) 'Political ecology and ecological resilience: an integration of human and ecological dynamics', *Ecological Economics*, vol. 35, pp. 323–336

Pickles, J. and Smith, A. (eds) (1998) *Theorising Transition: the Political Economy of Post-Communist Transformations*, Routledge, London

Pickles, J. and Unwin, T. (2004) 'Transition in context: theory in post-socialist transformations', in B. Van Hoven (ed.) *Europe: Lives in Transition*, Pearson, Harlow, pp. 9–28

Pielke, R. (2006) '"What just ain't so": it is all too easy to underestimate the challenges posed by climate change', *Nature*, vol. 443, pp. 753–754

Pinkerton, T. and Hopkins, R. (2009) *Local Food: How to Make it Happen in your Community*, Green Books, Totnes

Pirsig, R.M. (1974) *Zen and the Art of Motorcycle Maintenance*, Corgi Books, London

Porritt, J. (2007) *Capitalism as if the World Matters*, Earthscan, London

Potter, C. and Burney, J. (2002) 'Agricultural multifunctionality in the WTO: legitimate non-trade concern or disguised protectionism?' *Journal of Rural Studies*, vol. 18, pp. 35–47

Potter, C. and Tilzey, M. (2005) 'Agricultural policy discourses in the European post-Fordist transition: neoliberalism, neomercantilism and multifunctionality', *Progress in Human Geography*, vol. 29, no. 5, pp. 1–20

Povellato, A. and Ferraretto, D. (2005) 'Desertification policies in Italy: new pressures on land and 'desertification' as rural-urban migration', in G.A. Wilson and M. Juntti (eds) *Unravelling Desertification: Policies and Actor Networks in Southern Europe*, Wageningen Academic Publishers, Wageningen (NL), pp. 101–130

Prändl-Zika, V. (2008) 'From subsistence farming towards a multifunctional agriculture: sustainability in the Chinese rural reality', *Journal of Environmental Management*, vol. 87, pp. 236–248

Pretty, J.N. (1995) *Regenerating Agriculture: Policies and Practice for Sustainability and Self-Reliance*, Earthscan, London

Pretty, J.N. (2002) *Agri-Culture: Reconnecting People, Land and Nature*, Earthscan, London

Pretty, J.N. (2007) *The Earth Only Endures: on Reconnecting With Nature and Our Place in it*, Earthscan, London

Pretty, J.N. and Ward, H. (2001) 'Social capital and the environment', *World Development*, vol. 29, pp. 209–277

Przeworski, A. (1995) *Sustainable Democracy*, CUP, Cambridge

Putnam, R. (1993) *Making Democracy Work*, Princeton University Press, Princeton

Ray, C. (2000) 'The EU LEADER Programme: rural development laboratory', *Sociologia Ruralis*, vol. 40, no. 2, pp. 163–171

Read, R. (2004) 'The implications of increasing globalisation and regionalism for the economic growth of small states', *World Development*, vol. 32, no. 2, pp. 365–378

Redclift, M. (1987) *Sustainable Development: Exploring the Contradictions*, Methuen, London

Redford, K. and Sanderson, S.E. (2000) 'Extracting humans from nature', *Conservation Biology*, vol. 14, no. 5, pp. 1362–1364

Reichert-Schick, A. (2010) '"Dying villages?": the effects of demographic change on rural settlements in West Pomerania', in I. Mose, G.M. Robinson, D. Schmied and G.A. Wilson (eds) *Globalization and Rural Transitions in Germany and the UK*, Cuvillier Verlag, Göttingen, pp. 149–166

Resilience Alliance (2007) 'Assessing resilience in social-ecological systems: a workbook for scientists', www.resalliance.org/3871.php

Resilience Alliance (2009) 'Urban resilience', www.resalliance.org

Reynolds, L.T. (2002) 'Wages for wives: renegotiating gender and production relations in contract farming in the Dominican Republic', *World Development*, vol. 30, no. 5, pp. 783–798

Rhodes, R.A. (1997) *Understanding Governance*, Open University Press, Buckingham

Richards, M.D. (2004) *Revolutions in World History*, Routledge, New York

Rigg, J. (2006) 'Land, farming, livelihoods, and poverty: rethinking the links in the rural South', *World Development*, vol. 34, no. 1, pp. 180–202

Rigg, J., Law, L., Tan-Mullins, M. and Grundy-Warr, C. (2005) 'The Indian Ocean tsunami: socio-economic impacts in Thailand', *The Geographical Journal*, vol. 171, no. 4, pp. 374–378

Rigg, J., Veeravongs, S., Veeravongs, L. and Rohitarachoon, P. (2008) 'Reconfiguring rural spaces and remaking rural lives in central Thailand', *Journal of Southeast Asian Studies*, vol. 39, no. 3, pp. 355–381

Rival, L. (2009) 'The resilience of indigenous intelligence', in K. Hastrup (ed.) *The Question of Resilience: Social Responses to Climate Change*, Det Kongelige Danske Videnskabernes Selskab, Viborg (DK), pp. 293–313

Robertson, R. (1992) *Globalization: Social Theory and Global Culture*, Sage, London

Robertson, R. (1995) 'Glocalization: time-space and homogeneity-heterogeneity', in M. Featherstone, S. Lash and R. Robertson (eds) *Global Modernities*, Sage, London, pp. 45–65

Robinson, G. (2004) *Geographies of Agriculture: Globalisation, Restructuring and Sustainability*, Pearson, Harlow

Robinson, G. (ed.) (2008) *Sustainable Rural Systems: Sustainable Agriculture and Rural Communities*, Ashgate, Aldershot

Rofe, M.W. (2009) 'Globalisation, gentrification and spatial hierarchies in and beyond New South Wales: the local/global nexus', *Geographical Research*, vol. 47, no. 3, pp. 292–305

Rogers, E. (1995) *Diffusion of Innovations* (4th edn), Free Press, New York

Rotmans, J., Martens, P. and Van Asselt, M.B. (2002) 'Introduction', in P. Martens and J. Rotmans (eds) *Transitions in a Globalising World*, Swets and Zeitlinger, Lisse (NL), pp. 1–16

Sabatier, P.A. and Jenkins-Smith, H.C. (1993) *Policy Change and Learning: an Advocacy Coalition Approach*, Westview Press, Boulder (Col.)

Sachs, J. (1992) 'Building a market economy in Poland', *Scientific American*, March 1992, pp. 34–40

Salamanca, E.F. (2010) 'Improvement of coastal areas through mangrove enhancement initiatives in the Turks and Caicos Islands (Caribbean)', Paper presented at the Hazards Mitigation Workshop, 13–15 October 2010, University of Plymouth, UK

Sarkissian, W., Hurford, D. and Wenman, C. (2010) *Creative Community Planning: Transformative Engagement Methods for Working at the Edge*, Earthscan, London

Savage, M., Bagnall, G. and Longhurst, B. (2005) *Globalization and Belonging*, Sage, London

Scarfetta, N. and West, B.J. (2004) 'Multiresolution diffusion entropy analysis of time series: an application to births to teenagers in Texas', *Chaos, Solution and Fractals*, vol. 20, pp. 179–185

Schama, S. (1995) *Landscape and Memory*, Fontana Press, London

Scheffer, M., Westley, F. and Brock, W.B. (2003) 'Slow response of societies to new problems: causes and costs', *Ecosystems*, vol. 6, pp. 493–502

Schreuder, G.F. and Anderson, E.T. (eds) (1988) *Global Issues and Outlook in Pulp and Paper*, University of Washington Press, Seattle

Schultz, P.W., Zelezny, L.C. and Dalrymple, N.J. (2000) 'A multinational perspective on the relation between Judeo-Christian religious beliefs and attitudes of environmental concern', *Environment and Behavior*, vol. 32, pp. 576–591

Seaver, K. (1996) *The Frozen Echo: Greenland and Exploration of North America ca. AD 1000–1500*, Stanford University Press, Stanford (Cal.)

Seyfang, G. (2006) 'Ecological citizenship and sustainable consumption: examining local organic food networks', *Journal of Rural Studies*, vol. 22, pp. 383–395

Seyfang, G. (2009) *The New Economics of Sustainable Consumption: Seeds of Change*, Palgrave-Macmillan, Houndmills

Sheingate, A. (2000) 'Agricultural retrenchment revisited: issue definition and venue change in the United States and European Union', *Governance*, vol. 13, pp. 335–363

Sheller, M. and Urry, J. (2006) 'The new mobilities paradigm', *Environment and Planning A*, vol. 38, pp. 207–226

Shepard, P. (1969) *English Reaction to the New Zealand Landscape Before 1850* (Pacific Viewpoint Monograph No. 4), Wellington University, Wellington (NZ)

Shortall, S. (2008) 'Are rural development programmes socially inclusive? Social inclusion, civic engagement, participation, and social capital: exploring the differences', *Journal of Rural Studies*, vol. 24, no. 4, pp. 450–457

Shucksmith, M. (1993) 'Farm household behaviour and the transition to post-productivism', *Journal of Agricultural Economics*, vol. 44, pp. 466–478

Siegle, L. and Borden, H. (2011) 'The town of the future', *The Observer Magazine*, 6 February 2011, pp. 28–31

Simmons, I.G. (1996) *Changing the Face of the Earth* (2nd edn), Blackwell, Oxford

Simms, A. (2005) *Ecological Debt: the Health of the Planet and the Wealth of Nations*, Pluto Press, London

Smit, B. and Wandel, J. (2006) 'Adaptation, adaptive capacity and vulnerability', *Global Environmental Change*, vol. 16, pp. 282–292

Smith, A. and Swain, A. (1998) 'Regulating and institutionalising capitalism: the micro-foundations of transformation in Eastern and Central Europe', in A. Pickles and A. Smith (eds) *Theorising Transition: the Political Economy of Post-Communist Transformations*, Routledge, London, pp. 25–53

Smith, E.A. and Wishnie, M. (2000) 'Conservation and subsistence in small-scale societies', *Annual Review of Anthropology*, vol. 29, pp. 493–524

Söderholm, P. (2010) *Environmental Policy and Household Behaviour*, Earthscan, London

Staeheli, L.A. (2008) 'Citizenship and the problem of community', *Political Geography*, vol. 27, pp. 5–21

Stark, D. (1992) 'Path dependencies and privatization strategies in East Central Europe', *Eastern European Politics and Societies*, vol. 6, pp. 17–51

Steinberg, M.K. and Taylor, M.J. (2009) 'The direct and indirect impacts of population growth and economic development on maize (Zea Mays L) diversity in highland Guatemala', *Area*, vol. 41, pp. 72–81

Stiglitz, J. (2002) *Globalization and Its Discontents*, W.W. Norton, New York

St Martin, K. (2005) 'Disrupting enclosures in New England fisheries', *Capitalism, Nature, Socialism*, vol. 16, no. 1, pp. 63–80

Stokes, E. (2002) 'Contesting resources: Maori, pakeha, and a tenurial revolution', in E. Pawson and T. Brooking (eds) *Environmental Histories of New Zealand*, OUP, Oxford, pp. 35–51

Stryker, S. (1980) *Symbolic Interactionism: a Social Structural Version*, Benjamin Cummings, London

Stump, D. (2010) ' "Ancient and backward or long-lived and sustainable?" The role of the past in debates concerning rural livelihoods and resource conservation in Eastern Africa', *World Development*, vol. 38, no. 9, pp. 1251–1262

Swyngedouw, E. (1997) 'Neither global nor local: "glocalization" and the politics of scale', in K. Cox (ed.) *Places of Globalization*, Guildford Press, London, pp. 137–166

Swyngedouw, E. (2001) 'Elite power, global forces, and the political economy of "glocal" development', in G.L. Clark, M.P. Feldman and M.S. Gertler (eds) *A Reader in Economic Geography*, OUP, Oxford, pp. 541–558

Tan, Y., Hugo, G. and Potter, L. (2005) 'Rural women, displacement and the Three Gorges Project', *Development and Change*, vol. 36, no. 4, pp. 711–734

Teich, M. and Bebi, P. (2009) 'Evaluating the benefit of avalanche protection forest with GIS-based risk analyses: a case study from Switzerland', *Forest Ecology and Management*, vol. 257, pp. 1910–1919

Tews, K. (2005) 'The diffusion of environmental policy innovations: cornerstones of an analytical framework', *European Environment*, vol. 15, pp. 63–79

Thampapillai, D. and Uhlin, H.E. (1997) 'Environmental capital and sustainable income: basic concepts and empirical tests', *Cambridge Journal of Economics*, vol. 21, pp. 379–394

The Economist (2009) 'Onwards and upwards: why is the modern view of progress so impoverished?', *The Economist*, 19 December 2009, pp. 35–38

The Economist Technological Quarterly (2010) 'Power to the people', *The Economist*, 4 September 2010, pp. 20–21

Thomalla, F. and Klocker Larsen, R. (2010) 'Resilience in the context of tsunami early warning systems and community disaster preparedness in the Indian Ocean Region', *Environmental Hazards*, vol. 9, pp. 249–265

Thompson, J.B. (1981) *Critical Hermeneutics*, CUP, Cambridge

Thoreau, H.D. (1851) *Walden, or Life in the Woods*, Collier, New York

Thornes, J.B. and Brunsden, D. (1977) *Geomorphology and Time*, Methuen, London

Thrift, N. (1999) 'The place of complexity', *Theory Culture and Society*, vol. 16, pp. 31–69

Thrift, N. (2005) 'But malice aforethought: cities and the natural history of hatred', *Transactions of the Institute of British Geographers*, vol. 30, pp. 133–150

Tomlinson, J. (2007) *The Culture of Speed: the Coming of Immediacy*, Sage, Los Angeles

Tönnies, F. (1963) *Community and Society* (4th edn), Harper, New York

Tudge, C. (2005) *The Secret Life of Trees*, Penguin, London

Turner, B.L., Clark, W.C., Kates, R.W., Richards, J.F. and Mathews, J.T. (eds) (1990) *The Earth as Transformed by Human Action: Global and Regional Changes over the Past 300 years*, CUP, Cambridge

Turner, B.S. (2009) 'Citizens, communities and conflict: surviving globalization', *Citizenship Studies*, vol. 13, no. 4, pp. 431–437

UNDP (United Nations Development Programme) (annual) *Human Development Report*, OUP: New York

Vandermeulen, V., Verspecht, A., Van Huylenbroek, G., Meert, H., Boulanger, A. and Van Hecke, E. (2006) 'The importance of the institutional environment on multifunctional farming systems in the peri-urban area of Brussels', *Land Use Policy*, vol. 23, pp. 486–501

Van Hoven, B. (ed.) 2004: *Europe: Lives in Transition*. Harlow: Pearson.

Van Hoven, B., Unwin, T. and Jansen, A. (2004) 'Introduction', in B. Van Hoven (ed.) *Europe: Lives in Transition*, Pearson, Harlow, pp. 1–8

Van Rheenen, T. and Mengistu, T. (2009) 'Rural areas in transition: a developing world perspective', in F. Brouwer and C.M. Van der Heide (eds) *Multifunctional Rural Land Management: Economics and Policies*, Earthscan, London, pp. 319–334

Veek, A. and Veek, G. (2000) 'Consumer segmentation and changing food purchase patterns in Nanjing, PRC', *World Development*, vol. 28, pp. 457–471

Vitaliano, D.B. (2007) 'Geomythology: geological origins of myths and legends', *Geological Society London (Special Publications)*, vol. 237, pp. 1–7

Von Bertalanffy, L. (1968) *General Systems Theory: Foundation, Development, Application*, Allen Lane, London

WADE (World Association for Decentralised Energy) (2003) *World Survey of Decentralised Energy*, WADE, Edinburgh

Wade, N. (2009) *The Faith Instinct: How Religion Evolved and why it Endures*, Penguin, London

Walker, B.H. and Salt, D. (2006) *Resilience Thinking: Sustaining Ecosystems and People in a Changing World*, Island Press, Washington (D.C.)

Walker, B.H., Anderies, J.M., Kinzig, A.P. and Ryan, P. (2006) 'Exploring resilience in social-ecological systems through comparative studies and theory development: introduction to the special issue', *Ecology and Society*, vol. 11, no. 1, article no. 12 (online) www.ecologyandsociety.org/vol. 11/iss1/art12/

Walker, G. (2008) 'What are the barriers and incentives for community-owned means of energy production and use?', *Energy Policy*, vol. 36, pp. 4401–4405

Ward, C. and Styles, I. (2006) 'Evidence of the ecological self: English-speaking migrants' residual links to their homeland', *International Journal of Applied Psychoanalytical Studies*, vol. 4, no. 4, pp. 319–332

Waters, M. (1995) *Globalization*, Routledge, London

Weiß, W. (2006) 'Zur Entwicklung einer Residualbevölkerung infolge lang anhaltender selektiver Abwanderung in Mecklenburg-Vorpommern', *Zeitschrift für Bevölkerungswissenschaft*, vol. 31, no. 3–4, pp. 469–506

Welford, M. and Bossak, B.H. (2010) 'Revisiting the mediaeval black death of 1347–1351: spatiotemporal dynamics suggestive of an alternate causation', *Geography Compass: Environment and Society*, vol. 4, no. 6, pp. 561–575

Western, J., Stimson, R., Baum, S. and Van Gellecum, Y. (2005) 'Measuring community strength and social capital', *Regional Studies*, vol. 39, no. 8, pp. 1095–1109

Whatmore, S. (2009) 'Mapping knowledge controversies: science, democracy and the redistribution of expertise', *Progress in Human Geography*, vol. 33, pp. 587–598

White, L. (1967) 'The historical roots of our ecological crisis', *Science*, vol. 155, pp. 1203–1207

Williams, M. (1989) *Americans and their Forests: a Historical Geography*, CUP, Cambridge

Wilson, G.A. (1990) 'Aspekte der Waldrodung in Neuseeland', *Die Erde*, vol. 121, no. 2, pp. 73–85

Wilson, G.A. (1992) *The Urge to Clear the 'Bush': a Study of Native Forest Clearance on Farms in the Catlins District of New Zealand, 1861–1990*, University of Canterbury Press, Christchurch (NZ)

Wilson, G.A. (1993a) 'Irrational forestry policy: the timber industry and forest clearance on farms in the New Zealand Catlins District, 1870–1950', *Forest and Conservation History*, vol. 37, no. 3, pp. 120–131

Wilson, G.A. (1993b) 'The pace of indigenous forest clearance on farms in the Catlins District, SE South Island, New Zealand, 1861–1990', *New Zealand Geographer*, vol. 49, no. 1, pp. 15–25

Wilson, G.A. (1997) 'Selective targeting in Environmentally Sensitive Areas: implications for farmers and the environment', *Journal of Environmental Planning and Management*, vol. 40, no. 2, pp. 199–215

Wilson, G.A. (2001) 'From productivism to post-productivism … and back again? Exploring the (un)changed natural and mental landscapes of European agriculture', *Transactions of the Institute of British Geographers*, vol. 26, no. 1, pp. 77–102

Wilson, G.A. (2007) *Multifunctional Agriculture: a Transition Theory Perspective*, CABI, Wallingford

Wilson, G.A. (2008) 'Global multifunctional agriculture: transitional convergence between North and South or zero-sum game?' *International Journal of Agricultural Sustainability*, vol. 6, no. 1, pp. 3–21

Wilson, G.A. (2009) 'The spatiality of multifunctional agriculture: a human geography perspective', *Geoforum*, vol. 40, pp. 269–280

Wilson, G.A. (2010) 'Multifunctional "quality" and rural community resilience', *Transactions of the Institute of British Geographers*, vol. 35, no. 3, pp. 364–381

Wilson, G.A. and Bryant, R.L. (1997) *Environmental Management: New Directions for the 21st Century*, UCL Press, London

Wilson, G.A. and Hart, K. (2000) 'Financial imperative or conservation concern? EU farmers' motivations for participation in voluntary agri-environmental schemes', *Environment and Planning A*, vol. 32, no. 12, pp. 2161–2185

Wilson, G.A. and Juntti, M. (eds) (2005) *Unravelling Desertification: Policies and Actor Networks in Southern Europe*, Wageningen Academic Publishers, Wageningen (NL)

Wilson, G.A. and Memon, P.A. (2005) 'Indigenous forest management in 21st century New Zealand: towards a "postproductivist" indigenous forest-farmland interface?', *Environment and Planning A*, vol. 37, pp. 1493–1517

Wilson, G.A. and Memon, P.A. (2010) 'The contested environmental governance of Maori-owned native forests in South Island, Aotearoa/New Zealand', *Land Use Policy*, vol. 27, pp. 1197–1209

Wilson, G.A. and Rigg, J. (2003) '"Post-productivist" agricultural regimes and the South: discordant concepts?', *Progress in Human Geography*, vol. 27, no. 5, pp. 605–631

Wilson, G.A. and Wilson, O.J. (2001) *German Agriculture in Transition: Society, Policies and Environment in a Changing Europe*, Palgrave, Houndmills

Wilt, A.F. (2001) *Food for War: Agriculture and Rearmament in Britain Before the Second World War*, OUP, Oxford

Winter, M. (2003) 'Embeddedness, the new food economy and defensive localism', *Journal of Rural Studies*, vol. 19, pp. 23–32

Winter, S. (1990) 'Integrating implementation research', in D.J. Palumbo and D. Calista (eds) *Implementation and the Policy Process: Opening Up the Black Box*, Greenwood Press, Westport (Conn.), pp. 19–38

Woo, M.J. (2006) 'North Korea in 2005: maximising profit to save socialism', *Asian Survey*, vol. 46, no. 1, pp. 49–55

Woods, M. (2005) *Rural Geography: Processes, Responses and Experiences in Rural Restructuring*, Sage, London

Wynn, G. (1979) 'Pioneers, politicians and the conservation of forests in early New Zealand', *Journal of Historical Geography*, vol. 5, no. 2, pp. 171–188

Ye, J.Z. and He, C.Z. (2008) *Lonely Sunsets: the Elderly Left Behind in Rural China*, Social Sciences Academic Press, Beijing

Young, O.R., Berkhout, F., Gallopin, G.C., Janssen, A., Ostrom, E. and Van der Leeuw, S. (2006) 'The globalisation of social-ecological systems: an agenda for scientific research', *Global Environmental Change*, vol. 16, pp. 304–316

Zhao, Y.H. (1999) 'Leaving the countryside: rural-to-urban migration decisions in China', *American Economic Review*, vol. 89, no. 2, pp. 281–286

Index